INTERNATIONAL EXPRESS

UPPER-INTERMEDIATE
Student's Book

Adrian Wallwork

OXFORD
UNIVERSITY PRESS

Contents

ii

Welcome

to International Express
Upper-Intermediate

STUDENT'S BOOK	There are ten main units and five Review units in the Student's Book. Each unit has four main parts: Language focus, Wordpower, Focus on functions, and Skills focus. The unit begins with an Overview of the contents.
Language focus	This section presents and reviews grammar through authentic listening exercises and reading texts. You work out the grammar rules by yourself and apply them in short written exercises and then in speaking activities.
Wordpower	This section is designed for you to develop strategies to consolidate and increase your range of active and passive vocabulary. Most sections are introduced with a reading or listening activity which sets the context of the vocabulary that you are going to review and learn.
Focus on functions	In this section you learn the typical phrases and language you will need in various work and social situations, for example, on the telephone or at a restaurant. You will also learn key phrases and strategies to help you make your point clearly and understand others.
Skills focus	This is the final section of each unit. It aims to improve above all your listening and speaking skills, but also suggests ways of improving your writing skills, for example, in emails and letters.

🎧 **A note on the listening exercises**

About half of the listening exercises in this book are authentic: either they are interviews with real people or they are improvisations carried out in a recording studio. This means that you will hear people as they really speak. This is a difficult and challenging task, and you will certainly not be expected to understand every word you hear. You will learn strategies for deciphering natural speech in order to build up your listening skills. Those activities marked 🎧 **Understanding natural speech** are not contained in the Student's Book, but only in the Teacher's Book.

Review units	There is a Review unit after every two units. You choose what to revise and complete the review exercises. You can use the Self-check boxes to plan and check your learning.
Listening scripts	The scripts of the listening material are at the back of the Student's Book.
POCKET BOOK	At the back of the Student's Book there is a mini grammar and phrase book. This contains additional information on the key grammar points covered in each unit along with summaries of useful social and functional expressions.
WORKBOOK	The Workbook, with its own Student's cassette or CD, is a separate book containing extra exercises on grammar, reading, writing, and listening. Such exercises not only revise the work done in the Student's Book, but can also help you to prepare, if necessary, for the First Certificate and Business English Certificate examinations.

Needs and requirements analysis

1 What do you need English for?

- [ ] work
- [ ] holidays
- [ ] other (specify) _____
- [ ] meeting new people
- [ ] chatlines

2 If you need English for work, which of these areas will you use it most in?

- [ ] phone
- [ ] emails
- [ ] presentations
- [ ] meetings
- [ ] with visitors
- [ ] writing letters and documents
- [ ] customer support
- [ ] travel

3 How long have you been studying English?

- [ ] less than two years
- [ ] three years
- [ ] four years
- [ ] more than four years

4 Which area of English do you find the most difficult, and would most like to improve?

- [ ] speaking
- [ ] pronunciation
- [ ] grammar
- [ ] reading
- [ ] vocabulary
- [ ] writing
- [ ] listening

5 How much of your English lesson do you think should be spent on the following?

speaking _____   writing   _____

listening _____   vocabulary _____

grammar _____

6 When should the teacher spend time talking during a lesson?

- [ ] only to give instructions and explain grammatical rules
- [ ] to talk about himself/herself and his/her experiences
- [ ] to give general information about his/her culture

7 When you are having a discussion in your group should the teacher:

- [ ] interrupt you every time you make a mistake?
- [ ] interrupt you only if you keep making the same mistake?
- [ ] never interrupt, but note down the mistakes for explanation later?

8 Which do you think is better?

- [ ] to speak slowly and very accurately
- [ ] to speak more fluently but making quite a few mistakes

9 If you are given a course book, do you expect to:

- [ ] do every exercise in the book?
- [ ] do most exercises?
- [ ] use the book principally as a reference point?
- [ ] whatever the teacher thinks is best?

10 How much homework do you think you should do and how much do you think you will really do?

- [ ] an hour or more a day
- [ ] three to six hours a week
- [ ] two hours a week
- [ ] none

Unit 1

Roles and relationships

OVERVIEW
● Present tenses review
● Present Perfect Simple vs Continuous
● Techniques for learning new
   vocabulary
● False friends
● Adjectives – personal characteristics
● Introductions and greetings:
   levels of formality
   putting yourself in context
● Conversation conventions:
   breaking the ice
   building rapport

LANGUAGE FOCUS   Present time

1 Do men really have more advantages than women in the world of work? With a partner, discuss whether or not you agree with these statements.

1　Generally speaking, men have a better deal than women.

2　In all age groups, men earn more than women.

3　Women have fewer choices in life than men.

4　On the basis of time spent working inside and outside the home, women work more hours than men.

5　The worst jobs are generally done by men.

6　In the modern world, men need to take on both masculine and feminine traits and roles.

7　Women who work full time shouldn't have children.

8　Men's life expectancy has increased at the same rate as women's.

9　For many years more money has been spent on research into women's health than research into men's health.

10　The idea of the man being the sole provider for the family is no longer acceptable.

2 🔊 **1.1** Listen to two people talking about the role of men in today's society. Which of the points in **1** do they mention? Do they agree?

3 🔊 **1.1** Listen again.

1　According to the speakers, what is:
   the main difficulty that men have to face?
   the main choice facing working women?

2　Are the speakers' opinions different from yours? How?

 **Understanding natural speech**

2

4 You are going to read an article about changes in the number of women in employment.

1 In pairs, discuss these questions.

    a Are there more men than women in your workplace?

    b Is the number of women in your workplace increasing? Why, or why not?

    c How has women's influence in the workplace changed?

    d What effect has this been having on men?

2 Read the article. Does it support your answers to these questions?

The number of women working in the UK *has been rising*[1] steadily for several decades. In the mid-1960s, around 42% of women of working age were in employment; in the late 1990s, this number increased to nearly 70%. Today women *have actually overtaken*[2] men in the job market – men *have never been*[3] in such a position before and it now *appears*[4] to be affecting the way they view their role in life.

This phenomenon *is spreading*[5] rapidly around the world. The number of working women in the labour force in China *has increased*[6] from 49% in 1980 to nearly 60% today – the highest of any country in the world. At the other extreme, only about

'Times have certainly changed, Arthur.'

10% of women in Iraq and Saudi Arabia currently *work*[7].

Although their numbers *have been increasing*[8], only 3% of the directors of the UK's top 1,500 companies are female. Moreover, despite the fact that women *have made*[9] progress in areas such as child-care and increased flexibility in working hours, they *are still facing*[10] strong discrimination. Tina Knight, who *has had*[11] various jobs in industry and is now chair of Women Into Business, *is currently lobbying*[12] Parliament on these issues. 'One big mistake that successful women *make*[13],' says Tina, 'is to try to shut men out. We have to work alongside each other'.

The Guardian

Present tenses review

1 **Look at the verbs in italics in the article. Find one or more examples of:**

    a an action which takes place at the moment of speaking / a current trend

    b a completed action at an unspecified time in the past with a connection to the present

    c a permanent or usual situation / an action that happens repeatedly

    d an action that began in the past, is relevant now, and will continue into the future.

2 **Match each description with one of these tenses: Present Simple, Present Continuous, Present Perfect Simple, Present Perfect Continuous.**

3 **Look at the verbs in italics again. In which cases, if any, could you replace:**

    a the Present Simple with the Present Continuous?

    b the Present Continuous with the Present Simple or the Present Perfect Continuous?

    c the Present Perfect Simple with the Present Perfect Continuous?

    d the Present Perfect Continuous with the Present Continuous or the Present Perfect Simple?

📖 Pocket Book page 16

5 How has the role of a secretary changed over the last twenty years? What has led to this change? Think about the duties secretaries have to fulfil, and the assets, skills, and qualifications they need to have.

6 Read the article and put the verbs in brackets into an appropriate form. If more than one form seems possible, choose the best one.

GONE are the days when young women spent long, boring hours typing and taking notes.

The 21st-century secretary is still more likely to be a woman, but there the similarities end. Today she's a key part of any working team, making decisions, running vital parts of a company and keeping everyone in line – especially when it comes to new technology. In exchange she **1**_____ (earn) more money than ever before.

Recruitment director Philip Ayling, whose company **2**_____ (place) hundreds of secretaries into the highly skilled area of banking and IT in the City of London in recent years, **3**_____ (say): 'In the banking field you need technology skills and academic qualifications, often to degree level. Secretaries have to understand what their team **4**_____ (do), and be prepared to fit in by working long hours and undertaking many duties.'

The basic salary for such a banking job **5**_____ (range) from £20,000 to £30,000 in the City, with overtime up to £6,000 a year and often bonuses. Samantha Estrin, 23, **6**_____ (work) in the City since she graduated with a degree in English literature and language. 'The image of a secretary as a put-upon, worthless individual **7**_____ (disappear) entirely,' says Samantha. 'I **8**_____ (work) very much as part of a team. My boss, who is a director, couldn't carry out his job without me. I feel needed and I know that I **9**_____ (make) a valuable contribution to the team.'

The big change, says Ayling, is due to the arrival of new technology. 'For several years now, bosses **10**_____ (do) a lot of their own correspondence.'

Now men, too, **11**_____ (enter) the profession. 'But senior males still have this feeling that they couldn't have a man working for them in a secretarial role,' says Janet Crawford, founder of Angel Human Resources, which **12**_____ (place) senior secretaries, administrators and PAs across the UK.

The Mirror

THEN AND NOW

Duties then: 'Take a note Miss Jones'; buying the boss's wife a birthday card; making tea.

And now: diary management; arranging and minuting meetings; organizing travel; preparing presentations; typing letters and reports; helping analysts with research.

Assets then: shorthand and typing skills; good looks.

And now: computer skills; ability to make important decisions; willingness to work hard.

---

7 Work in pairs and discuss these questions.

1 Do secretaries in your organization have similar qualifications and roles to those of Samantha Estrin?

2 In your organization, how much of their written communication do people assign to secretaries?

3 What qualifications do you need to do your job? How much overtime do you have to do? Do you get bonuses?

4 What other jobs have changed significantly over the last fifty years?

8 1.2 Listen to an extract from an interview with Anthea Fraser, a self-employed businesswoman who started her own recruitment consultancy two years ago.

1 What evidence is there that the business is successful? Make a note of what she says about:
   a client companies
   b new staff
   c new offices
   d a web-based recruitment service.

2 What are the main advantages and disadvantages of her situation?

More about the Present Perfect Simple and Continuous

We use the Present Perfect to link past actions and events with the present.

1 Listen to the interview again and look at the script on page 124. What is the difference between the highlighted forms in this sentence? Why does Andrea use two different forms?

… I've been running my own business for just over two years now, and in that time we've attracted about a hundred and twenty client companies, …

What other similar examples can you find in the script?

2 Complete these sentences.

1 We normally use the Present Perfect _____ to refer to the length of time an activity has lasted, if it is still going on now.

2 We normally use the Present Perfect _____ to refer to the whole activity, or to give a sense of completion.

Pocket Book page 13

9 Work in pairs. Put the verbs in italics into an appropriate form. Choose some of the questions to ask your partner.

1 What field of work or study are you in? How long you *work/ study* in that field?
2 You *work/ study* long hours?
3 What project(s) you *work* on? How long you *work* on it/ them?
4 What subject(s) you *study*? How long you *study* them?
5 Which areas of your work or study do you think *go* particularly well over the last few months?
6 You ever *think* about changing your line of work or study completely?

Talking point **10** Prepare a short talk about one of these topics.

1 A key aspect of your life or career. Include information about:
   – things you are involved in at the moment
   – regular or constant activities
   – important achievements
   – a situation or process which started in the past and is still going on.

2 An important issue or development in your field of work, or a key social, cultural, or political issue in your country. Include information about:
   – the general situation
   – current developments
   – recent and long-term changes.

Work in pairs or small groups. Listen to each other's talks and ask appropriate questions.

Learning vocabulary, adjectives to describe people

Learning new words

Learning tip

1 associate new words with a sound, a picture, or an experience
2 repeat new words aloud
3 learn a certain number of new words a day
4 learn words in useful phrases or sentences
5 practise using new words in sentences
6 associate new words with similar words you already know
7 associate new words with similar words in another language
8 select words to learn from objects in a room
9 try to visualize the way a new word looks
10 write lists of words and review them regularly

1 How often do you try to learn new words? Do you have a favourite technique? How many words do you try to learn at once? Look at tips 1–10 for learning new vocabulary. Which ones have you tried? Compare your techniques with a partner.

2 🎧 1.3 Listen to three people outlining the techniques they use to learn vocabulary in foreign languages. They are:

— Timothy Mitchell, an American businessman, on learning Italian
— Ruth Glassock, a refugee worker, on learning Arabic
— James Lewin, a professional translator, on learning Russian and German.

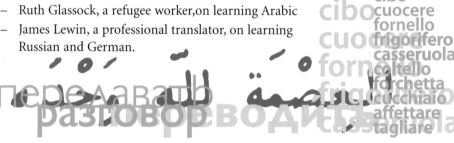

Which techniques from the Learning tip in **1** does each of them use?

3 With a new partner, decide on the most effective techniques in the list in **1**.

4 Here are some new words that have entered the English language very recently. Try learning them, using a technique you have not tried before. Test yourself in the next lesson.

docusoap *n* a television programme that combines the styles of a documentary and a soap opera

outsource *vb* to buy services from a source outside an organization

hot-desking *n* the activity of sharing desks or workstations in an office based on need, as a way of saving space and resources

stressed out *adj* very tired and nervous as a result of stress

sorted *adj* well-organized or under control

dress down *vb* to dress informally and casually at work (often on Fridays)

False friends

5 Remember that although a word in English looks similar to a word in your language, it might mean something completely different. These words are often called 'false friends'. Many false friends share the same origin in an older language (e.g. 40% of English words originate from Latin), or are borrowed by one language from another. For example:

actually   In English, does this mean *currently, happening now*, or *in fact, in reality*?
library   In English, is this a shop where you buy books, or a place where you can borrow books?
sympathetic In English, does this describes someone who is *nice* or *pleasant*, or someone who shares another person's feelings?

6 Japanese is one language that has borrowed a lot of words from English – about 50,000. These are some of them.

erebeta – *elevator*	mansion – *flat*
boss – *leader of gang of criminals*	bata – *butter*
terebi – *television*	happening – *unexpected incident*
famicon – *family computer*	pension – *guesthouse*
intelligent – *computerized*	intelibiru – *high-tech office*
waishattu – *white shirt*	sabotage – *be absent from school / work*

Do you know any words in your language that have been borrowed from English? Have the spelling and pronunciation changed? Has the meaning changed?

Adjectives – personal characteristics

7 These adjectives are often used to describe people's characters.

adventurous	creative	hard-working	outgoing	sensitive
aggressive	demanding	honest	passive	serious
agreeable	determined	independent	quiet	shy
ambitious	efficient	intelligent	reliable	sincere
aware	flexible	introvert	responsible	stubborn
boring	friendly	lazy	selfish	sympathetic
competent	fun	lively	self-motivated	talkative
confident	funny	meticulous	self-reliant	tolerant
conscientious	gentle	organized	sensible	warm

1   Check that you know what they all mean, using a dictionary.
2   Divide them into groups, depending on whether you think they are
    (a) mainly positive, (b) neutral, or (c) mainly negative.
3   Which words could be used to describe the way someone approaches their work?
4   Which techniques from the list in **1** would you use to memorize them? How
    would you deal with the false friends?

8 Add some more adjectives for describing people's characters to the words in **7**.
Choose three adjectives to describe the qualities of an ideal friend or partner. In
some cases you may want to use the noun form, e.g. *honesty, sensitivity* (see page 83).

Pronunciation Word stress

1 **Look back at the adjectives in 7. Which ones have the main stress on the first
    syllable? Mark the main stress in the others. Say them out loud.**

2 **Most two-syllable English nouns and adjectives have the main stress on the
    first syllable. Sometimes the stress doesn't shift when a word changes from an
    adjective to a noun, even if a syllable is added:**

honest (adjective) / **hon**esty (noun), **ser**ious (adjective) / **ser**iousness (noun)

Sometimes, though, the stress does change:

sensitive (adjective) / sensi**tiv**ity (noun), sympa**thet**ic (adjective) / **sym**pathy (noun)

**Look at script 1.3 on page 124. Mark the main stress of the words in italics.
1.3 Listen and check your answers.**

---

9 Work in groups and discuss
these questions.

1   What characteristics make
    an ideal (a) boss,
    (b) colleague, (c) employee?
2   What characteristics do
    men and women look for
    in (a) a friendship,
    (b) a relationship?

Formal and informal greetings

❶ How do you greet people in your country? What differences are there between formal and informal greetings? Do you have more than one form of *you*? Do you use titles when addressing certain people? When do you use first names?

❷ Work in groups. Read the text and decide whether it refers to a country in Europe, North Africa, Latin America, or South-East Asia. Then discuss which country it might be.

If you hurry introductions with an _____, whether with the man at the roadside food-stall or the head of a major corporation, it will be interpreted as disrespect. On first introduction (both for *hello* and *goodbye*), _____s shake hands with a very light touch, slightly bow their heads and smile. Although the clasp is very gentle (nearly limp by American standards), it's of long duration, ten to fourteen seconds; firm grips aren't appreciated here. Afterwards, _____s often bring their hands back to their chests to show that the greeting is from the heart. After this, handshakes are only used to offer congratulations, to bid farewell to someone leaving on a long voyage, or conversely, to welcome them back again.

Because physical contact between the sexes (except between married and engaged couples) is near nil in Muslim and Hindu cultures, women should shake hands with an _____ man only if he initiates it. Otherwise a slight bow is appropriate. Traditional Muslims say *As salaam aleikum* (Peace upon you) when greeting each other and when entering a store or office. Older generation Hindus offer a *namaste*, a slight bow with the palms of the hands together.

Passport Guides

❸ Look at these greetings and introductions.

    a Hi, Bill, how are *you doing*?
    b How *are you*?
    c Pleased to *meet you*.
    d Hi, Kate, good to *see you* again.
    e May I *introduce myself*?
    f Hello, Sal, this is Riccardo.
    g Good morning, I'm Angus Brogdon.
    h Peter, this is Kim. Kim, this is Kate.
    i Hi there!

  1 Decide whether they are formal (F), informal (I), or neutral (N). Then decide whether you would use them face to face, or on the phone, or both. Could any of them be used in an email?

  2 Which could you use when you have not met someone before?

 Pocket Book page 32

Pronunciation

Which of the words in italics in phrases (a) to (e) should take the main stress?
🔊 1.4 **Listen and check your answers.**

As a general rule, pronouns don't usually take the main stress, unless:

    you want to show interest – *And* **you**, *how are* **you**?
    you want to specify one person rather than another – *I gave it to* **her**, *not to* **him**.

🔊 1.5 **Listen and compare the difference.**

4 You're going to hear four short conversations where people greet and introduce each other. Before you listen, read the information and decide whether you think each one will be (a) informal, (b) formal, or (c) neutral.

1 A client phones a company he knows well, but talks to someone he has never spoken to before.

2 A lawyer meets a very important client for the first time. They both introduce themselves and their colleagues to each other.

3 A manager leaves a message for a person she has never met with someone at a company she's never contacted before.

4 Two colleagues who know each other well meet for the first time in several weeks. One of them introduces a new colleague to the other.

🎧 **1.6** Listen and check your ideas. Is the level of formality the same as you would expect in your country? What do the speakers say to:

– introduce themselves and put themselves in context?

– introduce another person and put them in context?

Note When you are greeting or introducing yourself to someone, especially for the first time, it is important to use the right level of formality. It is a good idea to put yourself in context when you are meeting someone for the first time, or if you have not spoken to them for a long time. It helps to tell them what you do or where you work (*I work for CPMD, I'm calling from CPMD in London*), or remind them of your last contact (*We met last year at the conference in Frankfurt, We spoke on the phone ... , I sent you an email ...*).

5 🎧 **1.6** Listen to extracts from two of the conversations again. Compare the ways in which the speakers:

– address and greet each other

– introduce their colleagues

– ask about a journey / trip

– put themselves and their colleagues in context.

Turn to the listening scripts on pages 124–5 to help you.

6 Work in pairs.

1 Look at the following scenarios and decide what kind of language should be used, formal or informal, and why. Would it be appropriate to use first names, or not?

a You are at **an exhibition.** You want to **introduce yourself** to the Sales Manager of an American company you have **never met before.** You want to **find out more** about his company because you are interested in working for them.

b You are on a **fact-finding** visit to a **Korean company.** There is the possibility of a joint venture. You want to **introduce your (female) colleague** to a technician from the Korean company.

c You need **to contact an English person** you have only met once before, **socially,** about a year ago. They were very friendly last time you met, but you aren't sure if they'll **remember you.**

d You have been **working in a German company** for several months. You want to say **goodbye** to the CEO (Chief Executive Officer) who, until today, you haven't met since **your first week.**

2 Act out each scenario.

1 What are your views on the rules of conversation? Look at these statements and decide if you agree or disagree with them. Tick the appropriate box.

		Agree	Disagree
1	I'm happy to start a conversation with anyone.	☐	☐
2	I usually wait for someone else to start a conversation with me.	☐	☐
3	Long silences during a conversation make me uncomfortable.	☐	☐
4	Silence during a conversation is OK – it's thinking time.	☐	☐
5	If someone talks for too long, it shows a lack of respect.	☐	☐
6	It's important to show interest when someone is speaking.	☐	☐
7	It's sometimes OK to interrupt someone who is speaking.	☐	☐

Compare your answers with a partner.

2 The Athabaskans and the Western Apaches are native North Americans. Work in pairs. Read these two articles and discuss the questions.

The Western Apaches do not feel obliged to 'introduce' people who don't know each other. Eventually, it is assumed, 'strangers' will begin to speak. 'Introductions' or other verbal routines are viewed as unnecessary.

'Strangers' who are quick to start a conversation are viewed with suspicion. A typical reaction to such individuals is that they 'want something' – money, labor, or transportation. Another common reaction to talkative 'strangers' is that they are drunk.

If a stranger is an Anglo, it is assumed that he 'wants to teach us something' (i.e. give orders or instructions) or that he 'wants to make friends in a hurry'. The second response is especially revealing, since the Western Apaches are extremely reluctant to be hurried into friendships with Anglos, or with each other. They believe that the establishment of social relationships is a serious matter which calls for caution, careful judgement and plenty of time.

K H Basso, *Speech and Situated Action*

'Be careful of this one, he talks too much.'

Among Athabaskan groups speech is avoided if there is doubt about social relationships and about how one should behave. And quite lengthy silences are readily tolerated. In interethnic communication, therefore, the English speakers start the conversation, because they want to set about establishing social relations and because the Athabaskans have remained silent. When there is a pause, the English speakers become uncomfortable about the silence well before the Athabaskans do, and therefore start speaking again.

The result is a 'conversation' where English speakers hold the floor for most of the time and control what topics are talked about. The Athabaskans go away from the conversation thinking that English speakers are rude, dominating, superior and self-centred. The English speakers, on the other hand, find the Athabaskans rude, superior, and withdrawn. In fact, hostility arises simply as a result of a failure by both parties to recognize that different groups of people have different norms concerning when and how language is used.

Peter Trudgill, *Sociolinguistics*

1 Are there any similarities between the Western Apache and Athabaskan attitudes to conversation, and attitudes in your own culture? Do you know any other cultures that have similar attitudes to theirs?

2 What is the effect of contrasting attitudes to norms of conversation like those illustrated in each of the articles?

3 What lessons about making conversation can be learned from the articles?

Social exchange

❸ 🔊 1.7 Two people are meeting for the first time before a training course. Listen to the conversation and answer the questions.

1 Do you think the man's behaviour is acceptable? Why, or why not?
2 What impression do you think the woman has of the man by the end of this conversation? Why do you think she formed this impression?

❹ 🔊 1.8 Listen to a different conversation. It takes place in the same situation.

1 What makes it better than the first one?
2 How do the two speakers take responsibility for the development of the conversation? How do they keep the conversation going?
3 How do the speakers show interest in what the other person is saying?

Pronunciation

❶ 🔊 1.9 **Listen to these responses. Does the speaker's intonation rise (↗) or fall (↘) at the end?**

Oh, are you?	That's excellent.	OK, right.
Oh, is it?	Oh, really?	How interesting.

❷ 🔊 1.9 **Listen again and repeat the responses. Try to use the same intonation as the speaker.**

---

❺ Work in pairs and act out a similar scenario. You have both arrived for the first day of a seminar. You have not met before. Coffee is provided. Make sure you:

– exchange greetings and introduce yourselves to each other
– try to keep the conversation going
– show interest in what the other person is saying.

Use this framework to help you.

Student A	Student B
Open the conversation with a question.	
	Respond – add a comment or information.
Respond positively and show interest.	
	Ask a question.
Respond – add a comment or information.	
	Respond positively and show interest.

❻ Two other people are meeting before the seminar. This time, they have met before, but haven't seen each other for a few months. Work in pairs. Make a list of things they might talk about, then improvise a dialogue with your partner. Make sure you:

– take equal responsibility for keeping the conversation going
– introduce any new topics in a natural way, i.e. don't jump from one topic to another indiscriminately, but link what you say to what the other person has just said
– show interest in what the other person is saying.

❼ 🔊 1.10 Listen and compare the dialogue with yours. What questions did the speakers ask each other? How did they keep the conversation flowing?

❽ Work in pairs and act out a similar scenario. You have met each other before, but not for some months. Last time you met, one of you was about to work abroad for three months, the other one was about to be promoted to a new job. Try to keep the conversation flowing naturally, and remember to sound positive.

Looking back

LANGUAGE FOCUS   **Talking about the past**

1 Who are your country's most famous national heroes, (a) from the past, (b) from the present? What fields do they come from (e.g. politics, the arts, science, sport)?

Many of the heroes of recent times come from the world of sport. What are your country's most popular sports? Who are its most famous sporting heroes?

2 2.1 You are going to listen to an interview with Sir Bobby Charlton, one of Britain's best-known sporting heroes. He was a star player for Manchester United, England's most successful football club, in the 1950s and 1960s.

Before you listen, decide whether you think the statements below are true (T) or false (F). Then listen and check your ideas.

1 Footballers used to get paid about the same as other people. ☐
2 Footballers were famous but not generally recognized in the street. ☐
3 There are more pressures now on footballers than there used to be. ☐
4 There was no critical analysis after football matches. ☐
5 Admission prices to football matches were discussed in Parliament. ☐
6 The media didn't use to hound the players like they do today. ☐
7 Footballers in the past used to have fairly normal working lives. ☐
8 Fans today are very affectionate towards players. ☐
9 Bobby Charlton was part of the England team that won the World Cup. ☐
10 Bobby Charlton is not involved in football any more. ☐

3 2.1 Listen to the interview again.

1 How does Bobby Charlton think the role of football has changed since he first got involved?
2 Have similar changes taken place in other sports?
3 Do you think sportspeople today have easier or more difficult lives than in the past?

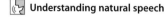 **Understanding natural speech**

4 Bobby Charlton referred to Munich as the worst moment of his career. Read this account of what happened at Munich.

1 Why were the Manchester United team in Munich?

2 What was the probable reason for the crash?

On the afternoon of 6th February 1958, eight members of the Manchester United football team died tragically in a plane crash in Munich. The team, including the young Bobby Charlton, and their manager, Matt Busby, were travelling home to England from Belgrade. Having won the English football championship the previous year, they were competing in the European Champions' Cup competition, and had just won an important match against Red Star Belgrade.

The flight left Belgrade in fine weather, but conditions in Germany were not so good; it had been snowing and the temperature had fallen to below zero. The plane landed at Munich airport to take on more fuel, but the pilot had been having some problems with the engines, and there was a delay while some checks were made. After he had completed the refuelling, he radioed the control tower to say he was ready for take-off.

The pilot made two unsuccessful attempts to take off, but couldn't get enough power from the engines. As he was trying to take off for the third time, the disaster happened. The plane was increasing speed and had almost reached the end of the runway when it seemed suddenly to lose power. Out of control, it crashed into some buildings, and then burst into flames.

A total of 23 people lost their lives, including eight of the players, management staff, journalists, and aircrew. Matt Busby's dream of Manchester United becoming European Champions died that day in Munich, along with most of the team he had created. It was another ten years before that dream was finally realized.

Past tenses review, *used to / would*

1 Highlight the past tense forms in these sentences.

a After the pilot had completed the refuelling, he radioed the control tower.

b The pilot made two unsuccessful attempts to take off.

c As he was trying to take off, the disaster happened.

d The plane crashed into some buildings, and then burst into flames.

e The temperature had fallen to below zero.

f The pilot had been having some problems with the engines.

2 Which past tense form do we use to describe:

1 something in progress at a particular time in the past?

2 a past action or situation that happened earlier than another past action or situation?

3 a longer action or situation that began at one point in the past and continued until a more recent point in the past?

4 completed or repeated actions and situations in the past?

Used to and *would*

3 Look at these sentences based on the interview with Sir Bobby Charlton.

*I remember when I **used to** go and watch Newcastle United playing.*

*Footballers **didn't use to** get paid very much, not like today.*

*You **would** go home, and you **would** do a little bit of some recreation … and you'd play the game on a Saturday.*

***Used to** and **would** can both refer to actions or habits in the past.*

1 Which form contrasts the way things were in the past with the way they are now?

2 Which form refers to a sequence of actions in the past?

3 We usually put adverbs before *used to*, but after *would*. Compare:

*I **never** used to get up for breakfast on Sundays, I **always** used to sleep late.*

*I would **never** get up for breakfast on Sundays, I would **always** sleep late.*

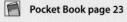 Pocket Book page 23

 Pocket Book page 15

5 Underline the correct verb form, using the information in italics.

1 I didn't know she (skied / was skiing). *I didn't think she knew how to ski.*

2 I remembered that Jack (lived / had lived) in London. *Jack doesn't live in London any more.*

3 She (had been sitting / had sat) at the computer all day. *Her eyes were tired and her back hurt.*

4 He realized someone (was / had been) in the next room. *He wasn't alone in the house.*

5 I (left / was leaving) the room when Ann came in. *I met Ann in the doorway.*

6 When I got home I realized I (had lost / had been losing) my keys. *They weren't in my bag or my pockets.*

6 How much time do you spend on leisure activities, compared to ten years ago? Make notes in the table below and then discuss your answers with a partner. Explain why things have changed.

Example: *I used to spend at least two hours a day reading, but now I only spend about twenty minutes. I'm just too busy.*

When I was younger, I would go out four or five nights a week – I'd go to bars with friends, and I would always go to clubs on Friday and Saturday nights. Now I just don't have the energy.

activity	time spent 10 years ago	time spent now
reading		
going out in the evening		
doing sports and exercise		
having lunch		
listening to music		
sleeping		
seeing friends		
travelling		
working / studying		
doing exactly what you want		

7 Complete the sentences and then discuss them with your partner.

1 Until I was about 18 I had never realized / noticed that …

2 I used to think that …

3 This time last year I was …

4 Until recently I had never been to …

5 People didn't use to …

6 While I was travelling to work this morning …

7 When I was younger I would …

8 Before I started my present job …

Remembering the past

8 2.2 Listen to four people talking about their childhood memories. Were their experiences mainly positive or negative?

Verbs + infinitive or gerund

Some common verbs can be followed either by the infinitive form (*to* + verb) or the gerund (verb + *-ing*). The choice of infinitive or gerund affects the meaning.

Compare these pairs of sentences from the four extracts. Listen to the extracts again and explain the difference in meaning.

a I really **liked going** to parties and clubs.
b My father always **liked to keep** going.
c I **remember having** to do a lot of sport at school.
d I always **remembered to put** them all back.
e It just seemd cruel, so I **stopped going**.
f Sometimes we didn't even **stop to have** lunch.
g I certainly don't **regret giving up**.
h I **regret to say** it never worked.
i My father would **try to entertain** us with stories and jokes.
j Sometimes I would **try pretending** I was ill.

📖 Pocket Book page 7

9 Underline the most appropriate form in these questions. Then ask and answer the questions with a partner.

1 What things would you like *doing / to do* that you don't have time for?
2 Which things that you liked *doing / to do* as a child have you stopped *doing / to do* now?
3 If you were on an eight-hour car journey, how often would you stop *eating / to eat*?
4 What things do you have to remember *doing / to do* before going on holiday?
5 What do you remember *doing / to do* in your first English lesson?
6 Is there anything in the past that you regret *to say / saying* to someone?
7 What should you try *to do / doing* if you feel stressed at work?
8 Have you ever tried *to give up / giving up* something that is bad for you (e.g. smoking)?

Talking point

10 Work in groups and discuss these topics using your own ideas and experience of the past.

– a time when you didn't remember to do something important
– something you did in the past and now regret doing
– something you still do that you wish you had stopped doing
– something you tried to do and succeeded.

11 Look back at the article narrating the events of the Munich air crash on page 13. Think of a news story from the past, or an event which you witnessed or were involved in, perhaps when travelling. It does not need to be a disaster. Work in pairs or small groups. Take turns to narrate your story.

Before you start, spend a few minutes reviewing the use of the different past tense forms.

Understanding unfamiliar words

Learning tip

1 First, always try to establish what the word is – a noun, a verb, or an adjective. Then match it with possible words from your own language that seem to make sense.

2 Guess the meaning of an unknown word from its context. Find clues to its meaning in the sentences before and after it.

3 Many writers dislike using the same word twice, so they use a synonym. See if the problem word has an equivalent in the previous or following sentences.

4 If a word you know seems to be in completely the wrong context, this might be because it is a false friend.

5 Note down new words that have a similar meaning to words you already know. Find examples which differentiate between these similar meanings.

1 Michael White works as a translator for the British government in London. He speaks five different languages fluently. Read his tips on what to do when you meet a new word when reading a text.

Do you already use any of these techniques? Which ones do you think would work for you?

2 Look at the text. Which of Michael's tips would you use to work out the meanings of the highlighted words? Which ones would not be useful? Why?

> Translating is an enormously **costly** and time-consuming business. A third of all administration costs in the European Union are **taken up** with paying translators and interpreters. In fact, one in three employees in the EU is engaged in translating papers and speeches. A compelling reason for an international language is the frequency and **gravity** of misunderstandings **owing to** difficulties of translation. The 1905 **draft** of a treaty between Russia and Japan, written both in French and English, treated the English *control* and French *contrôler* as synonyms when in fact the English form means 'to dominate or hold power' while the French simply means 'to inspect'. The treaty nearly **fell apart** as a result.
>
> Bill Bryson, *Mother Tongue*

What other techniques do you use when you meet a new word?

3 2.3 As part of the interviewing process for his job as an interpreter for the British government, Michael White was visited at his home by a man from Security. Listen and answer the questions.

1 What did Michael do before the man from Security arrived?
2 Why did he remove some books, and then move the other books together?
3 What two things did Michael think he could be doing when the man arrived?
4 What did he expect the man to do during the visit?
5 What did the man actually do?
6 How did Michael feel? How did his feelings show?

How do you act when people visit your home? How do you feel?

Look, sound, seem

4 Read script 2.3 on page 126. Find all the examples of *look*, *sound*, and *seem*.

How do we normally use *look (like)*, *sound (like)*, and *seem (like)*? Which goes with (a) an adjective (phrase), and (b) a noun (phrase)?

📖 **Pocket Book page 24**

SOUTHERN IRELAND

Beautiful stone-built farmhouse set in spectacular countryside in County Cork. Close to Kinsale and Cork, yet within easy reach of the rugged mountains and unspoilt beaches of the south-west coast. The main house sleeps 6–8 people, plus space for 4 more in an annexe if required. Heated swimming pool, mature gardens, etc. £300 per week.

Pronunciation

① 🎧 **2.4 Listen to two people discussing the advertisement. Underline the words they stress in these sentences. Mark the places where they pause. Why do they pause in the places marked?**

    A I think it sounds fantastic and it's just what we've been looking for.

    B Well, it certainly looks like a lovely place but it seems really expensive.

② **Mark where you think the stresses and pauses will come in these sentences.**

    a It looks like a really interesting job and it's very well paid.

    b She seems very nice but there's something about her I don't quite trust.

    c It sounds like the perfect house for us and it's got lots of space and a huge garden.

③ 🎧 **2.5 Listen and check your answers. Then repeat as closely as possible what the speakers say.**

More about infinitives and gerunds

① **Look at these sentences based on the interview with Richard Smith. Two of them are wrong. Which ones, and why?**

    a I even considered to remove everything personal.

    b I didn't want to risk creating the wrong impression.

    c Should I offer to show him round the house?

    d I managed making him a coffee, …

② **A number of common verbs are normally followed *either* by a gerund (verb + *-ing*) or an infinitive form (*to* + verb). Put these verbs into the correct box.**

admit	avoid	decide	enjoy	finish	imagine	miss	*refuse*	suggest
agree	consider	deny	expect	hope	manage	offer	risk	want

verb + … -*ing*	**verb + *to* …**
admit	refuse

③ **Choose six of the verbs in ② and invent questions to ask your partner. For example:**

*Have you ever **admitted making** a really bad mistake?*

*Have you ever **refused to obey** an instruction?*

📖 **Pocket Book page 7**

❺ Complete the quiz. Underline the correct word, or words, in italics and put a cross on the line to indicate your estimated percentage.

How much of what you *hear / listen to* and *see / watch* on TV do you believe?	What proportion of your evenings do you spend *seeing / watching* TV or *listening to / hearing* the radio?	How much do you *look / look like* your mother?	To what extent do you think your English accent *seems like / sounds like* a real English accent?	What percentage of the ideas generated in your company *seem / sound* good or *seem / look* good on paper, but in reality don't work?
0% 100%	0% 100%	0% 100%	0% 100%	0% 100%

Work in pairs. Think of similar questions to add to questions 1 to 5. Then interview another pair.

① Look at these phrases used on the phone. Decide which would be said by the person answering the phone (A), and which would be said by the person making the call (C).

a Can I speak to Jamie Bush?

b This is Neil Wood returning your call.

c Could you put me through to Hilary Cotton?

d Can I give her a message?

e Would you like me to take a message for her?

f Sorry, what did you say your name was?

g Shall I get her to phone you back?

h Would you like her to call you?

i I'll phone again later.

j OK. I'll get back to you later.

k What's your name?

l Who's calling?

m Nate Hancock, please.

n I'll try to connect you.

o I'll put you through.

p Can I ask who's calling?

Which phrases seem easiest to use or most familiar to you? Are there any you would not use? Why? (e.g. too complicated, not polite enough)

📖 Pocket Book page 36

Giving information

② Read the dialogue. At each stage, what else could / should the person answering the call say? Fill the gaps with a suitable phrase.

A Good morning. Could I speak to Roberta Lee, please?

B She's not in today _____

A Well, do you think you could tell me where I could reach her?

B I don't know where she is _____

A Has she got a mobile phone?

B I'm not sure _____

A Is there anyone else I could talk to?

B Everybody is at lunch at the moment _____

A Well, can I leave a message?

B Yes _____

A Could you tell her that Gavin Milsom called. That's M-I-L-S-O-M. From Mediatech in Dublin. And if she could ring me after ten o'clock your time.

B OK _____

A Thank you for your help.

B _____ Goodbye.

③ 🔊 2.6 Listen to the complete conversation and compare your answers. Discuss whether or not the extra things the secretary says in the recording are important.

> ## Pronunciation
>
> ① 🔊 2.7 Listen again to these phrases from the conversation. Mark the words that are stressed. Why are these words stressed?
>
> a ... I could find out from a colleague.
>
> b ... let me just check – no, I'm afraid she hasn't.
>
> c ... if you give me your name and number, I'll get someone to call you.
>
> d ... and you want her to call you after ten o'clock our time.
>
> ② Practise saying the phrases, paying attention to the stressed words.

④ Work in pairs. Improvise two telephone conversations. Student A should turn to page 112. Student B should turn to page 116.

Choosing the right register

Note Typically, a more formal register uses more complete sentences, is less direct and idiomatic, and uses more impersonal forms. An informal register uses shorter sentences, more direct and idiomatic phrases, and is more personal.

⑤ 🔊 2.8 Listen to these two telephone conversations. The content of both conversations is the same, but the register is different. Decide which one is:

a informal, between two people who have frequent contact

b formal, between two people who are speaking for the first time.

⑥ 🔊 2.8 Listen again and write down the key words and expressions that helped you to decide the level of formality or the relationship between the two people. Then look at the scripts on page 126.

⑦ Work in pairs. Use the outline dialogue below to improvise:

1 an informal conversation between two people who have frequent contact

2 a formal conversation between two people speaking for the first time.

SWITCHBOARD	Tecno PLC.
JONES	Val Jones. Nic Smith?
SWITCHBOARD	OK.
SMITH	Smith.
JONES	Jones. We need to discuss the project. Monday OK?
SMITH	No, Monday I'm busy. Thursday?
JONES	Ten o'clock?
SMITH	Two o'clock.
JONES	OK. Two o'clock. Bye.
SMITH	Bye.

Interrupting and clarifying

⑧ What phrases could you use on the telephone to let someone know:

1 you can't hear what they're saying?

2 you don't hear a particular word?

3 you didn't catch their name?

4 you want the them to spell their company's name?

5 you understand everything that they have said except for the first part?

📖 Pocket Book page 36

⑨ 🔊 2.9 Listen to this conversation. The operator is having some difficulty in understanding the caller.

1 What phrases does she use for the five problems listed in ⑧?

2 How does she signal that she wants to interrupt?

⑩ Work in pairs.

1 Invent and practise your own telephone conversations, deciding who you are and what the scenario is. The conversation must be very formal; some complicated message must be taken; one of the speakers must speak too fast or too quietly at first.

2 Now invent a similar conversation with a different partner. This time the conversation is informal; a series of arrangements must be made; there is some misunderstanding over times, days, etc.

Conversation topics

1 What topics do you think are suitable for making conversation with acquaintances from another country? Is there a difference between what you can talk about in a work-related context (e.g. before a meeting) and in a social context like a dinner party? Are there any topics you would definitely avoid?

2 Roger E. Axtell is the author of a series of books giving advice to business travellers. In *Do's and Taboos of Hosting International Visitors*, he outlines what are good and bad topics of conversation.

Work in groups. Look at the table and decide which country or countries in each group the topics refer to. Check your answers on page 120.

	Good topics	Countries			Bad topics	Countries	
1	history architecture gardening	☐ Australia ☐ England	☐ France ☐ Nigeria	6	religion Northern Ireland money	☐ Canada ☐ Ireland	☐ the UK ☐ the USA
2	culture history religion	☐ Israel ☐ Lebanon	☐ Peru ☐ the Philippines	7	personal questions religion politics	☐ Finland ☐ France	☐ Hungary ☐ Ireland
3	politics soccer family	☐ Argentina ☐ Brazil	☐ Italy ☐ Japan	8	political unrest secondary role of women	☐ China ☐ Pakistan	☐ South Korea ☐ Turkmenistan
4	children criticizing politics the Royal Family	☐ Belgium ☐ England	☐ the Netherlands ☐ Thailand	9	politics religion sex	☐ Iran ☐ Iraq	☐ Jordan ☐ Lebanon
5	religion natural beauty wildlife	☐ Kenya ☐ Poland	☐ Singapore ☐ South Africa	10	employment salary social status	☐ Norway ☐ Portugal	☐ Uganda ☐ Vietnam

3 🎧 2.10 Listen to these four people talking about what are and are not acceptable topics of conversation at a dinner party. Make a note of the topics they mention. Do they refer to any of the topics from **2**? Do they consider them acceptable or not?

Speaker 1 (Ireland)   Speaker 3 (Australia)
Speaker 2 (India)   Speaker 4 (Germany)

One speaker mentions that there are differences between formal and informal situations, another says that forty years ago people didn't use to talk about certain topics. Can you think of similar examples from your own culture?

4 Complete these sentences. Then discuss them with your partner.

1 When I'm listening to someone speaking, I spend most of the time …
2 I find it difficult to talk about (e.g. politics, religion, personal matters) …
3 I like talking about …
4 I find it quite difficult to listen to someone who …
5 Interrupting to ask questions when someone is speaking is …

How is listening to someone in a work-related context different from a social context?

Social exchange

5 🎧 2.11 Listen to two social conversations between colleagues at work. In each case, make a note of the topics they discuss.

6 🎧 2.11 Listen again. How did the speakers:

1   initiate a new topic?   3   return to the topic?
2   change the topic?   4   respond positively and show interest?

Make a note of the phrases they used.

📖 Pocket Book page 33

7 Work in pairs. Improvise a social conversation following this framework. Try to keep the conversation going as long as possible.

Student A

Open the conversation by initiating a topic.
Try to maintain the discussion of this topic.

Student B

Listen to A and respond positively.
At a suitable moment, change the topic to something you want to talk about.
Try to maintain the discussion of this topic.

Listen to B and respond positively.
Try to change the topic back to what you were talking about before.
Try to maintain the discussion of this topic.

Listen to A and respond positively.
Try to change the topic back to what you were talking about before.
Try to maintain the discussion of this topic.

8 Work in pairs or groups. Begin a conversation about one of these topics. As you speak, check that your listeners understand you. As you listen, show the speaker that you are following them.

– how you got your first job and what it was
– how you met your husband / wife / partner
– the worst holiday you've ever had
– the most expensive meal you've ever had
– an embarrassing episode at work
– the most frightening experience you've had
– your first English lesson

📖 Pocket Book page 33

9 Work in groups. Imagine a social situation in which some of you are the hosts and some of you are visitors. Decide what the context is, and who you are.

Improvise a conversation. The aim is to keep the conversation going, with a good atmosphere. Change or maintain the topic of conversation as appropriate. Show interest in what the other speakers are saying by asking questions and making positive comments.

Review Unit **A**

Present tenses

❶ Work in pairs. Compare these pairs of sentences and decide why one tense is used in the first sentence and a different tense is used in the second sentence.

1 I'm living here for six months.
   She's been living there for six months.
2 This is the first time I've eaten Chinese food.
   I eat Chinese food about once a month.
3 The *Financial Times* index has gone up 6% in the last three months.
   Prices have been going up steadily all year.
4 Ouch! I've cut my finger.
   We've been cutting down on expenses.
5 We're manufacturing far more cars this year.
   We manufacture mainly for the Far East.

Past tenses

❷ Put the verbs in brackets into the correct past tense.

1 I only _____ (ski) for five minutes when I _____ (break) my leg.
2 She _____ (meet) him while she _____ (stay) in a hotel in Paris.
3 They never _____ (go) to the US before, that's why they _____ (want) to go.
4 As I _____ (get on) the train, I _____ (realize) I _____ (leave) my briefcase in the taxi.

used to and would

❸ Underline *would* where it is possible to use it in place of *used to*.

1 My father *used to / would* have an old MG sports car. He *used to / would* spend hours working on it. At weekends, he *used to / would* sometimes take it out for a drive, but he *used to / would* never take it out in the rain.
2 Until a few years ago we *used to / would* do all our work over the phone, or we *used to / would* write a letter or send a fax. It *used to / would* take us hours to do the simplest task. Now we just use email.

Infinitive or gerund?

❹ Match the beginnings of these sentences with a suitable ending.

1	I stopped to look at shop windows	a	from beginning to end.
2	I stopped looking at shop windows	b	when I realized how late it was.
3	I remembered seeing her	c	to play tennis more often.
4	I remembered to see her	d	while I was walking round town.
5	I really love	e	playing tennis.
6	I'd really like	f	even the exact clothes she was wearing.
7	I heard her tell the story	g	as I was passing her office door.
8	I heard her telling the story	h	and tell her about your proposal.

Which of these verbs are normally followed by a verb in the gerund (*-ing*) form, and which by a verb in the infinitive form with *to*? Write a sentence using each verb.

admit	consider	deny	manage	offer	risk	want

Introductions and greetings

❺ Work in groups of three (A, B, and C), and improvise the scenarios. Put each person, in context. For example, *This is Peter. He works in the Marketing Department.*

1 A introduces B to his/her new boss (C), who is considerably older.
2 B is working on a project with a foreign partner (C). B introduces C to a colleague (A). You are all the same age, with the same level of responsibility.
3 C has just returned from one year abroad. A asks C a few questions before introducing B, a colleague. B then asks C some further questions.

Making contact by phone

6 Write two conversations, one formal and one informal, for each of these situations.

1 Alex Jones, please.
   Your name?
   Spelling?
   Message?
   Hold?
   Call later.

2 Marianne Walter, please.
   In a meeting. Message?
   Yes. Paul Martin called.
   Number?
   Yes. Call back?
   Give her message.

Giving information

7 Work in pairs and improvise a phone call. Think of a fictitious name for yourself and for a person you want to contact, and a reason why you want to contact them. Your partner is a colleague of the person you want to contact. Invent a short message to leave for them. Give them a fictitious phone number or email address, or both. Then change roles and improvise another phone call.

Student A Make the call – leave your details and the message. Try to speak fast, as if you are in a hurry.

Student B The person Student A wants to talk to is unavailable (give a reason why). Take Student A's message and make sure you repeat all the details. Ask for clarification where necessary.

Interrupting and clarifying

8 What phrases would you use on the phone when:

1 someone is speaking very quietly?
2 you don't understand their name?
3 you aren't sure how the name of their company is spelled?
4 you aren't sure exactly what they mean?

Initiating, changing, and returning to topics

9 Work in pairs. Choose one of these topics to talk about:

– the last film you saw
– a recent holiday
– violence in sport

– adult material on the Internet
– a new project you're working on
– something you heard on the news.

Student A Initiate the conversation and politely try to keep the conversation going on your topic.

Student B Show that you are following what A is saying and show interest, but try to change to your topic.

Vocabulary

10 Write two sentences for each group of words, that clearly show the difference between them.

1 *actually* and *currently*
2 *control* and *check*
3 *sensitive* and *sensible*

4 *library* and *bookshop*
5 *watch* and *look at*
6 *look like*, *seem like*, and *sound like*

Self-check box

	YES	NO	📖		YES	NO	📖
Present Simple	☐	☐	16	Introductions and greetings	☐	☐	32
Present Continuous	☐	☐	16	Making contact	☐	☐	36
Present Perfect	☐	☐	13,16	Messages	☐	☐	36
Present Perfect Continuous	☐	☐	13,16	Interrupting and clarifying	☐	☐	36
Past Simple	☐	☐	13	Initiating, changing, and			
Past Continuous	☐	☐	15	returning to topics	☐	☐	33
Past Perfect	☐	☐	15	Vocabulary: false friends	☐	☐	26
Past Perfect Continuous	☐	☐	15	*watch, look at*	☐	☐	26
used to, would	☐	☐	15	*look, seem, sound (like)*	☐	☐	24
Verbs + infinitive or gerund	☐	☐	7				

Travel and time

OVERVIEW
- Future forms review
- *If + will/going to/could/may*
- Collocations with *travel/trip/journey/ flight/tour*
- Verb + noun collocations
- *miss/lose/waste*
- Expressing attitudes to time
- Arranging meetings
- Asking and dealing with questions

LANGUAGE FOCUS	**Plans and predictions**

1 How often do you travel abroad for holidays, or on business? Where do you usually go? Do you take a guidebook with you? Why, or why not?

In groups, discuss which countries you:

- have already visited
- are planning to visit at some time in the future
- are going to visit this year
- will probably never visit.

2 Look at the covers of these travel guides and read the information. What type of person do you think they appeal to? For example, business travellers, backpackers on a limited budget, independent travellers with money to spend, members of organized tour groups.

In the summer of 1982,
Mark Ellingham set out to travel around Greece. However, he was surprised to find that none of the existing travel guides provided all the information he wanted.

He decided to write his own guidebook, one which not only gave a comprehensive account of historical sites and monuments, but also provided information about the people, politics, and contemporary culture, and with practical details about places to stay, where to eat, nightlife, and how to find the best beaches. It was intended to be entertaining as well as informative.

So the first *Rough Guide* was published, and from then the list grew rapidly. Today, Mark Ellingham is still travelling and writing, and Rough Guides publish over 100 titles, aimed at providing up-to-date information for independent-minded travellers of all ages, on all budgets.

3 [🎧] 3.1 Listen to this interview with Mark Ellingham, series editor and founder of Rough Guides. Answer the questions.

1 What aspects of a country does a travel guide writer have to be interested in?
2 Which countries has Mark written books about?
3 Which areas of the world would he like to visit?
4 Which countries is he going to visit this year, and why?
5 Which area of the world will he probably never visit?
6 For which country does Rough Guides *not* publish a guide, and why?
7 Which European country is going to become a more popular tourist destination, and why?
8 Which other country will see an escalation of European travellers, and why?
9 What projects are Rough Guides planning for the near future?
10 What approach do the Rough Guides take in the way they are written?

[👂] **Understanding natural speech**

Future forms review

1 Analyse the ways of talking about the future shown in the examples and answer the questions.

1 In which case has Mark probably already made some plans?
   a **I'll go** to Morocco in a month or two.
   b **I'm going** to Morocco in a month or two.

2 Which form indicates that a definite arrangement has been made?
   a **I'm travelling** to Morocco next month.
   b **I'm going to travel** to Morocco next month.

3 Which form indicates that there might already be signs of this trend happening?
   a **I think there will be** more tourism in southern India.
   b **I think there's going to** be more tourism in southern India.

4 Why is *will* used in a and *going to* used in b?
   a **I'll check** that information for you as soon as I can.
   b **I'm going to spend** this afternoon planning my trip to Croatia.

5 Which form is not possible here? Is there any real difference in meaning between the other two?
   a There are some countries that **I'll probably never visit**.
   b There are some countries that **I'm probably never going to visit**.
   c There are some countries that **I'm probably never visiting**.

2 Which future forms can be used to talk about:

1 plans and intentions   2 arrangements   3 predictions?

[📖] **Pocket Book page 6**

4 1 How would you talk about these topics to a friend or colleague? Think carefully about which future forms you would use.
   a Your predictions about changes to your work situation.
   b Any arrangements or plans you have made for the next few weeks.
   c Some changes you believe or hope may happen in your country.
   d Any holiday or business travel plans you have made for the next few months.

2 How could you find out similar information from someone else? Use your ideas from 1 as a basis for questions to ask a partner.

5 Read this short article about the impact of climate change on some tourist destinations.

1 What predictions are made about the effects on:
 – tropical islands and low-lying coastal areas?
 – mountainous regions?

2 Do you think the events predicted are likely or unlikely to happen? Will they affect your own region?

Paradise THREATENED

If current changes to the global climate continue, some of the world's most beautiful holiday destinations **may vanish forever**[1].

For a tropical island paradise like the Maldives, with an average height above sea level of less than two metres, the effects of global warming **will be disastrous**[2]. If the western Antarctic ice shelf melts, **which seems likely**[3], then the world's water level **will rise**[4], and 50% of the Maldives **could disappear**[5].

The sea is predicted to rise by two metres over the next 100 years, or by two centimetres a year. If this happens, there **won't be much left**[6] of the fragile ecosystems surrounding many of the world's tropical islands – Tonga, the Seychelles, and the Cook and Marshall Islands among many others. Even low-lying coastal areas of Europe, such as southern France, the Netherlands, and south-east England, **may be seriously affected**[7].

Global warming **is also likely to have**[8] a catastrophic effect on the world's colder and more mountainous regions. According to experts, central and eastern Himalayan glaciers **could melt**[9] within 40 years, changing a landscape that attracts many climbers and trekkers. In Europe, melting glaciers **are likely to**[10] threaten the safety of mountain villages. A rise in winter temperatures there **will mean**[11] less snow, and this **may well have**[12] a serious impact on the future of major ski resorts.

The Guardian

Making predictions – *if + will, going to, could, may*

  Look at the phrases highlighted in the article. In each case, how certain is the writer that the event will happen?

 a he's absolutely certain
 b he think it's probable
 c he thinks it's possible, but not certain

2 In which sentences is there a condition attached to the prediction?

 Pocket Book pages 6, 12

6 When making predictions, the degree of certainty is expressed by the phrases and adverbs the speaker uses, not only whether they use *will* or *going to* or a modal verb.

Look at sentences 1–8. Decide whether the speakers are:

a   absolutely certain   b   reasonably certain   c   not very certain.

Write your answers in the left-hand box. Which phrases or adverbs helped you?

1   I guess the number of visitors to southern India will escalate.   ☐☐
2   I think Croatia is probably going to become a major destination.   ☐☐
3   We'll definitely see a rise in the number of business travellers.   ☐☐
4   Look! The flight's leaving – if we don't hurry we're going to miss it.   ☐☐
5   I think it's likely that prices are going to go up.   ☐☐
6   I'm not totally convinced that these climate changes will happen.   ☐☐
7   I'm quite sure that business travel is going to get cheaper.   ☐☐
8   I think it may well get more expensive.   ☐☐

📖 Pocket Book pages 6, 12

Pronunciation

🎧 3.2 **Listen to the sentences in ❻. Notice the intonation of the speakers. How certain do they sound? Do you want to change your mind about the level of certainty of any of the sentences? Write your new answers, (a), (b), or (c), in the right-hand box.**

Talking point

7 Mark Ellingham mentioned that he has various plans for Rough Guides. What plans does your company have for the future? In pairs, ask and answer questions about these points.

1   What products/services your company provides, and what different 'slant' you have in relation to your competitors.
2   What kind of brand image/coverage you are aiming for.
3   What new areas you are planning to move into.
4   What other areas your company is looking into, or going to look into.
5   What the next ten years will bring for your company.
6   What's going to happen to you personally in your company in the next few years.

8 Rough Guides are producing around fifteen new titles a year to respond to the rapid growth in the tourist industry, which is now the world's largest employer.

1   Work in groups. Imagine you are a project team with responsibility for developing tourism in your town, country, or region.
    Predict how tourism is going to evolve over the next few years, and discuss what you will do to improve, develop, and exploit your region's:
    – image
    – environment
    – infrastructure
    – accommodation
    – cultural heritage
    – entertainment facilities.

2   Form a new group with one person from each of the other groups. Report your original group's predictions, intentions, and plans. After you have heard each report, try to agree on the best solution.

**Collocations with *travel,*
*trip, journey, voyage, tour***

① Read about the origins of some English words connected with travel.

During the Middle Ages in England people who used to travel would read their **journal**, a traveller's guide outlining the distance that could be covered in a day (French: *jour*). In fact, over the centuries a **journey** changed its meaning from a day's **travel** or even a

day's work (French: *travail*) to the process of getting from A to B – hopefully on time!

The French also gave us the word **tour**, which originally meant a period spent doing one's job (also known as a **turn**). By the beginning of the eighteenth century, a **tour** had come to mean an **excursion** or circuitous **journey** including visits to a number of places in a particular order. Throughout this century, and in particular in the mid to late 1800s, rich English people used to go on the Grand Tour, an educational **journey** through France, Germany, Switzerland, and Italy. Today, many **travel** agents and airline companies organize package **tours** using charter **flights**.

The word **trip** originally meant a short **voyage** in a ship. Within a few decades it was also used to describe someone's experiences while **travelling** on land. Nowadays, a **trip** can be of any length (in terms of distance and time), and it

describes either the **journey** itself or the whole experience, i.e. the **journey** plus any sightseeing or business done in a place.

For the last two centuries, **travel** has generally been used as a verb (though sometimes as an adjective, as in **travel agent**, or as a noun, as in **first-class travel**).

② Underline the correct word in italics. Then work in pairs, asking and answering the questions.

1 Who makes your *trip / travel* arrangements – you, your secretary, your partner?
2 When was your last business *trip / journey / voyage*?
3 How do you *travel / journey* to work?
4 What's the longest *travel / journey* you have ever made?

📖 Pocket Book page 26

③ What is the difference between these pairs of words?

traveller / tourist   itinerary / schedule   guide / courier

What strategies do you use to remember the differences between words with similar meanings?

④ Read the Learning tip. Are the strategies for learning collocations similar to the ones you use? Which do you think is more effective?

Learning tip

1 Make a list of collocations with *travel* and *trip* – *travel agent, travel arrangement, travel expenses, round trip, business trip*. Then, when you have learned the collocations, remove the key words *travel* and *trip*. You're left with a new list which says *agent, arrangements, business, expenses,* etc. Use this new list to test yourself.

2 If you have a very visual memory, try to do drawings of things. For example, draw a ship with the word *voyage* written in it, a train with *journey* written in it, or write the word *trip* with a circle round it to remind you that a trip returns to where you started from.

Verb–noun collocations

⑤ Match the verbs and verb phrases in Box 1 with the nouns in Box 2.

1	
get into / out of	board
go / travel by	arrive at / in
fly with	go through
land in / at	get on / off

2		
an airline	(a) plane	a town / city / country
(a) taxi	an airport	your destination
a terminal	home	underground / metro
customs	a station	
(a) train	(a) ferry	

6 🔊 3.3 Listen to two people describing difficult journeys. As you listen, check the combinations you created in **5**. Which ones did they use? Did they use any combinations you didn't think of?

Miss, *lose*, **and** *waste*

7 🔊 3.4 Listen to this extract from the recording again and fill in the spaces, using an appropriate verb.

'When I got out of the taxi and had to pay, I realized I'd _____ my wallet, at least I thought I had. In fact, I _____ so much time trying to find it that I _____ my train.'

What does this tell you about the use of the verbs *miss*, *lose*, and *waste*?

📕 Pocket Book page 24

8 1 Which of these nouns collocate with the verbs *miss*, *lose*, and *waste*? Which nouns can combine with more than one of the verbs?

an appointment	energy	a job	a talent
confidence	faith	a lesson	a target
control	food	money	time
a customer	a friend	an opportunity	a train
a deadline	interest	resources	value

2 What is the difference between:
   a *waste* time and *lose* time?
   b *miss* an opportunity and *waste* an opportunity?

9 Complete the sentences with an appropriate form of *miss*, *lose*, or *waste*. In some cases, more than one verb might be suitable.

   1 In your working life, what pointless activities do you _____ the most time on?
   2 Have you ever _____ a very important meeting or appointment? Why?
   3 If you _____ an English lesson, what do you do?
   4 Which do you think is worse for a business – _____ a lot of money or _____ a lot of opportunities?
   5 How much of your company's resources and the staff's energy are _____ due to inefficiency?
   6 Which is easier to _____ – weight or your confidence?

Work in pairs. Ask and answer the questions.

10 Work in groups. Describe a difficult journey that you've made. Include details about how you travelled and what went wrong.

Attitudes to time

1 Read these short descriptions of different cultural attitudes to time. Which description most closely represents attitudes to time in your culture? Try to match each description with an appropriate geographical area:

1 the US, Britain, northern Europe
2 southern Europe, the Middle East
3 south-east Asia.

a *Schedules and punctuality aren't as important as human relationships. Time is flexible; it can be used to carry out more than one task or discussion, which may overlap. If a meeting starts late and extends beyond the scheduled finishing time, that's usually fine if the objective is achieved.*

c *Time flows fast in one direction. The past is finished, and the future is influenced by the present. It's best to do one thing at a time, concentrate only on that, and do it within an agreed timescale. Being on time for appointments is very important. Time equals money and should not be wasted.*

b *Time is viewed as cyclical. It comes and goes like the seasons, and is constantly being renewed. The concept of 'wasting' time is irrelevant. Issues are not dealt with in sequence, but considered and discussed for a period of days or weeks. Decisions are not made quickly – there must be time for contemplation of the whole picture.*

2 In your culture, how important is it to be on time for social and business appointments? How punctual do you need to be? Write down how many minutes you can be late for each event.

a business meeting	_____	an English lesson	_____
a business lunch	_____	a play	_____
dinner with friends	_____	a concert	_____
a party	_____	a wedding	_____

3 3.5 Listen to Mustapha Bakali and Clare Leavenworth Bakali talking about the concept of time in Morocco and the United States.

1 How late is it acceptable to arrive at a dinner party in Morocco? Why is it widely accepted?
2 Why should you be on time for a dinner party at an American's house?
3 What should you do if you are going to be twenty minutes late for a restaurant meal in the US?
4 Arriving late in Morocco is not fashionable. What is this to do with?
5 What is 'somewhat inconceivable' in the US?
6 Why is time so important in the business world in the US?
7 Which attitudes to time described in **1** do the speakers' views reflect?

Arranging a meeting

4  3.6 Listen to two people trying to arrange a meeting and make a note of the details of their meeting.

5 🔊 3.7 Listen again. Make a note of one or two phrases they use to:

1 suggest a day/time
2 respond positively
3 make an alternative suggestion
4 refuse politely
5 give an explanation.

Work in pairs. Make a list of similar phrases to do these things.

📖 Pocket Book page 34

Pronunciation

① 🔊 3.7 **When we are making a suggestion we normally allow the intonation to fall on or after the last stressed syllable. Listen to the suggestions again. Then practise saying them with the appropriate intonation.**

② 🔊 3.7 **Listen again to this extract from the phone call. Mark the words that are stressed. Work in pairs and practise reading the extract, paying attention to the stressed words.**

DANIEL So, would Wednesday morning at nine o'clock suit you? There's an early flight from Stockholm.

PAOLA Ah, I'm afraid Wednesday's going to be difficult. The problem is, we have a group of visitors from the UK. I think, you know, Tuesday would be better for me.

DANIEL Sorry, no, I can't make it on Tuesday. I'm afraid I have to be in Frankfurt all day. Now, let's see … Well, could you manage Thursday morning?

PAOLA Just a moment, I'll look in my diary … I'm sorry, it looks as if I'm going to be busy all morning. Could you make it in the afternoon?

6 Work in pairs. Make up short telephone conversations to arrange a meeting. Use this framework.

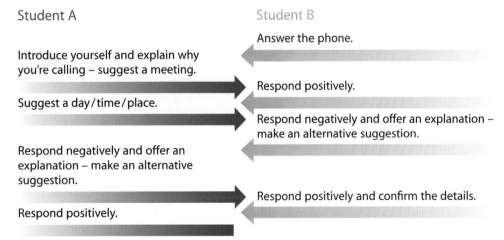

Student A

Introduce yourself and explain why you're calling – suggest a meeting.

Suggest a day/time/place.

Respond negatively and offer an explanation – make an alternative suggestion.

Respond positively.

Student B

Answer the phone.

Respond positively.

Respond negatively and offer an explanation – make an alternative suggestion.

Respond positively and confirm the details.

7 Work in pairs. Improvise two more phone calls to arrange a date, time, and place to meet. One call should be for a work-related event, the other for a social event. Use the appointments and commitments currently in your diary to say when you are not free, or invent them.

Direct and difficult questions

❶ In a social situation, is it acceptable to ask direct questions to people you don't know well? How do you feel if someone asks you a direct question about your culture?

❷ When someone mentions 'American culture', what do you think of? What aspects of American culture do you admire or dislike? For example, business, the movie industry, fast food, gang culture, race relations, economic power, optimism, freedom? Read these questions about aspects of life in the United States.

a Over half of mothers in the US work outside the home. Doesn't this threaten the unity and well-being of the family?

b I don't understand how you can have poverty and hunger and homelessness in the midst of such wealth. Why is this the case in the US?

c Why is there so much violence, so many cults and gang wars in America? What is there about your society that causes these to develop?

d The media in the US seems to play a strong role in the conduct of your government. It seems to be constantly searching for more and more scandal. Is this true? Is it a good thing?

e People in the US seem to know very little about world geography – names, places, locations. Why is this?

f Your newspapers don't carry much international news. How well-informed is the average US citizen about international politics and current events?

Roger E Axtell, *Do's and Taboos of Hosting International Visitors*

1 Imagine you are hosting a visitor from the US. Which questions do you think it would be acceptable to ask your guest?

2 Which questions would you most like to ask?

3 How would you respond to being asked similar questions about your country?

3 🔊 3.8 Listen to three extracts from a discussion in which an English woman is asking two people from the US how they feel about some of the questions in **2**. Which questions do they talk about?

4 🔊 3.8 Listen to the first two extracts again.

1 Is the English woman's tone initially:
   a confident   b critical   c hesitant   d neutral?

2 What phrases does the English woman use to soften the tone of her questions and to avoid being too direct and seeming too critical?

3 What does the man say about responding to this kind of question? Do you agree?

5 🔊 3.8 Listen to the third extract. Choose the best answers.

1 The American woman's first reply shows that she is:
   a slightly annoyed
   b quite angry
   c very angry.

2 The English woman's second question is intended to:
   a change the subject
   b reinforce her previous question
   c respond to the American woman's reply.

3 The two Americans:
   a accept what the English woman is saying
   b disagree with what she is saying.

4 The English woman's last comment shows that she:
   a feels she may have been misunderstood, and doesn't want to offend
   b is insensitive to the Americans
   c feels she is 100 per cent right.

6 Jeremy Paxman, the presenter of *Newsnight*, a current affairs programme on British television, once had to ask a senior politician the same question *eight* times before he received a satisfactory answer.

🔊 3.9 What can you do if you don't want to answer a direct question? Listen to five people being asked questions they don't want to answer.

1 Which ones:
   a refuse to answer the question   b avoid answering the question?

2 How did they do this? Match the strategies (a–e) to the extracts (1–5). Make a note of the phrases they used.
   a turn the question back to the other person
   b say they don't know much about the subject
   c make a generalization
   d refuse to talk about the subject
   e ask the questioner what they think the answer is.

📖 Pocket Book page 28

Social exchange   **7** Write two lists of questions that people might ask you about your country. The first list should contain questions that you would find relatively easy to answer (e.g. about food, family life, the general economy, leisure and sports activities). The second list should have questions that might be more difficult or embarrassing to answer (e.g. religion, politics, crime, money, sexual attitudes).

8 Work in pairs. Improvise two conversations in which you are a guest in your partner's country, and vice versa. Ask and answer questions from your lists, using appropriate phrases to introduce the questions, and to avoid or refuse to answer them.

Unit 4

Communication

OVERVIEW

- Use and non-use of articles
- Indirect speech
- *say/tell/speak/talk*
- Sentence patterns with reporting verbs
- Verbs + prepositions
- Understanding rapid speech
- Interrupting and clarifying, showing understanding
- Writing simply and clearly

LANGUAGE FOCUS   **Articles, indirect speech**

❶ How has the way we communicate changed over the last fifty years? How will it change in the future? Think about:

- human communication (e.g. between parents and children, employer and employee, the state and the individual)
- technological developments (e.g. satellites, mobile phones, the Internet).

❷ Read these extracts about different aspects of communication. Work in pairs and discuss the answers to the questions.

1 Almost every modern form of communication, from satellites to the Internet, is being intercepted by a multi-billion dollar global surveillance operation, according to a report for the European Parliament. The report says that a previously unknown international organization called ILETS plans to force manufacturers and operators of new communications systems to include monitoring capacity for use by national security or law enforcement organizations.
Which two countries do you think are dominating this 'surveillance operation'?

2 Fiorello La Guardia, who was Mayor of New York from 1933 to 1945, was fluent in three different languages: English, Italian, and Yiddish. Researchers who studied films of his speeches could tell which language he was speaking with the sound turned off.
How could they tell?

3 Sidney Jourard, an eminent social psychologist, once watched people having lunch together in various restaurants in San Juan (Puerto Rico), Gainesville (Florida), Paris (France), and London (UK). He wanted to see in which cultures people touched each other the most.
Within the space of an hour, how many times do you think the people touched each other in the four cities?

4 The mobile phone has changed the way we communicate. The percentage of mobile phone users is highest in Finland, Sweden, and Norway (an average of fifty per cent of the populations of these countries own a mobile phone).
Which of these countries do you think also has a very high percentage of users: Germany, Italy, the United Kingdom, or the United States?

5 One particular religious group, known for its pacifist beliefs, has no organized ritual, no priests, or prepared sermons. During worship, members communicate through spiritual silence, or at least until someone is moved to speak.
Who are these people?

34

③ 🔊 4.1 Listen to two people discussing the questions in **②** and make a note of the answers. Compare your ideas with their answers.

④ 1 In your culture, how important is body language? Are there any specific gestures you use to communicate? When is it acceptable to touch someone when you are speaking to them?

2 Why do governments spend large amounts of money on surveillance technology? What do they hope to find out? What other uses could this kind of technology have?

Use and non-use of articles – *a/an*, *the*, or no article

① Look at the six extracts in **②** and highlight all the examples of *a* or *an* (the indefinite article). Which ones refer to:

1 a specific item which is being mentioned for the first time?
2 a non-specific item, one example of many?

② Now highlight all the examples of *the* (the definite article). Match each to one of these uses.

1 It's clear from the context who or what is being referred to.
2 This is the only one in existence, or in this context (including superlative forms).
3 This has already been mentioned in this context.
4 This is a generalization about all of these items.

③ We normally use no article with generalizations using uncountable or plural nouns, and with the names of people and places (but there are many exceptions). Find examples in the six extracts of nouns which fit into these two groups.

④ Test yourself. Do we normally use *a/an*, *the*, or no article when we talk about:

1 the names of shops/restaurants/towns/cities/lakes/regions/(most) countries/continents?
2 the names of museums/art galleries/mountain ranges/rivers/seas/oceans?
3 the usual purpose of institutions like hospital/school/home/university/work?
4 jobs and occupations in general?
5 specific jobs within organizations or institutions?
6 sports and activities – jogging/swimming/football/aerobics/yoga, etc.?
7 entertainment and places of entertainment – theatre/cinema/opera/ballet?

📖 Pocket Book page 1

 The way we communicate is to a a large extent determined by the way we perceive things. When looking at a map of the world, for example, we will probably recognize the shape of Africa but not the shape of the Atlantic Ocean.
Look at the picture. What do you see?

Pronunciation

① Are these phrases preceded by *a* or *an*?

1	_____ educated guess	5	_____ European thing
2	_____ university friend	6	_____ one-off study
3	_____ incredible amount	7	_____ unusual thing
4	_____ hour	8	_____ old woman

🔊 4.2 **Listen and check your answers. Notice how the speakers link the words together. Practise saying the phrases in the same way.**

② 🔊 4.3 **Listen to these sentences and notice the different ways *the* is pronounced.**

a So **the** answer to **the** first one is **the** US.
b This was **the** easiest one.
c Oh yes, mobiles are definitely **the** accessory to have.
d **The** interesting aspect is that they're not as common in Germany.
e I think answer four is **the** one I find **the** most surprising.

What often happens to the pronunciation of *the* before a vowel?

5 Complete this story with *a/an*, *the*, or no article (Ø).

It was **1**_____ rush hour, and **2**_____ long-distance commuter train was full. Every seat was taken and **3**_____ passengers were standing crowded together in **4**_____ aisles. In **5**_____ corner seat, **6**_____ young man in **7**_____ blue suit was talking loudly into **8**_____ mobile phone, to **9**_____ obvious annoyance of **10**_____ passengers around him. 'I don't care what they say,' he shouted. 'Tell them it's ten million or we don't have **11**_____ deal.' And he switched off his phone.

At that moment, **12**_____ elderly man standing near **13**_____ door clutched at his chest and collapsed. For a moment there was **14**_____ silence as **15**_____ people stared at him in **16**_____ horror. Then **17**_____ woman stepped forward to help him. 'It's all right,' she said, 'I'm **18**_____ doctor.' She turned to **19**_____ young man in **20**_____ blue suit. 'Quickly,' she said. 'He's having **21**_____ heart attack. Phone for **22**_____ ambulance to meet us at **23**_____ next station.' 'I can't,' said **24**_____ young man. **25**_____ woman was furious, and some of **26**_____ passengers started shouting, 'It's **27**_____ emergency!'. But **28**_____ man still refused to use his phone.

Meanwhile, **29**_____ conductor arrived to find out what all **30**_____ noise was about. He instructed **31**_____ driver to radio ahead for **32**_____ medical assistance. Once her patient

was safely on his way to **33**_____ hospital, **34**_____ doctor went up to **35**_____ young man. 'So,' she said, 'Why wouldn't you use your phone?' He looked very embarrassed …

To find out the reason, turn to page 120.

6 Look at the photo. What do you think is happening? Who are the people? What are the advantages of this kind of communication?

7 ▷)) 4.4 Listen to two people discussing a TV report on video-conferencing. What do they say about:

1 what people mainly use video-conferencing for?
2 the main benefits to businesses?
3 how to behave during a video-conference?
4 what technology is available?

8 The most common verb used for reporting speech is *say* (*He said …, She said …*), but other verbs are also used.

1 ▷)) 4.4 Listen to the discussion again. Match the following verbs with the aspect of video-conferencing they refer to.

1	admit	a	the next generation of mobile phones
2	reckon	b	the technology
3	explain	c	meetings
4	make the point	d	the lighting
5	predict	e	flexibility
6	touch on	f	people appearing more polite

2 ▷)) 4.4 Why does the speaker use the phrases in italics?
a *He reckons* he can now have four meetings …
b *According to him*, it's important to sit up straight …
c … but *apparently* subtle body language just gets lost on screen.
d And *it seems that* the software already exists …

9 Discuss these questions with a partner.

1 Have you ever used video-conferencing? Would it make your job easier? Why, or why not?
2 What do you think are the disadvantages of video-conferencing?

Indirect speech

1. **Look at these examples of indirect speech. What were the actual words used?**

   a She said that she conducted most of her meetings from home.

   b He said it allowed him to take on cases that would otherwise cost him money.

   c She said she'd flown over a hundred times in the previous year.

   d He predicted that the next generation of mobile phones would allow video-conferencing on the move.

   c He said that the software already exists.

   d He said that the software already existed.

   e She said she conducts most of her meetings from home.

   f She says she conducts most of her meetings from home.

2. **Which aspects of speech need to change when we report what someone says? Which aspects stay the same?**

3. **Compare these pairs of sentences. Does the difference in tense affect the meaning?**

   a He said he used it for meetings with colleagues.

   b He said he had used it for meetings with colleagues.

4. **Look at these ways of reporting questions. What were the actual words used?**

   a They asked an American woman if she had used it.

   b He wondered how he had managed without it.

   c We enquired when the connection would be available.

   d She wanted to know why we didn't have the software.

   How does the word order change when reporting questions?

    Pocket Book page 9

10. Rewrite these questions and answers in indirect speech. For example:

    'Have you spoken to Maria about dinner tonight?' 'Not yet, I haven't had a chance.'
    I asked whether she had spoken to Maria, and she said that she hadn't had a chance.

    1 'Are you coming to the meeting?' 'Yes, I'll be there in a few minutes.'
    2 'Have you seen the weather forecast?' 'Yes, it's going to be stormy again tomorrow.'
    3 'Will you give me a hand with this rubbish?' 'Yes, but could we do it later?'
    4 'Could you finish this by tomorrow?' 'OK, I'll get it to you by 9.00.'
    5 'Did you enjoy the trip to Ireland?' 'Well, Dublin's a great city, but it rains a lot!'

11. 4.5 Listen to two people taking three messages for a colleague, Sue Lindley. Make notes on each message. Write an email reporting the messages using indirect speech.

Talking point

12. Do the quiz on your own. Then work in pairs.

    1 Choose five of your answers and discuss them with your partner.
    2 Change partners. Report your first partner's answers to your new partner. Pay attention to any tense changes. For example:
    *Alice said that communication **had changed** the most between parent and child, and that in the future it **would change** between employer and employee.*

1> To be an effective communicator, which factor do you need the most?
a a nice voice
b a nice face
c a good brain
d a capacity for listening

2> Which language is probably the easiest for foreigners to learn?
a English
b Chinese
c Esperanto
d your own language

3> Which country would you most like to live in?
a Australia
b Great Britain
c South Africa
d the US
e another (your choice)

4> Which place would you most like to visit?
a the Nile
b Niagara Falls
c Mount Everest
d the moon
e the South Pacific

5> Which was the greatest invention?
a the wheel
b the Internet
c the motor car
d the laser
e another (you decide)

6> If the pay was the same, which would you most like to be?
a an artist
b a university professor
c a top sports player
d a politician

7> So far in your life, where have you spent most of your time?
a at home
b at work
c at college
d in a bar
e at the cinema

8> Which would like to have more time for?
a playing an instrument (e.g. the piano)
b listening to the radio (or watching TV)
c having lunch (or dinner)
d doing charity work (e.g. visiting people in hospital or in prison)
e your family and friends

1 Do you believe animals are capable of using 'language' to communicate? Do you have any experience of animals that understand human speech?

2 Read the article and find out the answers to these questions.

1 How did Panbanisha first learn to communicate?
2 How does she communicate using a computer?
3 What does this tell us about animals' language skills?

The chimp who says just what she thinks

She looks and behaves like any other mischievous chimp – in every respect except one. For 14-year-old Panbanisha has the language skills of a 4-year-old child.

According to her keepers she has a vocabulary of 3,000 English words, and speaks through a computer voice synthesizer. If she is hungry, she will say 'Please buy me a burger'. If she is enjoying a hot drink, she will say 'Good coffee' to her guests.

Scientists have been teaching apes sign language for decades, and this was Panbanisha's first method of communication. Then a few months ago she was given a specially-designed keyboard. It has 400 buttons, each marked with a symbol standing for a word such as 'orange', 'up', or 'coffee', or an abstract concept such as 'good' or 'give me'. As she types the symbols, the words appear on a computer screen and are spoken aloud by the computer voice.

Another ape – a 20-year-old orang-utan from nearby Atlanta Zoo – is also learning to use the keyboard. Recently, during a heatwave, she saved money she had been paid in return for carrying out tasks, then told scientists in sign language that she wanted to buy a pool.

Duane Rumbaugh, Professor of Biology and Psychology, said: 'This is exciting research. The animals can understand the spoken word and give appropriate replies. It shows that language skills are not confined to humans and implies that, like us, apes have the power of thought and reasoning.'

Panbanisha's abilities have raised disturbing questions about using apes in laboratory experiments. Campaigners say that if they have the intelligence of children, it is wrong to subject them to the pain of research into Aids and cancer.

Daily Mail

Sentence patterns with *say* and *tell*

3 *Say* and *tell* are generally used in these sentence patterns.

1 *say (that)* something	2 *say* something *to* someone
Prof Rumbaugh *said (that)* the research had been very exciting.	Panbanisha will *say* 'Good coffee' *to* her guests.

3 *tell* someone *(that)* something	4 *tell* someone *(not) to do* something
She *told* scientists *(that)* she wanted to buy a pool.	The chimp *will tell* me *(not) to* bring him a banana.

Group these verbs according to the sentence pattern they follow. In some cases, they may fit more than one pattern.

admit	agree	ask	encourage	insist	persuade	remind	urge
advise	answer	describe	explain	order	reply	request	warn

📖 Pocket Book page 25

❹ 🔊 4.6 What are the main difficulties of trying to research language acquisition in animals? Listen to part of a radio interview with Dr Harold Burrell, a specialist in animal behaviour.

1 What were the findings of the studies carried out in the 1960s and 1970s?
2 Why were these studies criticized?
3 What sort of changes were made to the way later studies were conducted?
4 What is one of the most exciting discoveries for Dr Burrell?
5 How do some chimps acquire language in the same way as children?
6 What sort of conditions do the chimps live in?

❺ 1 Look at these sentences from the interview with Dr Burrell. Notice which prepositions follow the verbs or phrases in **bold**. Are they equivalent to those used in your language?

*… who's **responsible** for the Department of Animal Behaviour …*
*… thanks for **taking part** in the discussion today.*
*I think many studies have **benefited** from past criticisms …*

2 Cross out any verbs in each group which are not followed by the preposition on the right. Add them to the correct list(s). Follow the example.

a	apologize, hope, investigate, pay, search, wait	**for**
b	~~be accustomed~~, be inherent, believe, participate	**in**
c	be lacking, distinguish, listen, play, study	**Ø (no preposition)**
d	concentrate, depend, focus, insist, refer	**on**
e	agree, associate, conflict, communicate, object, sympathize	**with**
f	belong, choose, coincide, select, suffer	**from**
g	be allergic, contrast, subject (someone), *be accustomed*	**to**

3 Which verbs can be followed by more than one of the prepositions?

📖 Pocket Book page 19

❻ How do you memorize prepositions? What technique do you use to record them? Read the Learning tip on memorizing prepositions. Which technique would be the most effective for you?

❼ Choose ten verbs from ❺. Invent a question for each. For example:

*Do you **belong to** any clubs? Are you **allergic to** anything?*

1 Work in pairs and ask each other your questions.
2 Exchange questions. Try to memorize your partner's questions.
3 Form new pairs. Ask your new partner your first partner's questions.

Learning tip

a If words can take more than one preposition (*think of* or *think about*, *consist in* or *consist of*), write examples which show the difference in meaning.

b Always write a verb with its related prepositions. To test yourself, sort them alphabetically into two columns, verbs in the first column, prepositions in the second. Cover the second column and see how many prepositions you can remember.

c Make your own tapes. For example, record yourself saying 'to depend', then leave a pause. Then record yourself saying 'to depend *on*'. So when you listen, you first hear the infinitive. Say the preposition, then check if you were right.

Understanding rapid speech

1 What accents and dialects in your country do you find particularly difficult to understand? What strategies do you use when talking to people from those regions? Do you feel embarrassed if you don't understand each other?

2 Andy Crisp works for an international company in London. He has quite a strong Essex (north-east London) accent, and speaks rather fast.

   1   4.7 Listen to Andy explaining the difficulties his foreign colleagues have understanding his English. What three things does he identify as making him difficult to understand?

   2 How difficult do you find it to understand Andy? In your opinion, which of the three things he identifies in 1 creates the most difficulty?

   Understanding natural speech

3 Do you think other native English speakers would find Andy difficult to understand?

   1 4.8 Listen to one of Andy's American colleagues, Tim Mitchell from Dallas, Texas, talking about the problems he has understanding Andy. How does he feel about it? Are you surprised? Do you now feel reassured?!

   2 4.8 Listen again and make a note of Tim Mitchell's tactics for understanding Andy.

   3 Work in groups. Which of Tim Mitchell's tactics do you think is the most useful, and why? Brainstorm a list of other tactics you can use to help you understand native English speakers.

4 In November 2000 Joan Blake did a survey for the EU (European Union) on how funding is allocated for intra-EU projects. She found that many managers said they preferred not to deal with British companies due to the language factor. Her research paper, entitled 'Whose English is it anyway?', concluded that the British are (ironically) probably the worst users of the language. Many of them have little idea of the difficulties their listeners have understanding them.

   1 Read this transcript of part of an interview with Joan Blake (JB) by an Italian journalist (I). What strategies does she suggest for actively improving your understanding?

'What did he say?'

'I don't know - he was speaking English!'

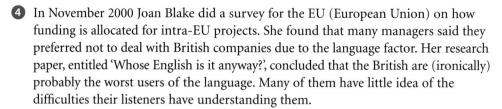

I Supposing I want to do business with a British company. What can I do to improve my understanding?[1]

JB I think the most important thing is to accept that it's all right not to understand. You know, I myself have quite a bit of difficulty in following people from Essex. And people from Newcastle are even more difficult – about fifty per cent of what they say seems incomprehensible to me.

I Fine. But how does accepting that it's OK not to understand help me?[2]

JB It helps you because it means that it's also acceptable to interrupt the speaker, to try and understand or to clarify what she or he is saying.

I So, typically, what could I say?[3]

JB Well, obviously you can ask them to slow down or speak up, or just repeat what they've said. But the problem is that they may just say the same thing again more loudly. Or the gap between each word will be longer but the words themselves will still be said at the same speed.

I So I still won't be able to understand them anyway?[4]

JB Right. What you have to learn to do, and this applies to any language, is to repeat back to the speaker what they've just said.

I But using my own words, I suppose?[5]

JB Exactly. This means they are aware that you may not be following them, and you can check whether you really are following them or not.

I So you're saying that I should rephrase any sentences that I think I may not have understood?[6]

JB That's right, as you have just done. You can also focus on particular things they've said.

I You can also what, sorry?[7]

JB Focus on things they've just said, by saying 'Sorry, *what* can you do?' like you just did. Or you can say something like 'Could you say that first part again?'. Another crucial thing is to ask relevant questions. This enables both parties to test whether they are talking about the same thing or not. But the main thing is not to be afraid, and not to feel inferior just because you don't understand. Remember that communication is a two-way process, which means the responsibility is not just with you, but with the other person too.

2   Which of the journalist's questions:
  a   clarifies what Joan has just said? _____
  b   indicates that he didn't catch one particular word that Joan said? _____
  c   shows Joan that he is following her because he makes a relevant suggestion?
       _____
  d   shows Joan that he is following her because he asks for an example of what
       she has just said? _____
  e   summarizes what Joan has just said? _____

5   Work in pairs or groups. Create your own checklist of strategies you can use to
improve your understanding of rapid speech. Refer back to the interview if you
need to.

**Interrupting and
clarifying**

6   4.9 Listen to a telephone call between two people discussing some new
technology.

  1   What is the purpose of the call?
  2   Was Jackie Rymell expecting the call?
  3   How does she sound? (e.g. interested, cautious, enthusiastic?)
  4   What exactly is the new technology Paul Gold is describing?
  5   When do they arrange to meet?
  6   What is Paul's phone number?

Does this technology already exist? How useful do you think it would be?

7   4.9 Listen again and note down what Jackie says to:

  1   check the name of the woman Paul Gold mentions
  2   check what Paul is talking about
  3   indicate that she thinks the technology is already available
  4   show that she is not following
  5   indicate that she has understood
  6   interrupt Paul
  7   resume the conversation
  8   make sure that Paul said 15 and not 50.

How does Paul make sure that the meeting is on Tuesday and not Thursday?

Pocket Book page 29

8   Work in pairs. Improvise a phone call. Student A should turn to the information on
page 112. Student B should turn to the information on page 116.

9   Prepare an explanation of how to do one of the following:

  –   save money
  –   rob a bank
  –   play a particular card game
  –   play a particular sport
  –   buy a house
  –   undertake some research
  –   have a long-term relationship (e.g. business, love, friendship).

Now sit back to back with a partner and explain your chosen topic. Make sure both
you and your partner use some of the phrases for interrupting and clarifying
practised in this section.

1 Work in groups. Discuss these questions.

1 What kinds of documents do you find particularly difficult to read (e.g. computer manuals, contracts, tax forms, EU directives)?

2 What makes them difficult to read? How could they be improved?

3 What progress has been made in your country or organization towards simplifying documents?

4 What kind of documents do you personally have to write?

5 When you're writing, how much do you think about the reader?

2 Read these four possible versions of a text from a manual for computer programmers. They describe EDITMENU, a program that creates and maintains file menus. It's not important if you don't understand the exact meaning of every word.

Put the versions in order, from the easiest to understand to the most difficult to understand. Think about which version is most similar to your own style of writing.

a   The operation of **EDITMENU** takes place on a dedicated workfile. Therefore, during the maintenance of a Menu file, no changes to the original file are effected until such time as the session comes to an end or the operator accesses another Menu file. The implication of this is that the original file will remain without alteration if, for some unforeseen reason, the operating session does not come to a normal termination.

b   **EDITMENU** operates on a workfile of its own. So, when you are maintaining a Menu file, your original is not changed until either you finish your session or you access another Menu file. In this way, you keep your original safe, even if your session does not terminate normally for any reason.

c   **EDITMENU** operates on its own workfile. Accordingly, when you are maintaining a Menu file, none of your changes is made until either you finish your session or you access another Menu file. So the original files remain safe if, for some reason, your session does not end normally.

d   **EDITMENU** operation is on a dedicated workfile. Thus, during Menu file maintenance, no change in the original is performed until session termination or alternative Menu file access. Original file safety in the event of abnormal session termination is thereby ensured.

John Kirkham, *Good Style*

3 The four versions of the text in **2** were part of two surveys done in the UK. Groups of technical and non-technical people were asked to judge the best way to write scientific and technical documents. The results were almost identical for both groups: version B was considered best by around 40% of those surveyed, version C 20%, version D 5%, and version A 3% (in the original survey there were six versions).

1 Why do you think version B was considered the best? Think in terms of:
   – passive vs active structures   – technical vs non-technical vocabulary
   – impersonal vs personal structures   – short vs long sentences/words.

2 What are the advantages of using *you* rather than an impersonal structure, such as *the user* or *the operator*? What are the disadvantages of using *the user* or *the operator*?

3 Version B contains more verb-centred phrases than noun-centred phrases (e.g. *when you are maintaining a Menu file* rather than *during Menu file maintenance*). What are the advantages of this?

4 The other versions use words or phrases such as *therefore, hence, consequently, accordingly, thereby, the implication of this is* – what alternative words or phrases does version B use?

5 Should it make any difference to the style of a manual if the user of the manual is an expert or non-expert?

4 Look at these guidelines for writing clearly and effectively.

1 Put yourself in the reader's shoes.
What does he or she already know about the subject? Then decide exactly what message you are trying to get across, and why. Is it to inform, sell, persuade, or explain?

2 Use short sentences.
The shorter the sentence, the stronger the message, and the less room for ambiguity and confusion. This is why most advertisers use short sentences,

even when they are aiming at a highly educated market. The *New York Times* has a reputation for good writing, yet it is written so that it can be read easily by a 17-year-old.

3 Use active verb forms.
One way to shorten sentences is to use active verb forms rather than passive forms. Another good idea is to use personal pronouns wherever it's appropriate.

4 Include just one main idea per sentence.
This avoids the possibility of confusion or ambiguity, particularly when the subject matter is complex.

5 Remove all unnecessary words or phrases.
This will not only help to shorten sentences, but also makes the language more forceful and direct.

1 Work in pairs. Do you agree with all the guidelines? Can you think of any other ideas to add to the list?

2 Look at these extracts and decide what kind of document each one comes from – e.g. a report, a formal letter, a technical manual, etc. Rewrite each extract, implementing the writing guidelines above. Then compare your revisions with your partner, and with the suggested answers on page 120.

a It is hoped that all the reports will have been returned to us by the end of this financial year or at least by the start of the next financial year at the very latest.

c In an attempt to make things more professional in relation to the overall efficiency of the department, staff are requested to answer enquiries, reply to letters from customers, and deal with all correspondence within a total of FIVE DAYS of the receipt of such items.

b If your payment was in the form of a cheque, it will be necessary for me to seek confirmation from the bank that the cheque has been cleared before we can investigate this matter further.

d If **EDITMENU** updating is being performed on a file that is also the file currently under utilization by **STARTSYSTEM**, no change is effected in **STARTSYSTEM** until termination and subsequent re-start of **STARTSYSTEM**.

5 Write a short report or account (100–150 words) on one of these topics:
1 the current state of the project you are working on
2 an overview of your company's field of business
3 a meeting you recently attended
4 a recent film or play you have seen
5 a book you enjoyed reading.

6 Work in pairs. Exchange reports with your partner. Your task is to suggest changes to improve the clarity and simplicity of their writing. When you have both done this, return the reports. Discuss the suggested changes and implement those you think are most appropriate.

7 Work in groups. Discuss whether it is equally important for spoken language to be clear and concise. Can you apply the techniques outlined in this section to speech? What would you change?

Review Unit B

Future forms

1 Put the verbs in brackets into the most appropriate future form: the Present Continuous, *going to*, or *will*. More than one form may be possible.

1 A When _____ (you go) home tonight?
  B I'm not sure yet. I _____ (let) you know later.
2 A _____ (you use) that file later, or can I borrow it?
  B I _____ (use) it after lunch.
3 A I _____ (go) to the cinema tonight – do you want to come?
  B Yes, I _____ (come) with you. What _____ (you see)?
4 A I _____ (call) you around eleven p.m. if that _____ (be) OK?
  B Actually, I _____ (get) an early night, so I'd rather you called earlier.
5 A How _____ you (get) to the conference?
  B I _____ (fly) to Boston, then I _____ (probably rent) a car.

Future possibilities

2 Complete the sentences with *can* or *may*, and put the verbs in brackets into the Present Simple or future with *will*.

1 We _____ need some extra resources on this project – I'm not sure yet.
2 There is no doubt about it. If we _____ (not find) an answer soon, we _____ (miss) this opportunity.
3 I _____ help if you _____ (want).
4 If we _____ (do) it this way, there _____ well be some problems.

Articles

3 1 Put *a* or *an* before these words and phrases.

___ unidentified flying object   ___ UFO   ___ EU directive
___ European   ___ MEP   ___ honest citizen   ___ house

2 Complete the text with *a / an*, *the*, *his*, or nothing (Ø).

1___ business executive from 2___ US was asked to make 3___ after-dinner speech at 4___ important conference in 5___ England, which was being attended by 6___ group of (all male) business associates. He wanted to end 7___ speech with 8___ amusing story, but couldn't think of anything interesting to talk about. In 9___ end, he decided to tell 10___ rather risky story about 11___ sex, which went down very well.

When he arrived home after 12___ dinner, 13___ wife asked him how 14___ speech had gone. He replied that it had been 15___ huge success. 'But what did you talk about?', she asked.

Afraid that she might not be amused if he told her 16___ truth, 17___ man thought for 18___ few seconds, and then replied 'Oh, 19___ sailing'.

20___ following week, one of 21___ man's colleagues approached 22___ wife at a cocktail party and commented: 'That was 23___ marvellous speech 24___ your husband made 25___ last week.' 'I know,' replied 26___ wife. 'It's amazing. He's only done it twice in his life. 27___ first time 28___ hat blew off, and 29___ second time he felt so seasick that he had to go to 30___ hospital.'

Indirect speech

4 Put these sentences into indirect speech. Use a different verb in each case.

| admit | advise | ask | inquire | remind | say | suggest | tell |

1 Where have you been? I was worried about you.
2 If I were you I'd leave it till tomorrow.
3 Don't forget to turn off the lights when you leave.
4 Don't do it now, it can wait.
5 What about going out for a drink tomorrow?
6 You're right, I did steal the money.
7 When will it be ready?
8 I'm sure someone was in the other room.

Vocabulary

⑤ Complete the story with *travel, trip, journey, flight, tour, missed, lost,* and *wasted.* Use each word only once.

> I once went on a guided ¹_____ of Scandinavia, but it was probably the worst ²_____ of my life. The ³_____ there was terrible because we ⁴_____ the ⁵_____ and so we ⁶_____ several hours hanging around the airport waiting for the next one. Then, when we were already on the plane, I realized that I had ⁷_____ my passport ...

Verbs + prepositions

⑥ Write an appropriate preposition next to each verb. If no preposition is needed, don't write anything.

1 associate ___   3 focus ___   5 listen ___   7 suffer ___
2 depend ___   4 investigate ___   6 participate ___   8 wait ___

Understanding, clarifying, interrupting

❼ You are on the phone. Write down phrases you could use:

1 to check the name of the caller
2 to tell the caller that they are speaking too fast
3 to say you can't understand
4 to interrupt the caller
5 to resume what you were saying after an interruption
6 to check that you have understood what the caller has just said.

Arranging a meeting

❽ Work in pairs and improvise a phone call to arrange a meeting. Then change roles and improvise another call.

Student A Suggest a day, time, and location. When B refuses, make an alternative suggestion.

Student B Refuse A's first suggestion and give an explanation. Then accept A's second suggestion.

Asking and answering difficult questions

❾ 1 You are a guest in a foreign country. You want to find out more about the poverty, homelessness, crime, or drug situation in your host's country. You don't want to offend your host. Write down a 'soft' indirect way of finding out this information.

2 Work in pairs. Ask and answer the questions you have just prepared. Answer them in these three ways:

a turn the question back to your guest
b refuse to talk about it
c make a generalization.

Self-check box

	YES	NO	📖		YES	NO	📖
Present Continuous for future	☐	☐	7	Vocabulary: *travel, trip, journey, voyage, tour, miss, lose, waste*	☐	☐	26, 24
will, going to	☐	☐	6	Verbs + prepositions	☐	☐	19
First conditional for predictions + *can* and *may*	☐	☐	3, 12	Understanding, clarifying, interrupting	☐	☐	29–36
Articles	☐	☐	1	Arranging a meeting	☐	☐	34
Indirect speech	☐	☐	9	Asking and answering difficult questions	☐	☐	28

Unit 5

The Internet

OVERVIEW

- Defining and non-defining relative clauses + prepositions
- Internet vocabulary
- *make/let/allow/enable/permit*
- Phrasal verbs: *make/get/let*
- Avoiding ambiguity
- Making your point clearly
- Writing emails

LANGUAGE FOCUS   **Relative clauses**

1 Have you ever heard of an Internet site called lastminute.com? Look at this extract from their website. What services do you think they might offer?

demand our newsletter!

your email

select your version

➲ html ➲ text

uk home

what we do

flights ◄
hotels ◄
holidays ◄
entertainment ◄
auctions ◄
restaurants ◄

home   search   help   site map   contact us   my space   shopping basket

do something lastminute.com

our site is 100% secure

hello there!

to login or register, click here

Thought you could make it through the winter without going on a city break or escaping someplace hot? Well, take a look out the window, have a rethink

today's highlights

✈ From Flights ...

DUBLIN
Guinness, Joyce, U2...
and you?

from £67.30

2 Read this article about Martha Lane Fox, who founded lastminute.com with her partner, Brent Hoberman.

1 Why don't lastminute.com's offices seem like 'the nerve-centre of a multi-million-pound Internet business'?

2 Martha Lane Fox describes herself as 'about as technical as a peanut'. What do you think she means?

3 How did lastminute.com get started?

4 How did her friends react when they found out what she was doing? Why did they react like this?

5 What services does the company offer?

3 Work in pairs and discuss these questions.

1 Does Martha Lane Fox match your image of an Internet entrepreneur? Why, or why not?

2 Why do you think they chose the name lastminute.com? What do you think it says about the kind of customers the company attracts?

3 Would you use lastminute.com's services? Why, or why not?

46

Internet entrepreneur is 'as technical as a peanut'

THE offices of lastminute.com hardly seem like the nerve-centre of one of Britain's most talked about and potentially lucrative Internet concerns. The reception area, which is on the seventh floor of an anonymous office building behind London's Oxford Street, consists of a couple of scruffy sofas, a coffee table and a rug displaying a number of hard-to-shift everyday stains.

Sitting there with your coffee, you can watch casually-dressed twentysomethings tapping away at their workstations in a generally non-stressed kind of way. And Martha Lane Fox initially gives little indication that she is one of Britain's hottest young Net entrepreneurs as she arrives and leads me into a boardroom which contains a long table, a few chairs that don't match, and a pile of cardboard boxes.

'About as technical as a peanut', is how she describes herself, and perhaps in this she takes after her father, Robin, a celebrated classical scholar, who informed her only the other day that he had just used a cash machine for the very first time.

Her rise has been swift, although not without the odd wrong turning. She denies she was known as 'Fast-Lane Foxy' at Westminster School, but she was certainly quick and bright enough to win a place at Magdalen College, Oxford, where she read Ancient and Modern History.

On leaving in 1994, she decided to pursue an interest in the media, and landed a job at a management consultancy called Spectrum, which advised big companies on the uses of new technology. One of her first projects was a presentation for British Telecom called 'What is the Internet?'. Three years later, she moved to Carlton Television, and not long after that Brent Hoberman, a former colleague at Spectrum, told her about his idea for a new website. Ms Lane Fox responded by sending him a very long email explaining exactly why she thought it was such a bad idea.

But then she realized that it was, in fact, a very good idea. And like most very good ideas, it was a simple one: to offer last-minute deals on a whole range of items, including flights, hotels, holidays, theatre tickets, and gifts.

In early 1998, when the two first put together a business plan and sent it to three or four venture capital companies, their friends thought they were taking a risk. 'At that point the Internet was so untrendy,' she recalls. 'All my friends, who are now leaving their jobs to join Internet start-ups, said, "What are you doing?"'. Nevertheless, by June that year they had £600,000 in the bank, and by October they had a website. 'Then it just flew,' she says.

Lastminute's website was launched with five major European airlines, five hotel chains, and thirty upmarket independent hotels. It also included suppliers of unusual gifts, such as helicopter flying lessons, time in a professional recording studio, and even the chance to adopt a donkey. The section that I like the most is called 'Serious Money'. Here you can arrange unique and absurdly expensive treats, such as a trip in a Russian MiG-25 fighter aircraft to the edge of space, where you experience zero gravity.

Having started with a skeleton staff, the company now employs around 120 people in London and another 50-plus in the rest of Europe. The number of subscribers to the company's weekly email newsletter offering last-minute bargains has already reached 700,000. As an example of customer satisfaction, Ms Lane Fox tells the slightly alarming story of a gentleman whose honeymoon was arranged in an auction at the site forty minutes before he was due to get married. 'That is the perfect lastminute customer,' she says.

Independent; Wall Street Journal; Daily Telegraph

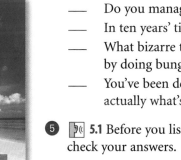

④ 🎧 **5.1** You are going to hear an interview with Martha Lane Fox. These are the questions she was asked. Put them in the order you would expect to hear them, and compare your order with a partner. Then listen and check your answers.

—— Did you have any idea that this [lastminute] was going to be so successful?

—— Do you manage to sleep at night?

—— In ten years' time how do you see yourself?

—— What bizarre things can I get? Supposing I want to get married this evening by doing bungee jumping off the Tower Bridge or something like that?

—— You've been described as a young and funky company. I just wondered actually what's the average age of the people working here?

⑤ 🎧 **5.1** Before you listen again, answer the following questions. Then listen and check your answers.

1 What's the average age of the staff at lastminute.com?

2 Can you name two bizarre things that lastminute.com can arrange for you?

3 What kinds of plans can they help you out with?

4 What, in Martha's opinion, is the key to being successful?

5 How much does Martha sleep?

6 Why can't she imagine what she will be doing in ten years' time?

7 What plans do they have at lastminute for the immediate future?

🎧 **Understanding natural speech**

Defining and non-defining relative clauses

Look at these examples of relative clauses (a–g) and answer the questions (1–3).

a She takes after her father, Robin, who informed her only the other day that he had just used a cash machine for the very first time.

b Ms Lane Fox tells the story of a gentleman who wrote to express his thanks.

c All my friends, who are now leaving their jobs to join Internet start-ups, said …

d The reception area, which is on the seventh floor of an anonymous office building, consists of …

e … she leads me into a boardroom which contains a long table …

f The section that I like the most is called 'Serious Money'.

g She landed a job at a management consultancy called Spectrum, which advised big companies on the uses of new technology.

1 Which sentences are examples of defining clauses (where the information is essential) and which are examples of non-defining clauses (where the information is additional and not essential)?

2 In which case(s) can the relative pronoun be omitted? Why?

3 Look back at the article on page 47 and find examples of other relative pronouns. Are they used in defining or non-defining clauses?

 Pocket Book page 17

Relative clauses and prepositions

In relative clauses, a relative pronoun can be the object of a preposition. In speech or informal writing (e.g. emails), we generally put the preposition at the end of the clause, otherwise it may sound very formal or awkward.

Compare the following sentences. Which sentence sounds more natural, and why?

a The people **with whom** I keep in touch are mainly friends.

b The people (**who**) I keep in touch **with** are mainly friends.

You can put quantifiers such as *all*, *each*, *some*, *several*, *many*, or *most* before *of whom* and *of which* to give extra information about the whole or a part of a particular group.

*Search engines find a lot of sites, **most of which** are generally irrelevant to your needs.*
*I've met a lot of people through chatlines, **some of whom** have now become my friends.*
*Newspaper websites, **the majority of which** are free, are a good source of financial information.*

 Pocket Book page 17

6 Underline the most appropriate form in italics (Ø = no pronoun). If both forms are possible, underline both.

> After leaving university in 1994, the year ¹*which / that* I was twenty-one, I took some time off to go travelling, ²*which / that* turned out to be the best decision of my life. I ended up in Thailand, ³*which / that* was where I met my business partner, Alex. We worked out the idea for a website company over dinner in the hotel ⁴*where / that* we were both staying in.
>
> We started the company in 1998, ⁵*which / Ø* was the year the Internet really took off. The place ⁶*which / where* we finally decided to base ourselves was Dublin, ⁷*where / Ø* there are lots of hi-tech companies. One of the things ⁸*that / Ø* I like best about this job is the freedom to experiment and explore new possibilities. I have to admit that I owe most of my success to Alex, ⁹*who / that* is the real 'ideas' person.

7 Change these examples of written forms into more natural spoken forms.

1 I have an excellent relationship with the people with whom I work.
2 AF1081 is the flight on which we will be arriving at 13.30 tomorrow.
3 This is the region from where most of the refugees are arriving.
4 This hotel, about which I told you in my last message, has excellent facilities.
5 Lastminute.com, about which everyone is now talking, is a very successful company.
6 The computer on to which I have logged can't access that information.

8 Match the two parts of these sentences. Then join them together using a quantifier (*all, some,* etc.) and *of which/whom.*

1 Our website gets over 200 hits a day …
2 I have a number of friends living abroad …
3 We started with a skeleton staff of five …
4 This job allows me to travel to new places …

a I email most of them regularly.
b I haven't visited some places before.
c Only a very few lead to new customers.
d They are all still with us.

Talking point   **9** Do the quiz and discuss your answers with a partner.

THE_INTERNET / AND_YOU

1_ How long have you been using email and the Internet? How much have they changed your life?
2_ How often do you check your email?
3_ How many messages do you send or receive each day?
4_ Do all your family have email?
5_ Do you use it for work or for your own private interest?
6_ How quickly do you find what you want on the Web?
7_ Which search engines do you use?
8_ What are your favourite Internet sites?
9_ What's the most unusual site that you've ever visited?
10_ Are there any companies whose sites you find particularly good or bad?
11_ Have you ever logged on to a chat room?
12_ If so, do the people you meet there have similar interests to yours?
13_ Do you know anyone who's met someone through the Internet?
14_ Should the Internet, which is now used by millions of children worldwide, be subject to censorship laws? Should these laws be international?

10   5.2 Listen to two people discussing some of the questions in the quiz. The first time you listen, tick the questions they discuss. The second time, note down their answers. What other aspects of the Internet do they talk about?

Verb–noun collocations

❶ Here are some key verbs and nouns associated with using the Internet.

browse	enter	hit	set up	use
download	hack into	log on to	surf	visit

chat room	homepage	information	provider	system
cybercafé	images	the Net	search engine	website

1 Which verbs can collocate with which nouns?

2 Choose six verb–noun combinations and make questions. For example:
   *How often do you **surf** the **Net**?*
   *Have you ever **visited** a **cybercafé**?*

3 Ask and answer the questions in pairs.

Make and let

❷ Look at these phrases and answer the questions.

*One effect of the Internet is to **make** companies change the way they operate.*
*There are computer services that **let** users compile 'buddy lists' of friends and family.*

1 Which verb is used when we have no choice about what happens?

2 Which verb can be replaced by *allow (to), enable (to),* and *permit (to)*?

📖 Pocket Book page 24

❸ 1 Complete these sentences with *make* or *let*.
   a I'll _____ you have an answer tomorrow.
   b She won't _____ me read her mail, so that _____ it difficult for me
      to answer your query.
   c You're really funny – you _____ me laugh a lot.
   d My laptop _____ me work at home, on the train – anywhere I want.
   e They don't _____ us work specific hours. They _____ us arrive at
      work whenever we want.
   f Being online _____ me keep in touch with my colleagues, even when
      I'm at home.

2 Which examples of *let* can be replaced by *allow (to), enable (to),* or *permit (to)*?
   What changes, if any, would you need to make to the sentence structure?

❹ Choose three or four words from the list and write a definition for each one.
Include information about what they *allow, enable,* or *permit* you to do.

bookmark	emoticon	firewall	mail filter	newsgroup	TCP/IP
browser	encryption	hyperlink	mailing list	shareware	viewer

Work in pairs. Take turns to read your definitions and see if your partner can guess
which word you have described.

Phrasal verbs

Learning tip

1 It's important to be able to understand phrasal verbs.

2 You can communicate quite effectively without using phrasal verbs.

3 Avoid using phrasal verbs with other non-native speakers of English – they may not understand you.

4 Phrasal verbs are being invented all the time, so it is impossible (and pointless) to learn them all.

5 Try to work out the meaning of a phrasal verb. Replace it with another verb and see if that makes sense – then check in the dictionary.

6 Note down a new phrasal verb with an English synonym next to it, plus an example of how it is used.

5 Look at these examples of phrasal verbs. What do they mean?

*Lastminute.com really **took off** in 1998 …*
*Nowadays you can **plug in** and listen to your home radio station …*
*Chat room users want to **get** their ideas **across** as quickly as they can …*

Work in pairs or groups and look at the suggestions in the Learning tip. Decide whether they are good advice or not.

📖 Pocket Book page 16

6 Sometimes there is some logic to the use of the prepositions used with a phrasal verb, especially with reference to movement. Here are some examples with *get*.

*He **gets up** at 8.00 every morning. He has breakfast then **gets in** his car and **gets out** at the station. He **gets on** the train and **gets off** at the second stop.*

Now complete the sentences with *down, in, off,* and *out*.

1 Can you let me —————, please? The door is locked and I'm getting cold.
2 I think the cat wants to go into the garden – can you let her —————?
3 Come on, have some fun. Let you hair ————— for once!
4 They let ————— an alarm to warn people of the danger.

7 Sometimes it is possible to work out the meaning of a phrasal verb from the context. In pairs, try to think of synonyms for the words in **bold**.

1 They knew all about it, but they didn't **let on**. In fact, they didn't tell anyone.
2 You can rely on me – I'll never **let** you **down**.
3 I don't believe your story – I think you're **making** it **up**.
4 She speaks so quickly that it's hard to **make out** what she's saying.
5 My company gave me a day off to **make up for** working at the weekend.
6 I really don't want to go to the meeting – I wish I could **get out of** it.
7 She's got so much work to do, it's really **getting** her **down**.
8 I really **get off on** this kind of music – it makes me feel so good.

8 Now match the phrasal verbs in **7** with these synonyms.

a be excited by
b disappoint or fail
c indicate your awareness of something
d make depressed

e understand
f compensate for
g avoid
h invent

9 Work in pairs. Ask and answer these questions.

How easily and how often do you really let your hair down?
Have you ever made up a really good excuse (e.g. for being late)?
What aspects of your job do you wish you could get out of?
What kind of things get you down?

1 Here are some extracts from real stories in newspapers and magazines in the English-speaking world. They all contain an example of *ambiguity* – they are intended to have one meaning, but because of the way they are written they can also mean something else.

Work in pairs. Match each extract with one of the cartoons, and say what makes them ambiguous.

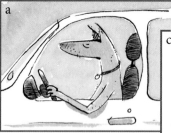

1   I bet I'm the only guy who's chased a rabbit on a motorbike round a field and caught the rabbit.

2   **The other motorist declared that Mr Howard smelled of drink. So did a policeman.**

3   They delivered 66 food parcels to the elderly residents living locally in a large box.

4   If you take your dog in the car don't let him hang out of a window while driving.

5   **Like Adela, he had dark brown hair, with enormous black eyebrows, a moustache, and a short beard.**

Denys Parsons, *The Best of Shrdlu*

2 Here are some tips for writing clear sentences, and avoiding ambiguity.

- Put the subject as close as possible to the verb.
- Put adjectives before the noun they describe.
- If there are several adjectives, follow this order:
  personal opinion + size + age + colour + origin + material + use.
- Be careful how you use participles –
  they usually refer to the subject immediately preceding them.

Rewrite the sentences in **1** so that the meaning is clear.

Pronunciation

1 **You're going to hear three versions of the same sentence, spoken three different ways. A different word is stressed in each to give a particular meaning.**

1   Decide which word would be stressed in order to produce the response.

   a   I went to Paris first.
       Oh, not to Rome?

   b   I went to Paris first.
       So you went, not Elena?

   c   I went to Paris first.
       So you went to Paris before you went to Rome?

2   **5.3** Listen and check if you were right.

3   Work in pairs. Practise saying the sentences and responding, stressing different words.

4   Work in pairs. One person should look at sentences a–c; the other should look at sentences d–f. Underline three different words in each sentence which can be stressed to give a particular meaning.

   a   He can play the piano extremely well.

   b   Her home number is 212664.

   c   Let's meet on Thursday the thirteenth.

   d   We're going to the Alps for a skiing holiday.

   e   His work address is 16 High Street, Oxford.

   f   She should be here before six.

2 **Take turns to read out your sentences, giving one word a particular stress. Your partner should respond, improvising as necessary.**

3 Work in pairs and improvise a telephone conversation. Student A should look at the information on page 113. Student B should look at the information on page 117.

4 Sometimes stress or intonation are not enough to emphasize a particular point. You are going to hear two extracts of people talking about the Internet.

    1   🔊 5.4 Listen to the two extracts. For each extract, what aspect of Internet business is being discussed? What is the speaker's key point?

    2   🔊 5.4 Listen again. Make a note of the phrases the speakers use to underline a point, and to make it clear what they mean.

5 Practise making your point clearly. Follow the framework and use the information in the table.

1 Make your point clearly

➡ 2 Use a clarifying phrase
     Let me explain what I mean.
     What I'm trying to say is …

  ➡ 3 Give examples
       To give you an example, …
       For example, …

    ➡ 4 Clarify your terms
         By X, I mean …
         that is, …
         or more specifically, …

      ➡ 5 Emphasize / summarize key information
           So, essentially …
           The point is …

	1	2
Key point	Internet chat rooms can be dangerous.	You can't run a business without a website.
Clarification	People can use them as a way of getting information about you.	People expect professional companies to have their own website.
Examples	• If you log on to a chat room, people can access information through the name you use. • If you're asked to enter an unfamiliar command, don't – someone could hack into your computer.	• More and more people are using websites to find out about companies' products and services. • A website is proof that you're serious about investing in your business.

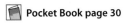 Pocket Book page 30

6 1 Read the three texts and think of two discussion questions related to each text.

      2 Work in groups and ask each other the questions. Each time you manage to emphasize your point using phrases and techniques from **5**, score one point. After ten minutes, see who has the highest score.

a A survey of Internet users in the United States found that advertisements online are effective. Around 27% of Internet users bought something online last year, and 39% of these made their purchases after clicking on an Internet advertisement. The main reason why web-based businesses aren't growing more quickly is that many customers are reluctant to transmit their credit card details over the Internet.

New York Times Almanac

b 'Adult' sites only account for between 2 and 4% of the total number of websites, but receive 10 to 20% of search requests. More than 25% of Internet users in the United States visit such sites. In 1996 a law was passed to control explicit material on the Internet, but in 1997 it was withdrawn because it went against the basic constitutional right of free speech.

New York Times Almanac

c Altogether, 78% of all websites are in English. But this figure is much higher (91%) for sites linked to secure servers. A total of 96% of all '.com' webpages linked to secure servers are in English.

The Economist

1> not making it clear who you are and why you are writing

2> assuming that all emails are informal and not responding with the same level of formality as the sender

3> not answering all the points raised by the sender

4> not making it clear which part of the sender's mail you are responding to

5> writing too much, or in sentences that are too long

6> not bothering to correct spelling mistakes

7> writing everything in UPPER CASE

8> sending attachments that the receiver may not be interested in, or may not be able to open

9> not making it clear what tone you are writing in (for example, if you intend your comments to be humorous)

10> not telling the reader what you expect them to do, and how you yourself will proceed

❶ Ask and answer these questions in pairs.

   1 How often do you use email?
   2 If you use email at work, how has it changed your working life?
   3 What do you use email for? Is it more appropriate for some work-related functions than others?
   4 To what extent do you think writing emails differs from writing letters or faxes? How much difference is there between a formal letter and a formal email?
   5 Do you think email has changed the way people address each other? How?

❷ A survey of typical 'mistakes' made in emails revealed that the ones listed here were the ten most common mistakes.

   1 Which of them do you think:
      a you make?
      b only non-native users of English are likely to make?
      c are the most serious?
      d are not really mistakes at all?

   2 What can you do to avoid some of these mistakes?

❸ Read these two emails. Both are authentic although the names have been changed. Decide which of the 'mistakes' listed in ❷ they contain.

   1 The sender of this email, a marketing manager, wishes to introduce his company, which produces information kiosks, to a potential Spanish client.
      a How suitable is his choice of communication for such an introduction?
      b Is an email the best format for giving company information? What would be better?
      c How appropriate is the first paragraph?
      d What mistakes in the use of capital letters does he make?
      e How could the last paragraph be made more concise?
      f What final salutation would have been more appropriate?
      g What fundamental information has Mr Badu omitted?

From:	**BADU, Giovanni**
Sent:	Tuesday, February15th, 11:55am
To:	'Javier Fernandez'
Subject:	kiosk technologies

Dear Javier Fernandez,

your mail address was given to me by way of my colleague Lucilla Rigobon. During your holiday in Brighton you said to Lucilla that it is possible that Your company is interested in the kiosk market.

To let you understand our activity in kiosk technologies, you'll find attached a brief description of our products and a file containing some references and samples.

Here is some info about our Company and marketing strategy.

- -
30 lines of info about the company then follow
- -

If interested and if you need more information, don't hesitate to contact me sending the address and reference of your Company, so that we can provide you some more information and presentation of our Company, its products and skills.

Regards,
Giovanni Badu

2   The sender of this email works on a help desk, giving support for clients who wish to connect to European electronic money markets. The email he is replying to automatically appears below his own, and is complete.

   a   What two mistakes does he make with the name (Mr Chelsea)? How could he avoid such a mistake?

   b   Are there any parts of the email that are unnecessary?

   c   Does he give all the information required?

   d   How appropriate is Chelsea Reeve's level of formality (i.e. no 'Dear ...', only essential information given)?

   e   Does the help desk's reply match the level of formality of Chelsea Reeve's message? Is this appropriate?

   f   What alternatives to the sentence 'Should you need any further information please do not hesitate to contact us' could have been used?

   g   Is 'Yours sincerely' an appropriate way to sign off?

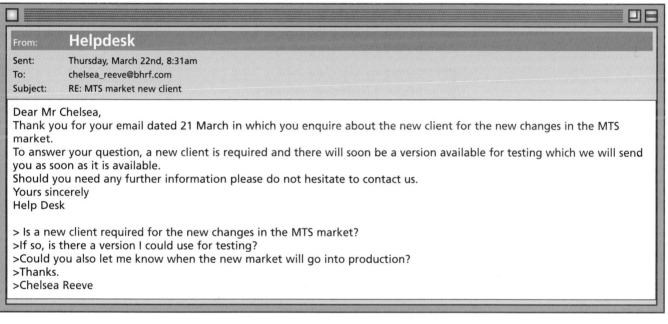

From: **Helpdesk**
Sent: Thursday, March 22nd, 8:31am
To: chelsea_reeve@bhrf.com
Subject: RE: MTS market new client

Dear Mr Chelsea,
Thank you for your email dated 21 March in which you enquire about the new client for the new changes in the MTS market.
To answer your question, a new client is required and there will soon be a version available for testing which we will send you as soon as it is available.
Should you need any further information please do not hesitate to contact us.
Yours sincerely
Help Desk

> Is a new client required for the new changes in the MTS market?
>If so, is there a version I could use for testing?
>Could you also let me know when the new market will go into production?
>Thanks.
>Chelsea Reeve

❹   Work in groups. Create a checklist of things to remember when composing an email. For example:

Do make it clear who you are and why you are writing.
Don't write in sentences that are too long.

When you have finished, compare your list with another group.

❺   Choose one of the emails in ❸ and rewrite it, using the checklist you created in ❹.

❻   How would you deal with these situations – by letter, fax, email, or phone?

   a   You forgot to go to a friend's birthday party.
   b   You made a minor mistake with a client's order.
   c   You wish to change a hotel booking.
   d   You want to change the date of a meeting for the second time.
   e   You want some information about a company's product or service.
   f   Your client is six months late in payment for something.
   g   A reply to an email you sent someone is very late.
   h   You receive an email whose tone appears to be rather angry or unfriendly.

   1   Choose two of the situations and write an appropriate email for each.
   2   Exchange emails with a partner, and write a reply to each other's message.
   3   Analyse each other's emails in terms of the 'mistakes' in ❷, and the checklists you created in ❹.

Unit 6

How much is enough?

OVERVIEW
- Expressing quantity
- Time clauses
- Collocations with *money raise/rise/arise*
- Describing increase and decrease
- Explaining consequences, trends, and statistics
- Presenting information

LANGUAGE FOCUS Expressing quantity and time

1 Test yourself. Which of these nouns are always uncountable (u)? Which are sometimes uncountable and sometimes countable (c/u)? Think of sentences to illustrate the difference. For example:

*My company does a lot of **business** in Latin America.*
*I'd like to start **a business** of my own.*

accommodation	entertainment	information	research
advice	equipment	interest	software
apparatus	fabric	knowledge	technology
business	furniture	machinery	traffic
competition	hardware	material	transport
economy	help	news	work

2 Which nouns from the list can be combined with these phrases?

1 *a piece of* 　　　　　2 *an item of* 　　　　　3 *some*

📖 Pocket Book page 4

3 Who really are the super-rich? These are some of the world's richest people. How many of them can you name?

1 You are going to listen to an interview with a journalist about some of the world's billionaires. What do you think he will say about:

a　the number of women billionaires?

b　the countries where there are most billionaires?

c　what businesses they have made their money from?

d　what they do with a lot of their money?

e　great philanthropists?

2 🔊 6.1 Listen and check. Do any of the answers surprise you?

Expressing quantity

1 Put these expressions in order, from most (1) to least (8).

a lot	several	hardly any	some
none	nearly all	most	not many

2 Which of these expressions can be used with uncountable nouns, and which with countable nouns? Which can be used with both? Think of a sentence for each example.

how many	a lot of	all of
a little	a huge amount of	not much
very few	a great deal of	every
hardly any	a number of	how much

3 What is the difference between these pairs of sentences?

a Our business made **a little** money last year.

b Our business made **little** money last year.

c There are **quite a few** billionaires in Europe.

d There are **very few** billionaires in China.

e One million dollars is **plenty** of money for one person.

f One million dollars is **enough** money for one person.

📖 Pocket Book page 4

4 Look at the results of a survey of rich and successful people who were each asked these questions. The chart shows the percentage that answered 'Yes' to each question. Make sentences about the results of the survey using an appropriate quantifier. For example:

Nearly all *of them said their success was mostly due to hard work.*

Do you consider your success to be mostly due to hard work? **97%**	Would you consider stopping working if you had enough money? **4%**	Do you think you are a control freak? **10%**
Do you consider your success to be partly due to luck? **63%**	Do you give more than ten per cent of your income to charity? **85%**	Do you have time to take long holidays? **79%**
Do you think you have enough money? **17%**	Do you feel a responsibility to give something back to the community? **98%**	Do you have your own private plane? **22%** Do you want to be a billionaire? **43%**

5 Look at these two graphs which show how three people spend their working days, and their monthly income.

Alicia
Stefan
Monika

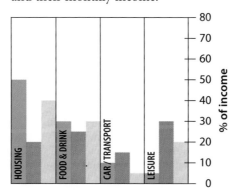

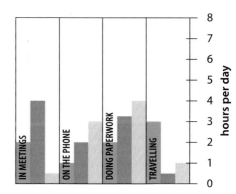

1 Make sentences about:

   a the amount of time each person spends doing the various work activities

   b the amount of their income each person spends in the four categories.

   Don't give exact figures – use an appropriate quantifier to give an approximate number.

2 Work in pairs. Ask and answer questions to find out approximately how much time your partner spends on the different work activities, and how much of their monthly income they spend in the various categories.

6 What is your image of a self-made American billionaire? Decide which of these characteristics they might have:

1 is completely focused on business interests
2 owns several homes and a private jet
3 gives very little money to charity
4 has very little free time to pursue other interests
5 is arrogant and not very likeable.

Read this article about Paul Allen, one of the richest men in the world. As you read, check your ideas for questions 1 to 5. Do you think Paul Allen is a typical billionaire?

A WEALTH OF INTERESTS

SO what do billionaires spend their money on? Paul Allen may not be a household name, but he is one of the world's richest and most influential men, with a wealth of interests and a gift for ideas.

Paul Allen is the computer genius who, with Bill Gates, launched Microsoft, the world's largest producer of software, in 1975. Since then, he has built up a fortune estimated at the turn of the century to be worth over $30 billion.

Allen was Vice-President in charge of research and product development when he was diagnosed with Hodgkin's disease, a form of leukaemia. He underwent radiotherapy successfully, but the experience forced him to evaluate his life and to rethink its direction. Until that point he had been wholly focused on his work with Microsoft, but decided to leave the company in 1983. Before moving on, however, he secured a seat on the Microsoft board. As he retained a seven per cent share of the company's stock, the money has continued to roll in.

Allen has dedicated much of his life since then to the causes he cares about. He gives away millions of dollars each year. He has established charitable foundations to boost the arts, save the trees, promote literacy, build swimming pools, and fund medical research. He has financed numerous development projects in and around the city of Seattle, and put $60 million into Aids research, and to modernizing libraries and theatres.

As soon as an idea is formed, it is translated into action. Typical of Allen's approach was his idea for saving and resurrecting the Cinerama Theater. While buying laser discs from a video store near where he had grown up, Allen noticed a 'Save the Cinerama' petition on the counter. The Cinerama was once a hugely popular entertainment center, but in recent years it had become sad and run down. After learning that it might become a dinner theater, a rock-climbing club, or even a parking lot, Allen signed the petition. Then he bought the theater – for $3.75 million. America's third-richest person owns a movie house. 'The Cinerama was part of my movie-going experience growing up here,' he says. 'I thought it was important to keep.'

In his free time, Allen enjoys surfing the Internet, scuba diving and reading science magazines. He has his own Boeing 757 jet, a yacht with a helipad and recording studio, and a fleet of cars. He owns homes in Beverley Hills, Manhattan, France and elsewhere. What he seems to like best, though, is playing guitar with his six-piece band, The Grown Men.

Because Allen is private and generally inaccessible, as billionaires tend to be, he is often described as 'shy and reclusive'. But he also has an outgoing lifestyle, rubbing shoulders with the rich and famous. His lavish parties are legendary, and his friends include tennis star Monica Seles and musicians Peter Gabriel and Dave Stewart.

Characterized by one friend as 'smart, modest and likeable', the man whose vision inspired the world's most successful company is using his great wealth not only to enrich his own life, but to improve the lives of thousands of others. As a biography of Bill Gates puts it, Allen is probably 'the nicest billionaire you'll never meet'.

Seattle Times

7 Read the article again.

1 Why do you think Paul Allen decided to leave Microsoft in 1983?
2 Why has the money 'continued to roll in' since then?
3 Why did Allen think it was important to keep the Cinerama Theater as a cinema?
4 Why do you think billionaires tend to be 'private and generally inaccessible'? How is this different from being 'shy and introvert'?

Time clauses

1 **What is the difference in meaning between these pairs of sentences?**

1 In which case is there a sense of urgency?
   a **When** he became a billionaire, he sold his company.
   b **As soon as** he became a billionaire, he sold his company.

2 Which sentence might indicate that he never changed roles at Microsoft?
   a **When** he left Microsoft, he was Executive Vice-President.
   b **Until** he left Microsoft, he was Executive Vice-President.

3 Which sentence suggests that she was/is a cause of problems for the speaker's business? What does the other sentence mean?
   a **While** she worked for us, everything was OK.
   b **Until** she worked for us, everything was OK.

4 Which sentence indicates that I won't need it after Saturday? What does the other sentence mean?
   a I'll need it **until** Saturday.
   b I'll need it **by** Saturday.

2 **In sentences like these, conjunctions of time (*when, as soon as, until, before, after*, etc.) normally behave like *if* and are not immediately followed by *will*, but by a present or past tense form.**

*I will let you know when I **have finished**.*
(not *when I ~~will finish~~*)

*As soon as she **comes**, I will call you.*
(not *As soon as she ~~will come~~*)

 Pocket Book page 18

8 Work in pairs. Underline any of the forms in italics that are not possible or are unlikely. Decide the difference in meaning, if any, between the remaining forms.

1 We didn't buy any stock *when/ as soon as/ until/ after* the merger was announced.
2 She worked for the same company *while/ when/ until/ before* she was working in Hong Kong.
3 He gave away millions *when/ as soon as/ until/ after* he became a billionaire.

9 Underline the correct forms.

1 I can't do anything *until/while* you *are/will be* here, so please come quickly.
2 I *will stay/stay* here *until/when/by* you *will get/get* back, but not for long.
3 If you *manage/will manage* to finish this *until/by* Friday, I *give/will give* you a bonus.
4 Don't worry, I *let/will let* you know *as soon as/when* I *have/will have* any news.

Talking point

10 How important are material possessions in your country?

🎧 **6.2** Now listen to an American, an Australian, and an Indian discussing the importance of money in their countries. Underline any of the words in the box that they use. Did they say anything that suprised you?

📱 **Understanding natural speech**

11 Work in groups and discuss these questions.

1 Is it acceptable to talk about how much money you have?
2 Should people be judged on the basis of their wealth and possessions?
3 In your country, is there a big divide between rich and poor? If so, what can be done to improve things?
4 Think about people that you know in your country, or the town you live in. Discuss how many of them:
   - love to talk about what they earn
   - are becoming very materialistic
   - have only one child
   - have more than four children
   - have a computer at home
   - have become rich from humble origins
   - use a mobile phone
   - don't have a car
   - have more than one job
   - own two homes
   - are middle class
   - are millionaires.

class struggle
corporation
corruption
dollars
earn
getting enough to eat
greed
jobs
lottery
luxury
materialistic
middle class
millionaire
money
penniless immigrant
possessions
poverty
stock exchange
success
successful
status
wealth

1 How good is your knowledge of vocabulary associated with money? Work in pairs and check that you know all the verbs in the box.

bet	finance	loan	pay	rent	spend
borrow	fund	lend	pay for	run short of	value
change	gain	lose	put aside	save	waste
deposit	hire	make	put into	secure	win
earn	invest	mint	raise	sell	withdraw

1 Which of these verbs <u>do not</u> collocate with *money*?

2 Some of these verbs are almost synonyms of each other. Which ones? What is the difference in meaning between them?

3 Which verbs are antonyms (opposites) of each other?

4 What noun or nouns can be formed from these verbs?

invest	lose	pay	raise	secure	sell	value	withdraw

Pocket Book pages 22–25

Raise, rise, and arise

2 Look at these headlines.

Commentators predict interest rate rise
Unions demand 10% raise
CHARITY APPEAL RAISES OVER $2M
Inquiry raises questions over police powers

WALL STREET'S LATEST STAR RISES TO TOP JOB

Questions arise over MEPs' expenses claims

House prices continue to rise
Central bank to raise lending rates

1 What is the difference between *to raise*, *to rise*, and *to arise*? Which one means:
  a to go up / to increase?
  b to put up / to cause to increase?
  c to bring up / to mention?
  d to get on / to achieve a higher position?
  e to come up / to occur?
  f to generate / to acquire (money, interest)?

  What is the past form / the past participle of each verb?

2 Complete these sentences with a suitable form of *raise*, *rise*, or *arise*.
  a Political parties often try to _____ support from business people.
  b A job opportunity has _____ at our office in Sydney.
  c Salaries only _____ by 2.5% last year.
  d It's likely that a few problems will _____ because of the delay.
  e The government is predicting that the cost of living will continue to _____ .
  f I plan to _____ the question of late payment at the next meeting.

Pocket Book page 25

3 Which of these words are (a) verbs only, (b) both verbs and nouns?

rise	decline	put up	improve	increase	go up
go down	raise	decrease	put down	reduce	fall

Group them into two sets of pairs: synonyms (words with the same or similar meaning) and antonyms (words that mean the opposite of each other). You may be able to use the same word in more than one pairing.

Increase and decrease

4 1 These adjectives are all used to describe increase and decrease (rise and fall).

considerable	dramatic	gradual	moderate
negligible	rapid	sharp	significant
slight	slow	steady	substantial

Which ones describe (a) the size of the change, (b) the speed of the change, or (c) both? Group the adjectives with one of the three graphs.

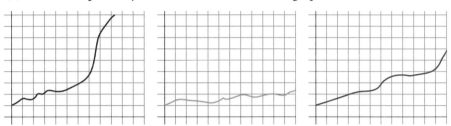

2 Which adjectives in 1 can be collocated with: *almost, barely, quite, rather, very*?

3 We can describe increase and decrease in two ways:

*There was a **steady rise** in house prices last year.* (adjective + noun)
*House prices **rose steadily** last year.* (verb + adverb)

Which sentence focuses on the process that took place? Which one focuses on the event, or the result of a process?

4 Look at the graph. Complete the text with some of the words from 1 (either as adjectives or adverbs). Do not use the same word more than once.

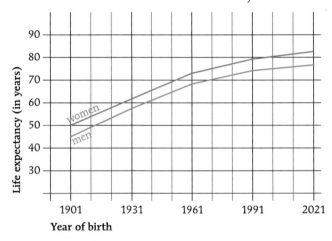

Generally speaking, the average woman lives longer than her male counterpart. The life expectancy of human beings went up 1_____ from 1901 to 1931. It then rose 2_____ over the next 30 years. There was then a 3_____ increase until 1991. Since then there has been a 4_____ increase every year. Increases from year to year are 5_____, but the life expectancy will go up 6_____ until that for men reaches an age of about 80, and for women about 83.

Sociology

5 Complete the following sentences. Use either an adjective + noun or a verb + adverb construction.

1 There's been _____ in my weight since I left school.
2 The value of my house/flat _____ since I bought it.
3 I've had _____ in my salary since I started my current job.
4 My car _____ in value since I bought it.
5 The time I can run a kilometre in _____ since I left school.
6 I've seen _____ in my company's profits over the last five years.
7 Shares prices in my country _____ in the last few months.
8 I've noticed _____ in my cost of living over the last five years.

6 Work in pairs and discuss the various changes in your lives in recent years, with reference to some, or all, of these aspects:

– your working hours
– your workload
– the amount of free time you have
– the level of responsibility you have
– your job satisfaction
– your standard of living.

1 Work in pairs. Before you read the article, look at the photographs and discuss these questions.

   1 What do you think ordinary working people spent most of their family budget on one hundred years ago?

   2 What do you think they spend most of it on today?

2 Read this extract from an article about the ways family spending has changed in the US since 1900. Check your answer to the questions in **1**.

THE BIGGEST CHANGE IN SPENDING has been in the amount spent on food, which has declined significantly from 46% of the total family budget in 1901 to 19% of current total expenditure. This is *due to the fact that*[1] people are now able to buy more and better foods at lower prices. *As a result of*[2] the growth in fast-food establishments (*for example*[3], MacDonald's, Kentucky Fried Chicken) more people are also eating out. *Thus*[4] about 30% of today's food budget goes on meals eaten outside the home, *whereas*[5] a hundred years ago it was only 3%.

At the beginning of the last century, few people owned their homes (only around 19% of worker families) and their own cars (at $1,000 per car this was well above the average family income of $650 per year), *as*[6] most people were unable to borrow money. But there was a rapid rise in both home and car ownership during the mid-1900s.

Leisure time increased considerably *following*[7] the shortening of the working week, *i.e.*[8] from six days to five, and from ten hours to eight hours a day. In fact, the car producer Henry Ford soon realized that the working day couldn't be too long, otherwise workers wouldn't have time to spend their money. The proportion of a family's budget spent on outside entertainment has increased from just under 6% in Ford's day to approximately 9% today. *On the other*

hand[9] we spend only a quarter of what our great-grandparents paid for reading materials.

It is difficult to make long-term projections on how our spending patterns may change in the future, as these are a result of trends in social and economic conditions, and of course demography. In the short term, we already know that our population is ageing and this will affect the amount of money we spend on medical care. *But*[10] the long-term consequences of new technologies *such as*[11] the Internet and genetically modified food are, like changes in tastes, unpredictable.

Monthly Labor Review

3 1 Look at the words highlighted in the text in **2**. Match them with words from the box that have a similar meaning.

because	due to	for instance	like	so	while
because of	e.g.	however	since	that is to say	

   2 Which words in the list can be used to:

     a give a reason?   c indicate a contrast?

     b state a consequence?   d specify or give an example?

   3 Which of the words in the text and the list are likely to be used in speech as well as in writing?

 Pocket Book page 30

4 Use the notes in the table to explain the three trends. Make sure you use appropriate words to give an example, give a reason, state a consequence, and indicate a contrast.

	1	2	3
Trend	More people are taking holidays to exotic locations	More people are eating out more than once a month	People in the West are having fewer children
Example	Southern India, SE Asia, and Latin America are all very popular destinations	Over 50% of 25 to 40-year-olds eat out twice a month	Average number of children per woman, 1995–2000: Spain 1.15, Italy 1.20, Yemen 7.60, Somalia 7.25, Uganda 7.10
Reason	Air travel is becoming much cheaper, people want more from their leisure time	People have more money and less time to cook, fewer women stay at home all day	More women are working, people want more freedom and choice in their lifestyles
Consequence	Changes to the economy and environment of destination countries	More restaurants are opening up (increase in choice)	In future there will be more older people and fewer tax-payers to support them (the average % of population aged over 65 in Europe is around 17%)
Contrast	Fewer people are taking holidays in their own country	More people are also buying frozen, ready-to-eat meals	Birth rate is still going up in developing countries, more children surviving infancy compared to 50 years ago

5 Look at graph 1 showing the spending of a typical UK family. How do you think it compares with family spending in your country?

1 Draw a curve on graph 2 to show:
   a how your expenditure (or the expenditure of a typical family from your country) on the items in the list has changed during your lifetime, and why
   b how you expect it to change in the short term (i.e. over the next couple of years), mid term, and long term, and why.

graph 1

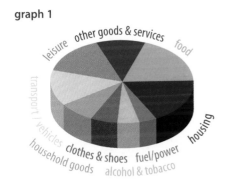

graph 2

- alcohol and tobacco
- education and training
- food
- housing
- leisure
- medical care

2 Compare your ideas with your partner. Make sure you explain the reasons for any changes and that you give examples.

6 Look at graph 3 which gives details about changes in the UK government's spending since 1900.

graph 3

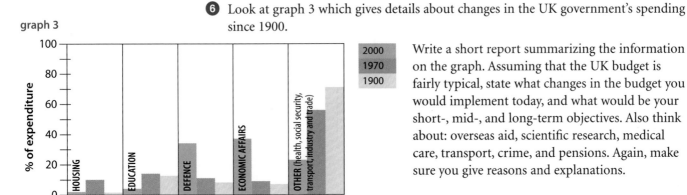

Write a short report summarizing the information on the graph. Assuming that the UK budget is fairly typical, state what changes in the budget you would implement today, and what would be your short-, mid-, and long-term objectives. Also think about: overseas aid, scientific research, medical care, transport, crime, and pensions. Again, make sure you give reasons and explanations.

❶ Have you ever had to give, or listen to, a presentation in English?

1   If the answer to this question is 'Yes', how successful was the presentation? What factors made it a good or bad presentation? Discuss your ideas with a partner.

2   If the answer to this question is 'No', how would you prepare to give a presentation in English? What information would you need to know in advance? Discuss your ideas with a partner.

3   Work in groups. Write a list of the key rules for making a good presentation. Here are some of the features you may wish to consider:
    –   research and preparation
    –   content and length
    –   organization and structure
    –   visual/aural aids
    –   delivery (e.g. voice, speed, appearance, gestures, use of humour)
    –   knowledge of audience.

    Compare your ideas with another group.

❷ How many hours per week do you work? Is this more or less than people of your parents' generation? How many hours a week did your grandparents work?

1   Draw a curve on the graph to show what you think was the general trend of the average working week in industry during the 20th century, and what you think it will be until 2020.

2   Work in pairs and describe your trends. Draw each other's curves on your own graphs.

3 Here are some initial notes for a brief presentation on working hours in 20th-century America. The presenter still has to find a number of statistics.

1 Put the notes into a logical order.
2 Decide what you would say to begin and end the presentation.

Notes for April presentation on working week

1930s predicted working week would be ? hours for white collar workers

highest paid workers work longer than lowest paid (1999) - in 1900?

agriculture 70 hours (1900)

industry 60 hours (1900), ? hours (1920), ? hours (1939), ? hours (1943), ? hours (1970)

average working week likely to be ? hours by 2020.

European blue collar workers want 35 hours.

4 6.3 Listen to the presentation and draw the curve that the presenter describes on to the graph in **2**. How similar is it to the curves you and your partner drew?

5 6.3 Listen again and answer the questions.

1 Did the speaker present the information in the same order as you did?
2 How did he introduce himself?
3 What technique does he use to summarize what he is going to say?
4 How quickly does he speak?
5 How does he make what he is saying sound interesting? Evaluate his presentation according to the key rules for good presentations that you discussed in **1**.

Pronunciation

Turn to page 132 of the Listening script.

1 Underline the words in italics that you think should receive the most stress. If you think they should have an equal stress, underline both.

2 6.3 Listen and check your answers.

6 You are now going to make a short presentation. Work in groups.

1 Choose one of the topics listed below and decide who the audience is.
2 Brainstorm some more factors to cover in your presentation.
3 Organize the factors into an appropriate order, discarding any irrelevant ones.
4 Give your presentation to another group.

	Present your ...	Some factors to consider:
a	company	– when it was founded – what the company originally did – location – number of employees
b	current project	– why it was initiated – when the deadlines are – who it's for – what has been achieved so far
c	country	– geographical location – history – GDP – tourism.

Pocket Book page 31

Review Unit C

This unit reviews the main language points from Units 5 and 6. Complete the exercises. Check your learning with the Self-check box at the end.

Defining and non-defining relative clauses

1 Complete the sentences with *who, whom, which, that,* or nothing (Ø). Add commas where you think they are necessary.

1 I take after my mother ___ like me has a passion for piranha fish.
2 She told me a joke about a man ___ thought he was a teapot.
3 All of my friends most of ___ are in therapy have three or more children.
4 The hotel ___ overlooks the zoo and is the only one ___ has over 200 rooms.
5 The part of the film ___ I liked best is when she falls off her bike and into the back of a truck.

Countable vs uncountable nouns

2 Decide if these words are countable (C), uncountable (U), or both countable and uncountable (C/U). For those that you have marked C/U, write pairs of sentences which clearly show the difference in meaning.

advice	coffee	furniture	information	paper
business	feedback	glass	knowhow	software

Expressing quantity

3 1 Write sentences about other members of your class or colleagues at work. Use a different quantity word from the list in each sentence. Follow the example.

a lot of	(not) much	(not) many	(a) few	(a) little	plenty of	most

speak English fluently   *Few people in my company can speak English fluently.*

a speak Chinese   d live in the city
b use a computer   e come to work by car
c play a musical instrument   f are married

2 Underline the word/phrase in *italics* which you think is more likely to be true.

a We founded our company last year and it's already made *little / a little* money.
b *Quite a / Very* few British people speak more than two languages.
c We've got ten minutes – that's *just enough / plenty of* time to have another coffee before the train leaves.
d I didn't answer *any / some* of the questions, two or three at the most.

Time clauses

4 Underline the correct word/phrase in *italics* and put the verbs in brackets into the correct tense form. More than one word/phrase and tense form may be possible.

1 *While / Until* I (live) in Tokyo, I (not realize) what being a commuter was like.
2 *When / As soon as* he (finish) the report, he (read) it through very carefully.
3 They said they (tell) me *by / until* the weekend if I (get) the job.
4 Call me *as soon as / when* you (arrive) at the hotel – I need to speak to you urgently.

Vocabulary

5 Underline the most suitable choice from the word(s) in *italics*. More than one choice may be possible.

1 My salary has gone up – I now *earn / gain / win* considerably more than before.
2 I want to stay in this job for another year to *earn / gain / win* more experience.
3 I'm going to ask my father to *borrow / lend / loan* me the money for a new car.
4 If we don't conclude this deal now, a lot of problems are likely to *raise / rise / arise*.
5 If the government *raises / rises / arises* interest rates, our mortgage payments will definitely *raise / rise / arise*.

Vocabulary

6 Complete the sentences with an appropriate form of a verb from the list.

earn	gain	win	borrow	lend	loan	arise	raise	rise

1 Just because you _____ more money doesn't mean your standard of living _____ .

2 She _____ ten dollars from me last month and still hasn't paid me back. I'm never going to _____ her money again.

3 He's _____ a lot more respect from everyone since he _____ that contract.

4 A problem _____ concerning the mortgage for your house. We are willing to _____ you the money, but only if you pay a 20% deposit.

Phrasal verbs

7 Match each phrasal verb with a suitable equivalent.

1	get down	a	avoid
2	get off on	b	pretend
3	get out of	c	become depressed
4	let down	d	deal leniently with
5	let off	e	disappoint
6	make out	f	be excited by

make, let, enable, allow, permit

8 Underline the correct verb in each sentence. More than one may be possible.

1 This programme *allows/ lets/ permits* you to download sound files.

2 This programme *enables/ lets/ permits* sound files to be downloaded.

3 They didn't *let/ make/ allow* me see her, so I don't know how she is.

4 They *made/ let* me tell them everything before they *made/ let/ allowed* me to go.

Describing statistics

9 Rewrite these sentences. Change the highlighted adjectives into adverbs. Find alternative words or phrases for those in *italics*. Follow the example.

There has been a **sharp** increase in house prices, and first-time buyers are *therefore* in great difficulty.
House prices have increased sharply in recent times, and because of this first-time buyers are in great difficulty.

1 Several countries, *for example*, Denmark, Sweden, and Finland, have seen a **steady** rise in the use of mobile phones.

2 Prices have *gone up* considerably in the last year – this has been the result of **higher** interest rates.

3 There has been a **negligible** increase in turnover this year. *On the other hand*, the value of the company has rocketed.

Writing emails

10 What were the last five emails you wrote in your own language? Choose two, and briefly outline the context so that your teacher can understand the background to the email. Then write an equivalent email in English.

Self-check box

	YES	NO	📖		YES	NO	📖
Defining and non-defining relative clauses	☐	☐	17	Phrasal verbs with *get, make,* and *let*	☐	☐	16
Countable vs uncountable nouns	☐	☐	4	*make, let, enable, allow, permit*	☐	☐	23, 24
Expressing quantity	☐	☐	4	Describing statistics	☐	☐	30
Time clauses	☐	☐	18	Writing emails	☐	☐	
Vocabulary: *earn, gain, win / borrow, lend, loan / raise, rise, arise*	☐	☐	22–25				

Unit 7

OVERVIEW
- Passives review
- *have/get something done*
- Education vocabulary
- Organizing information: *firstly, consequently, eventually*, etc.
- Giving and getting explanations
- Clarifying and paraphrasing
- Explaining a process
- Interviews

Education

LANGUAGE FOCUS   **Passives review,** *have/get something done*

1 Work in pairs and discuss these questions.

1   How important is a university education in your country?
2   How easy is it to get into university?
3   What are the most useful subjects to study?
4   Does a university qualification guarantee a good job?

2 Read this article about the relationship between university and getting a job in three different countries. Find the information to complete the table on page 69.

In many countries, having a university degree can give you a flying start in life. But where you were educated is often just as important. Attending the 'right' university can be a major factor in determining whether or not you are destined for a top-flight career.

In Britain, it is generally recognized that a degree from Oxford or Cambridge universities
10 opens doors when it comes to working in government, the media, banking, or the diplomatic service. America's equivalent is its Ivy League universities, for example Harvard, Yale, and Princeton. Most other countries have their élite institutions, too. France, for example, has the *grandes écoles*. In Italy, economists traditionally graduate from Bocconi in Milan, while in Japan most politicians have been educated at a top public university,
20 such as Todai, Waseda, or Keio.

So just how easy is it to get into university these days?

In Britain, most prospective students apply to the Universities and Colleges Admissions Service (UCAS), and their applications are passed on to the universities they have specified on their UCAS form. If successful, they are invited to an interview and may be awarded a place at the university of their
30 choice based on the grades they are expected to get in their core high-school subjects.

In Japan, competition for a place at one of the top national universities or private institutions (73 per cent of Japanese universities are privately run) has always

been intense, as a spokesperson from Japan's Ministry of Education, explains. 'It's very difficult to get into a national university, or a top private one, though it's quite easy to get
40 into a lower-level private institution. You must have a senior high-school diploma. Then you apply to each university separately, and take a different exam for each one. A nationwide standardized exam was recently introduced to screen applicants. If an applicant is recommended by his or her high school, he or she will probably be invited to attend an interview.'

In Italy, it is a similar story. Although it's
50 relatively easy to get into many Italian universities, says Professor Gabriele Azzaro of Genova University, for most students this means the one nearest to home. There's still fierce competition for places at the top institutions. 'You need to have passed your *Maturità*, which is like the *Baccalauréat*. Basically, you make a written application and pay the fees. But in some faculties, like dentistry or medicine, good grades in certain
60 key subjects may be required.'

So how useful are university qualifications when it comes to getting a job?

British students graduating from most universities after three or four years' study receive a Bachelor of Arts or Science, depending on their subject. For prospective employers, the class of the degree can be crucial. 'A second-class degree is an
70 indication that someone has achieved a good

general standard,' says Human Resources Manager Emma Harte. 'A first-class degree shows that they have something extra, an intellectual edge, and the ability to think creatively and independently. Since only a tiny percentage of students are awarded a first, having one gives you a significant advantage when applying for high-level jobs.'

80   In Japan it's somewhat different. You rarely hear a Japanese person say, 'I've got a BA or an MA'. It's more usual to hear 'I graduated from X University'. It depends on the company, but where you studied is often more important than what you studied when it comes to getting a job. There are no classes of degree. It's useful to have a

	Requirements for getting into top universities	What employers are interested in
Britain		
Italy		
Japan		

③ Read the article again. Work in pairs and discuss these questions.

1 In most countries, why are there some universities that are more prestigious than others?

2 Why does the university you attended seem to be more important to employers in Japan than what you studied?

3 Why is the class of degree so important to prospective employers in Britain?

4 What does this tell you about attitudes to education and employment in Britain and Japan?

relevant qualification, but big companies often have their own
90 entrance tests.'

And in Italy? According to Professor Azzaro, graduating from one of the major universities is inevitably an advantage. 'But employers will also look at your overall grade, a total score out of 110, which is based on your work over four or five years. Students are usually
100 examined by dissertation, or by oral exams. And getting a good reference from your professor is important, too.'

Passives review

① **Look at these sentences from the article and highlight the verbs in the passive. How do we form the passive in English?**

a In Britain, it is generally recognized that a degree from Oxford or Cambridge universities opens doors …

b If successful, they are invited to an interview …

c A nationwide standardized exam was recently introduced to screen applicants.

d If an applicant is recommended by his or her high school, he or she will probably be invited to attend an interview.

e …in Japan most politicians have been educated at a top public university …

f …in some faculties …good grades in certain key subjects may be required.

② **Compare these pairs of sentences. Why do we sometimes choose passive forms?**

a If an applicant **is recommended** by his or her high school …

b If his or her high school **recommends** an applicant …

c Students **are usually examined** by dissertation, or by oral exams.

d Universities **usually examine** students by dissertation, or by oral exams.

③ 1 In which sentences in **①** a–f is the agent of the action in the passive mentioned?

2 For the other sentences, decide if the agent is not mentioned because:

a the agent is unknown, or no one in particular

b the focus is on the action – the agent is not important

c the identity of the agent is obvious.

📖 **Pocket Book page 13**

4 Change these sentences into the passive. Decide whether or not to include the agent.

1 In Britain, about ten per cent of parents send their children to private schools.
2 Someone from the institute met us at the airport and drove us to our hotel.
3 Many universities have awarded Nelson Mandela an honorary degree.
4 The government funds most of the public universities in Japan.
5 Teachers will tell all students their grades at the end of the week.
6 After university, five prospective employers interviewed me, and they all offered me a job.

5 Work in pairs. Describe to each other the steps leading to your present job. Include information about your education, applications, interviews, and previous jobs or positions in your company. Try to use passive forms as much as possible.

6 7.1 Listen to three extracts from a conversation between three people.

1 Which countries are they from?
2 Where do they all work?
3 In each extract, what are they discussing?

7 7.1 Listen again.

1 In Extract 1:
   a what does Adriano say about his students' assignments?
   b what does he need to do about the
      i research data   ii field equipment   iii vaccinations?

2 In Extract 2:
   a How are some study fees paid in Italy and Japan?
   b According to Adriano, what are the advantages of living at home while you study?

3 In Extract 3:
   a What happened to a wallet, and a bicycle?
   b What is said about Akemi's accommodation, and about her books and personal possessions?

Have / get something done

1 Look at these pairs of sentences. In each case, what is the difference in meaning?

   a I have all the assignments marked.
   b I have marked all the assignments.

   c I had some money transferred from my bank account.
   d I had transferred some money from my bank account.

2 In which of these sentences does someone arrange for something to happen? In which sentence does something happen to someone?

   a I had my all my books shipped over from Japan.
   b My sister had her bike stolen from outside her flat.

3 In sentences 1a,c and 2 a,b you can use *get* in place of *have*. Which of these sentences sounds more informal?

   a I need to have my passport renewed.
   b I need to get my passport renewed.

 Pocket Book page 8

8 Complete these sentences using the words in brackets in the *have / get something done* structure.

1 My brother works for the diplomatic service in Kenya. He … (all his living expenses / pay for).
2 I think I should … (eyes / test). I can't read that poster on the wall from here.
3 Tom accidentally downloaded a virus into his computer. He … (all his files / corrupt).
4 We can … (the money / pay into) a special account – that way we won't be tempted to spend it.
5 Did you hear that terrible storm last night? The house next door … (part of its roof / blow off).

9 Look at these diary notes of a university research expedition that had some problems. Write two sentences for each note, one in the passive form, one with *have/get something done*. For example:

The visas have been extended.   We've had the visas extended.

> **DAY 4 – In the capital**
> Managed to extend visas - phew!
> Now we need to renew the trekking permits.

> **DAY 5 – On the road …**
> Trekking permits OK.
> Recording equipment damaged in transit - must repair.

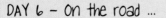

> **DAY 6 – On the road …**
> Bad storm at campsite last night - some clothing blown away.

> **DAY 8 – On the road …**
> Problem with visas - police confiscated our passports this morning.

> **DAY 7 – Near the border**
> Mike's tooth still a problem - checked by local dentist.

> **DAY 9 – Near the border**
> Disaster! Someone stole our camera equipment last night - police not interested.

10 Work in pairs. Combine appropriate nouns and verbs from the boxes to form questions. Ask your partner questions using a variety of tenses. For example:

How often do you have your eyes tested?   *When did you last …?*
Would you ever ….?   *Have you ever …?*

article / paper / book	hair
body	heart
car	house
clothes	idea
driving licence	portrait
eyes	wallet

break into	publish
dye	service
endorse	steal
make	tattoo
paint	test
pierce	wash

11 Work in groups. Choose one or more of these statements, and prepare to discuss it with your group.

1 In life, experience and ability are more important than qualifications.
2 Being successful depends more on *who* you know than on *what* you know.
3 Going to university is about doing things for yourself and finding out who you are.
4 The most successful people in life are not always the best educated.

❶ Excluding native speakers, around one billion people worldwide speak English.

1 How many people in your country speak one or more foreign languages?

2 At what age do children in your country start learning a foreign language?

❷ Read this article and find out:

1 why the writer is against teaching foreign languages in British schools

2 what serious errors he thinks are responsible for the failure of language teaching.

Let's take leave of French

ONE TOPIC is rarely mentioned in all the talk of improving standards in our schools: the almost complete failure of foreign-language teaching. Despite the compulsory teaching of French in secondary schools, our ability to speak it is minimal.

Take any random sample of the population, and barely half of them will be able to say more than a few words. Those who can speak more than this probably owe their skills not to school, but to other experience or training.

As a French graduate who has taught for more than twenty-five years in state schools as well as independent schools, I believe I have some idea of why the failure is so total. Apart from the faults already diagnosed in the education system as a whole – such as child-centred learning, the 'discovery' method, and the low expectations by teachers of pupils – there have been several serious errors which have a direct effect on language teaching.

The first is the removal from the curriculum of the thorough teaching of English grammar. Pupils now do not know a verb from a noun, the subject of a sentence from its object, or the difference between the past, present, or future.

Another important error is mixed-ability teaching, or teaching in ability groups so wide that the most able pupils are held back and are bored while the least able are lost and equally bored. Strangely enough, few head teachers seem to be in favour of mixed-ability school football teams or choirs.

Progress depends on memory, and pupils start to forget immediately they stop having regular lessons. This is why many people who attended French lessons at school, even those who got good grades, have forgotten it a few years later. Because they never need it, they do not practise it.

Most American schools have accepted what is inevitable and withdrawn modern languages, even Spanish, from the curriculum. Perhaps it is time for Britain to do the same, and stop wasting resources on a subject which few pupils want or need.

Daily Mail

❸ 1 What is the difference between a *state* school and *a public* school?

2 Complete the diagram:

Age 16–19	_____ education
Age 11–16	*secondary* education
Age 5–11	_____ education

a child-centred learning
b mixed-ability teaching
c the 'discovery' method

3 Match these teaching methods from the article with the most suitable definition.

i pupils of different learning capacity are taught together

ii pupils are not taught, but are given the opportunity to find out things for themselves

iii the focus of learning is on the pupil, not the teacher

What do you think about these methods of learning? Do you have any experience of them?

④ Test your knowledge of education vocabulary. Choose the best answer a–d. In some cases, more than one word may be possible. Check your answers in the article in ②.

ucation education education education educat

1 When you finish university you are a/an
- **a** aspirant
- **b** candidate
- **c** doctor
- **d** graduate

2 School is important for your
- **a** education
- **b** formation
- **c** upbringing
- **d** training

3 The people who teach at schools are known as
- **a** directors
- **b** pedagogues
- **c** professors
- **d** teachers

4 Children at school are called
- **a** fellows
- **b** pupils
- **c** scholars
- **d** students

5 Lessons at schools follow a
- **a** curriculum
- **b** programme
- **c** schedule
- **d** syllabus

6 Schoolchildren _____ lessons.
- **a** assist
- **b** attend
- **c** follow
- **d** frequent

7 If you do well at school you usually get good
- **a** grades
- **b** characters
- **c** notes
- **d** votes

8 Mathematics, geography, history, and English are all
- **a** arguments
- **b** materials
- **c** subjects
- **d** topics

Pronunciation

① 🔊 7.2 Listen to the way the words *graduate* and *estimate* are pronounced in these sentences. What do you notice about the difference in pronunciation between the noun and verb forms?

② Now practise saying these words in the two different ways.

associate	duplicate	graduate	separate
delegate	estimate	initiate	subordinate

③ 🔊 7.3 Listen to the differences in pronunciation between the verb and noun/adjective forms of *present/presented* and *progress/progressed*. How does the stress change?

④ Now practise saying these words in the two different ways.

conflict	export	object	progress	refund
contrast	import	permit	project	subject
defect	increase	present	record	transport

Learning tip

When the same word can have two different pronunciations it is clearly a good idea to note this down. If the pronunciation is different (as in the examples in **Pronunciation**, or in words like live – to *live* /ɪ/, a *live* /aɪ/ programme) use phonetic symbols (or your own system) to show the difference.

If the stress is different, simply mark the stress and note the part of speech (noun, verb, adjective): **re**cord (n), re**cord** (v). Writing the word in a context may help you to memorize it better. For example:

I've recorded it on to a mini disc.
The statistical records show that …

Organizing information

5 ▶ 7.4 Listen to an interview with Emilio Gonzales, who is trying to get English adopted as the only official language of the United States.

1 What has happened in schools in the US as part of the bilingual programme?
2 What happens to immigrants in the US who don't speak English?
3 What were the findings of the study conducted among children in New York?
4 What other negative consequences are there of the bilingual programme?
5 How large is 'US English', and what is its aim?

6 The words in List 1 were all used by the two speakers in the interview.

1 Which words are used to describe the sequence of events?
2 Match the words in List 1 with the word or phrase in List 2 closest in meaning.

List 1			
1 firstly		5 definitely	
2 consequently		6 eventually	
3 actually		7 subsequently	
4 ultimately		8 finally	

List 2			
a in reality, really		e so, as a result	
b certainly		f lastly	
c to begin		g in the last analysis	
d in the end (after some trouble)		h later	

7 ▶ 7.4 Listen to the interview again. Decide whether the way the words in List 1 are used matches the meanings you chose. If necessary, refer to the script on pages 132–3.

📖 Pocket Book pages 26, 35

8 Complete this story with suitable words from List 1 in **6**.

Learning any new skill

can be a painful process. Take my recent experience with snowboarding. 1_____, I learned, you have to forget everything you know about ordinary skiing. Snowboarding is more like surfing or skateboarding, so knowing how to ski is 2_____ a disadvantage. When I first started, I kept trying to lift one leg at a time, and always face downhill. 3_____, I spent a lot of my time falling over in the snow and feeling rather foolish. 4_____ I learned that it's the same for most people at the beginning, but at the time I seemed to be the only one. 5_____, after three or four days of embarrassment and frustration – mine and my instructor's – I worked out how to shift my weight in the right way. After that I was unstoppable. The rest of the holiday passed in a blur of blue skies, pine trees, and multi-coloured snowsuits. I've realized that, 6_____, it isn't important how proficient you look. It's having fun that matters, and I did. I'll 7_____ be coming back next year.

9 Work in pairs. Choose one of these options.

1 Describe your experience of learning a new skill.
2 Describe your experience of the primary or secondary education systems in your country.
3 Describe an interview or selection process you have been through.
4 Invent a story that contains at least six of the words and phrases from the two lists in **6**.

❶ Think about the typical order in which we do things in our lives – for example, school, university, job, marriage, children, retirement. Is this the best way to structure our lives and to make them interesting and dynamic? What alternative ways can you think of?

Clarifying and paraphrasing

❷ 🔊 7.5 Listen to Dr Karen Jones, a social psychologist, describing how she thinks the order in which we do things in our lives should be changed.

1 According to general agreement, what is the main purpose of education?
2 Why is the current 'education process' inadequate?
3 What kind of jobs could be learned by ten- and eleven-year-olds? Why would these jobs be suitable?
4 What is the advantage of young adults experiencing various different jobs?
5 Why does Dr Jones suggest people should go to university in their late thirties?

❸ 🔊 7.5 Listen again. Make a note of:

1 the expressions the interviewer uses to get Dr Jones to explain herself more clearly
2 the expressions Dr Jones uses to clarify and paraphrase what she has said, and to confirm what the interviewer has said.

📖 Pocket Book page 29

Explaining stages in a process

❹ The four boxes contain notes about some of the stages in four different activities.

1 Identify what the four activities are. Choose two of the activities and write down two different sequences of events in the process. In one case you should choose an unusual order.

buy house	advertise	amend and check	decide on budget
live together	find venue	circulate for comments	do research
get to know each other	confirm arrangements	collect information	negotiate deal
fall in love	reply to participants	define aims and objectives	select possible options
have children	fix date and time	distribute	test drive
marry	organize speakers	write rough draft	visit dealer(s)

2 Work in pairs and explain your processes to your partner.

Student A   As you explain, respond to your partner's questions or comments. Develop your explanation by rephrasing and adding more information.

Student B   As you listen to your partner's explanation, try to get more information using an appropriate phrase or question.

Use listening script 7.5 on page 133 to help you structure the discussion.

❺ Work in pairs.

1 Put the activities in the list in order, according to how difficult they would be for you to explain how to do them.

a apply for a study or research grant
b create an educational website
c obtain EU funding for a project
d organize a training session
e learn a language
f play a sport or game
g get residency in your country or town
h vote in a general election
i join or found a religious group
j become a billionaire

2 Choose one activity, and make notes on a four- to six-stage sequence to explain the process.
3 Change partners and see if your new partner can improve your sequence.
4 Write a full explanation of the whole process.

❶ What do you think are the most important things to consider when you are preparing for: (a) a job interview, (b) an appraisal or progress report?

❷ Before you prepare for a job interview, it's important to find out as much as possible about your prospective employer to see how your skills and personality are likely to fit in.

1 Work in pairs. Exchange information about your working environments in terms of:

a company culture   d top products
b management style   e customer base
c size of company and office layout   f future outlook.

2 Discuss how easy it would be for you to exchange work roles. If you are both employed by the same organization as your partner, imagine you work for a different company that you are very familiar with.

❸ Look at this list of the 'Twelve Most Common Interview Questions'.

1 >Describe your greatest strengths/weaknesses.

2 >Where do you see yourself in five years' time?

3 >Why should you be employed by this company?

4 >Describe your most recent accomplishments.

5 >Describe a recent situation at work which you found frustrating.

6 >In the past year, what have you been dissatisfied about in your performance?

7 >What do you think is the most important skill that a manager should possess?

8 >What major problem have you encountered recently, and how did you deal with it?

9 >In what ways could you be described as creative?

10 >Have you ever managed a conflict? How?

11 >Which is more important to you, money or job satisfaction?

12 >How has your recent project been going?

1 Match each question with one of the categories a–f. If you think that some of the questions don't fit into any particular category, invent your own categories.

a good points/bad points   d goals/plans
b achievements/disappointments   e business values/personal values
c likes/dislikes   f job progress/problems

2 Which of these questions are the most difficult to answer? How would you answer them?

❹ 🔊 7.6 Listen to these answers and match them to six of the questions in ❸.

a ___   b ___   c ___   d ___   e ___   f ___

How good, and how appropriate, were the individual answers?

❺ Work in the same pairs as in ❷. Decide whether you are going to practise a job interview or a job appraisal scenario. Choose three of the categories a–f in ❸ to ask and answer questions about. Use the information you exchanged in ❷.

Student A You are the interviewee / employee. Prepare some brief information about yourself on the categories you have chosen.

Student B You are the interviewer / employer. Think of two appropriate questions to ask Student A on each of the categories you have chosen. Try to make the two questions as different as possible.

1 Act out the interview.

2 Change roles and choose three different categories. Act out the second interview.

3 Discuss whether some questions were easier or harder to ask and answer than others, and why.

6 What sort of questions do you think it might *not* be appropriate to ask in an interview? The Data Protection Act in the UK has changed the type of questions that can be asked in a job application form.

1 Work in pairs. Look at these questions and decide which ones would be valid (✓) and not valid (✗), and which ones you are not sure about (?).

CANDIDATE'S DETAILS

☐ Name of applicant
☐ Sex
☐ Age / Date of birth
☐ Marital status
☐ Do you have a partner?
☐ If so, are they male or female?
☐ Do you have children / dependants?
☐ If so, how old are they?

EDUCATION

☐ Name of secondary school
☐ Qualifications obtained

☐ When were they obtained?
☐ Name of post-school institution
☐ Qualifications obtained

☐ When were they obtained?

WORK EXPERIENCE

☐ Name of employers and nature of jobs
☐ *dates in reverse chronological order*

☐ Current salary

HEALTH

☐ Current and recent health problems
☐ Absence record in last job
☐ Disabilities

HOBBIES AND INTERESTS

☐ Membership of clubs and societies
☐ *include union and political party membership*

PERSONAL STATEMENT

☐ Background aspirations, career intentions and personal qualities

People Management

2 Turn to page 120 and compare the questions with the information on UK legislation. What do you think is the rationale behind the UK law?

7 Asking good questions as an interviewee or employee also gives a good impression.

1 Decide which of these areas it would be acceptable to ask about in an interview and then write appropriate questions for each one you choose.

- appraisal system
- career prospects
- company history
- company structure
- courses / training
- future outlook of company
- holidays
- hours of work / flexitime
- level of responsibility
- luncheon vouchers
- overtime
- pension schemes
- perks
- reasons for working for the company
- salary
- social activities
- stock options

2 Which of the questions you have just written did you ask at the interview for your present job? What other questions did you ask?

8 Work in two groups: A and B.

Students in group A should turn to page 113.
Students in group B should turn to page 117.

When you have discovered your job, ask some questions from **7**. Your interviewer should improvise suitable answers.

Getting it right

OVERVIEW
- Hypothesizing: conditionals review
- Speculating about the present and past: modal auxiliary verbs
- Word-building (1): prefixes and suffixes
- Apologizing
- Meetings:
  managing interruptions
  keeping to the point
  asking for clarification
- Listening skills: listening without prejudice

LANGUAGE FOCUS	Hypothesis and speculation

1 Have you ever been the victim of a computer error or administrative mistake? To what extent do you think computer errors are man-made? How often do you check the information your bank sends you?

2 Look at the newspaper headline and the photo. What do you think the article might be about?

3 Read the article and letter, and check your ideas.

'Dear Madam, you owe us £121 billion'

A STUNNED **LIZ SEYMOUR** CAME home from holiday to find her bank account overdrawn – by a mind-boggling **£121 BILLION**.

And a letter from her bank accused HER of 'an oversight' for going into the red by the equivalent of a third of the national debt.

Liz, 24, an aerobics instructor from Yorkshire, was given a week to repay the incredible sum of £121, 318, 928, 560. And she was warned that interest was being charged at £2.5 billion per month.

She said yesterday, 'I nearly fainted. I knew that I could have been a little overdrawn – but not by £121 billion.'

Liz found the letter waiting for her when she arrived home in Hull after a week's holiday on the island of Gran Canaria.

She said, 'If I had known I was that much overdrawn, I would have stayed out there forever.'

Liz contacted her bank in Hull where officials admitted they had made a mistake.

A spokesman said, 'It was a one-off administrative error for which we apologize. Obviously she will get a revised statement.'

The Sun

Account number	3141526278718
Account balance	£ 121, 318, 928, 560.00 **DR**

Dear Miss Seymour

I note that your account is overdrawn by £ 121, 318, 928, 560 although there appears to be no prior arrangement.

I am sure that this is just an oversight and that you will shortly pay sufficient funds into your account to return it to order and cover cheques you may have issued.

If the overdrawn balance is not repaid within 11 days, your account may be transferred to our Collections Department in Brighton.

In the meantime, interest on the overdrawn balance is being charged at our rate for unauthorized borrowing, currently 2.20% per month, but variable.

Yours sincerely,

4 Work in pairs and discuss these questions.

1 How do you think the bank's mistake happened?
2 How would you have felt in Liz Seymour's situation?
3 What would you have done?

5 🔊 8.1 Listen to some people discussing Liz Seymour's situation and answer the questions.

1 What does the woman usually do if there is an error in her statement?
2 What would she have done if she had been Liz Seymour?
3 Why might Liz Seymour have sued the bank if she had been in America?
4 What would the American do if his bank inadvertently credited his account with a million pounds or dollars?
5 What did the woman who found the bag of used banknotes do?

Conditionals review   Hypothesizing

1 **What is the difference in meaning between these pairs of sentences?**

a   If I get a letter like that, I phone the bank.
b   If I get a letter like that, I will phone the bank.

c   If my bank phones me, I will tell them it's their mistake.
d   If my bank phoned me, I would tell them it was their mistake

e   If my bank made a mistake like that, I would phone them and complain.
f   If my bank had made a mistake like that, I would have phoned them and complained.

2 **Which of these sentences is a reference to:**

1   a possible future situation?
2   a hypothetical situation in the past which didn't happen?
3   something that is generally true?
4   a hypothetical situation which could happen?

3 **In each sentence try replacing *will* or *would* with *may* or *might*. What effect does this have on the meaning of the sentence?**

📖 Pocket Book pages 3, 12

---

6 What kind of conditionals are used in these sentences? Why is a particular conditional used in each case?

1 Your account may be transferred if the overdrawn balance is not paid.
2 If I had been Liz Seymour, I would have phoned the bank.
3 If I found a bag full of money, I would take it to the police.
4 I would have stayed there for good if I had known I was that much overdrawn.
5 If I find mistakes in my bank statement, I phone the bank immediately.
6 I would check your statements if I were you.

7 1 Complete these sentences, then compare your answers in pairs.

a If you want to get promoted in my department, you …
b I get very irritated if …
c You can live much more comfortably if you …
d If you visit my town in the summer …

2 Underline the most appropriate form in italics, then ask and answer the questions in pairs.

   a *Will/Would* you stop working, if you *inherit/inherited* $2 million?

   b If you *are/were* offered a job with a much better salary but in another part of the country, *will/would* you accept?

   c *Will/Would* you retire early, if you *have/had* the opportunity?

   d If your government *stands/stood* for re-election, *will/would* you vote for them?

8 Work in groups. Read the situations and discuss what you would have done.

   1 Suzanne found a new colleague of hers stealing a small quantity of office pens and paper. She said nothing, either to the colleague or her superiors.

   2 Peter was doing business in a foreign country. He got a parking ticket on his rented car. He didn't pay the fine.

   3 Cristina was asked by a friend to provide a job reference for him. She knew that he was not a great worker and that he had lost his previous job because of several mistakes he had made. She refused.

9 1 Why do you think Liz Seymour contacted a newspaper about the mistake her bank had made?

   2 Why did the woman in France take the bag of used banknotes to the police station?

   8.2 Listen to some people talking about Liz Seymour and the woman in France. Make a note of which woman they are talking about.

Modal auxiliary verbs Speculating about the present and the past

Look at the example sentences and answer the questions.

   a Well, I think she **should have** kept it.

   b She **may have** simply wanted to expose the bank.

   c I think she **must have** thought that someone had seen her.

   d It **must** be a bit of a shock …

   e She **must have** known she could make a lot of money … they **must** pay a lot for stories like that.

   f She **can't have** known who the money belonged to … she **could** be just a very honest person.

   g It **may not have** been because she was honest … she **couldn't have** kept that amount of money without someone finding out.

   h Of course, she **may** be regretting it now.

1 Which sentences refer to past events, and which to a present or general situation?

2 In which sentences do the speakers:
   i   feel certain about what they say?
   ii believe there is a strong possibility that they are right?
   iii think that it is possible they are right?
   iv refer to something that did not happen?

3 In which sentences can *might* or *might not* (*have*) be used in place of the highlighted modal verbs? How would the meaning of the sentence change?

 Pocket Book page 12

Pronunciation

1 8.3 Listen to these sentences. What do you notice about the pronunciation of *have, had, will,* and *would*?

   a If my bank gets it wrong, I'll be very surprised.

   b I'm not sure what I would have done.

   c If my bank had made a mistake like that, they wouldn't have admitted it.

   d What would you do if you found all that money?

   e I think she should have kept it.

   f She must have thought that someone had seen her.

   g She can't have known who the money belonged to.

   h It may not have been because she was honest.

2 8.3 Listen again and repeat the sentences. Try to pronounce *had, will, would,* and *have* in the same way as the speakers.

10 Complete these extracts from two conversations, using an appropriate form of a modal verb with the verb in brackets.

1 '... Everyone was in a hurry because the train was late, so I just grabbed it from the baggage shelf and headed for the taxi rank. When I got here I realized I had the wrong one – someone **1**_____ (take) mine by mistake. I **2**_____ (check) properly. I suppose I should have, but I was in such a rush. Whoever has mine **3**_____ (know) by now – it's got my diary and my mobile in it ...'

2

'... We were only out for about half an hour, so they **4**_____ (be) there long. I suppose they **5**_____ (be watching) the house. They smashed a window to get in so they **6**_____ (make) quite a lot of noise. They only took the TV and video, fortunately ... the police think they **7**_____ (be) the same ones who are responsible for a lot of break-ins in the area ...'

Talking point

11 Work in pairs or small groups. In your group make deductions and speculations about three or four of these facts. For example:

why the British drive on the left and continue to drive on the left
It may be because they want to be different from the rest of Europe.
They must have decided to be different from the rest of Europe.

1 why the Romans used such a strange numbering system
2 how they built the pyramids at Giza in Egypt, and why
3 why so many people claim to have seen UFOs
4 why no one has apparently found a cure for the common cold
5 how some people seem to learn English more quickly than others, and speak it so much better
6 why there are so many different religions in the world.

12 Ask and answer the questions with a partner.

1 If your house were on fire, what three things would you save?
2 If someone knocks on your door at home, do you open the door immediately?
3 If you could exchange your life for anyone else's, whose life would you choose?
4 If the weather is good this weekend, what will you do?
5 If you hadn't studied [subject] at school what would you have studied?
6 If you were the mayor of your town, what would you change?
7 If you hadn't found your current job, where would you have worked?
8 If you arrive late for work, what happens?

Apologizing

1 What do you understand by the term 'saving face'? Read the extract from an account by an American priest, temporarily living in South Africa. It describes how he first encountered the concept of saving face. What 'mistake' did he make?

Eunice,

a black South African, was employed to help my wife care for the house and the children. Eunice worked hard and was **trustworthy**[1]. We were delighted she was with us.

One day she had just cleared the table of some dishes when I heard a crash in the kitchen. With a voice that I hoped expressed **non-judgemental**[2] inquiry, I asked, 'Eunice, did you break a dish?' I even raised my voice just a touch at the end to be sure not to communicate anger or disgust.

Note my use of the active voice. I even called her by name so there would be no mistaking who I believed had broken the dish. I had no malice toward Eunice, and I certainly did not intend to sound **disrespectful**[3]; this is the way everyone spoke where I grew up. It was so very natural. Wasn't everyone like me?

'No, *Umfundise* [a term of respect]. The cup fell and it died.'

I thought, 'What do you mean, "the cup fell and it died"? What kind of answer is that?' Unhappy with her response and wanting some indication of **accountability**[4], I pursued the point.

'You mean that you dropped the cup?' Again I tried to use a tone that would show my desire to clarify. I was looking for a simple admission of guilt, but was not even aware of why that should be important. It was just the way things should be done.

'The cup fell and it died,' she said a second time with a more subdued voice, this time dropping the term of respect.

Still confused by her answer, but thinking that yet another attempt to get 'the real story' would probably be **unproductive**[5], I decided to drop the issue. 'Why can't she just give a straight answer?'

was the frustrating thought in my mind.

Eunice's answer, 'The cup fell and it died' struck me as evasive. 'Why isn't she willing to assume responsibility for her actions? She's an adult. Being willing to accept blame is mature adult behaviour. What is her problem?' I wondered, believing that my confusion had been produced by some deficiency on her part. In essence, I was wishing Eunice would be more Western, more like me, so I would not be forced outside of my comfort zone. If I could change her, I could avoid the **awkwardness**[6] of changing myself.

D H Elmer, Cross Cultural Conflict

2 Match the explanations with the words highlighted in the text.

   a not polite or concerned   d reliable

   b being responsible for something   e neutral, not critical

   c not useful or effective   f difficulty or inconvenience

3 Discuss these points.

   1 Why was Eunice so indirect? Why didn't she just apologize?

   2 Why did the author want Eunice to admit her guilt?

   3 Why did the author expect Eunice to behave in a certain way?

4 1 How many ways can you think of to apologize? Work in pairs and make a list.

   2 8.4 Listen to six people apologizing, and make a note of the expresions they use.

     Pocket Book page 28

   3 Work in pairs and play the Apology Game. Turn to page 121.

Prefixes and suffixes

5 Prefixes are often used to create opposites. Look back at these examples from the text: *non-judgemental*, *unhappy*. Which of these prefixes are used in the same way (with adjectives or verbs)? Write down two examples for each prefix you chose.

anti-	bi-	con-	dis-	ex-	il-	im-	in-	ir-	mis-	pro-	semi-

6 Create opposites of these words using a suitable prefix. If more than one prefix is possible, is there any difference in meaning?

  ___connect   ___do   ___lead   ___load   ___polite   ___tidy

  ___correct   ___interested   ___legible   ___mature   ___replaceable   ___well

7 Suffixes are used to create one class of words from another. For example, adjectives can be made into adverbs by adding *-ly* (e.g. *certain – certainly*). But some don't change their form when they become an adverb (e.g. *He's a fast runner – He runs fast*).

Underline the correct form in each sentence. Then write a sentence using the form you *didn't* underline.

1 Eunice worked *hard/ hardly*.
2 Your guests speak very *high/ highly* of you.
3 I haven't been to the cinema *late/ lately* – I've been too busy.
4 No wonder it's cold – the door is *wide/ widely* open.

Noun suffixes

8 Nouns can be made from many verbs and adjectives by using suffixes. The suffixes *-ion, -ity, -ment, -ance, -ness, -er, -ee, -ist,* and *-or* can be used to change verbs into nouns.

Change these verbs and adjectives into nouns using the suffixes. Some of the words can take more than one suffix, for example, to make them a personal noun (interview*er*, interview*ee*).

agree	attend	decide	interview	organize	responsible	useful
appear	communicate	employ	manage	polite	specialize	visit

Verb suffixes

9 Verbs can be created from nouns and adjectives using the suffixes *-ize* or *-ify* (e.g. *social – socialize; intense – intensify*)

1 Which verb ending in *-ize* means:
   a to bring a system or an organization up to date?
   b to change from a conventional system to a computer-based system?
   c to make a product fit someone's specifications exactly?
   d to permit something to happen legally?

2 Which verb ending in *-ify* means:
   a to correct a mistake?
   b to make something clear?
   c to say more precisely what you mean?
   d to make someone extremely frightened?

Adjective suffixes

10 Adjectives can be created from nouns and verbs using the suffixes *-able, -al, -ive,* and *-ous*.

1 How can these nouns and verbs be changed into adjectives using the suffixes?

attract	create	criticize	fame	humour	profession	regret	rely	understand

2 In which cases does the spelling need to change?

Pronunciation Shifting stress

1 Adding suffixes can sometimes change the main stress of a word. Try pronouncing these pairs of words.

analyse	method	responsible
analytical	methodical	responsibility
manage	organize	understand
management	organization	understandable

2 🎧 8.5 Listen and check your ideas. What do you notice about the change in stress?

Culture in meetings

1 There are several factors which can contribute to a successful meeting. With a partner, look at the following rules and arrange them in order of importance by writing numbers in the boxes. Exclude any you do not agree with. Discuss how each one might be achieved.

RULES FOR EFFECTIVE MEETINGS

- ☐ AN AGENDA SHOULD ALWAYS BE PREPARED AND DISTRIBUTED TO ALL PARTICIPANTS IN ADVANCE.

- ☐ BEFORE YOU START THE MEETING, IT IS SOMETIMES USEFUL TO AGREE ON GROUND RULES.

- ☐ A SPEAKER SHOULD MAKE SURE HE OR SHE HAS EQUAL EYE CONTACT WITH ALL PARTICIPANTS.

- ☐ IT IS IMPORTANT THAT SOMEONE CHAIRS THE MEETING.

- ☐ EVERYONE SHOULD HAVE THE OPPORTUNITY TO EXPRESS THEIR OPINION – NO ONE SHOULD DO ALL THE TALKING.

- ☐ CONSTANT INTERRUPTIONS SHOULD BE DISCOURAGED.

- ☐ PEOPLE SHOULD ONLY TALK ABOUT ITEMS ON THE AGENDA.

- ☐ IF YOU DON'T UNDERSTAND WHAT IS BEING SAID, YOU SHOULD ALWAYS SAY SO.

- ☐ IT IS IMPORTANT TO USE CLEAR AND CONCISE LANGUAGE.

- ☐ MEETINGS SHOULD BE KEPT SHORT AND TO THE POINT.

- ☐ A PROFESSIONAL MANNER SHOULD BE MAINTAINED AT ALL TIMES.

- ☐ IT IS USEFUL TO CONFIRM THE OUTCOME OF THE MEETING IN WRITING.

2 Read the text about meetings in Brazil. It focuses on different elements from those you discussed in **1**. Analyse how each stage in a Brazilian meeting compares with the way things are done in your country.

MEETINGS BRAZIL

You and your counterpart(s) will exchange business cards at the beginning of the meeting. Brazilians will often bend over a top corner of a card, in a gesture that 'personalizes' its presentation.

At first, the conversation will be informal. You'll start off by talking about other topics. Your counterpart will almost certainly ask if you would like a *cafezinho* (a glass of water and/or fresh juice), and enquire about your trip.

Brazilians are simultaneously emotional and shrewd. In the course of sizing you up, they'll observe not only the quality of your shoes, let's say, but also how *simpático* (nice, amenable) you seem.

Once the initial niceties have taken place, maybe after ten or fifteen minutes, you can start presenting your business – in a straightforward, pleasant manner.

Direct your comments to the whole group but particularly to the highest-ranking individual and decision-maker. Answer questions openly,

> **❝ Brazilians are simultaneously emotional and shrewd. ❞**

don't appear defensive, and never 'talk down' to anyone in the room.

If you (wisely) arranged your meeting for 10 a.m. or 3 p.m., you might find that, at its conclusion, everyone will go out to lunch, or drinks, or dinner together. If you're invited along, it's a good sign.

E Herrington, *Passport Brazil*

Christopher J. Hutton
Chief buyer
1016 Washington Av
Philadelphia, 94156 PA
cjhutton@usdimports.com
tel +1 600 421 2001
fax +1 600 421 2003

Managing discussion

③ 🔊 8.6 Listen to the first part of a meeting between three people in a company discussing the possibility of expansion in Brazil. Note the phrases they use to:

    1   emphasize a particular point
    2   get into the discussion
    3   manage an interruption.

📖 Pocket Book page 30, 34

④ 1   Work with a partner. You are in the middle of a discussion about a pay review. Follow the framework.

Student A   **Student B**

Join the discussion by suggesting a 2% increase in salary.

→ Emphasize the point that you think 2% is too high.

Start to suggest another figure, but stop when B interrupts you. ←

→ Interrupt A in the middle of a sentence.

Deal with the interruption and continue with what you were saying. ←

    2   Swap roles. Improvise a similar discussion about performance bonuses.

⑤ 🔊 8.7 Listen to the second part of the meeting. What phrases do the three people use to:

    1   ensure other people get to speak?
    2   keep to the point?
    3   ask for clarification?

⑥ Complete the following phrases to match the headings. For example:

To manage interruptions
Can I finish _what I was saying_ ?
We were _in the middle of discussing something._

To keep to the point
_____ the point?
I think we've _____

To ensure other people get to speak
Mark, _____ say something now?
Mark, what _____ ?

To ask for clarification
Could you be _____ ?
I'm sorry, but _____

⑦ 🔊 8.8 Listen to the final extract and make a note of the phrases used to:

    1   return to a subject
    2   move on
    3   summarize.

With a partner, brainstorm some more similar phrases.

📖 Pocket Book pages 30, 34

⑧ In addition to the phrases you noted in **③**, **⑤**, and **⑦**, there are simpler ways to communicate effectively in meetings. With a partner, decide what alternative methods you could use, not necessarily including language. Think about things you can say, and things you can do.

⑨ Work in groups. You are in the process of forming a new political party. You are in a meeting with three others to decide on some of your party's policies. Look at the information on page 122.

1 How much do you think misunderstandings between cultures are due to stereotypes? What stereotypes are associated with people from your country? How true are they?

2 When you listen to someone speaking, what things influence the way you listen? Which do you pay more attention to: *what* they say, or *how* they say it? Read these two extracts and discuss the questions.

A To be able to really listen, one should abandon or put aside all prejudices. When you are in a receptive state of mind, things can be easily understood. But unfortunately most of us listen through a 'screen of resistance'. We are screened with prejudices, whether religious or spiritual, psychological, or scientific; or with daily worries, desires, and fears. And with these fears for a screen, we listen. Therefore we listen really to our own noise, our own sound, not to what is being said.

L D Eigen & J P Siegel, *Manager's Quotations*

B RESEARCH reveals that although we spend so much of our time listening we don't necessarily remember all we're told. Shortly after a 10-minute oral presentation the average listener will have retained only half of what was said. After 48 hours they are likely to remember only 10 per cent. Research has also shown that far greater credence is given to non-verbal messages than to what is actually said: words 10%, tone 35%, non-verbal behaviour 55%. If a speaker's words are in conflict with his non-verbal behaviour, it is the latter that will invariably be assessed as genuine.

I MacKay, *Listening Skills*

1 What kind of people do you think the two extracts were written by? Which contains the most useful information for a work context, and why?

2 What are the implications of the 'screens' described in extract A? Do you think these influence your relationships with people from other countries, with people from a different social background, or from a different level in the company hierarchy?

3 What are the implications of extract B for people who use English at work?

3 Do you listen through a 'screen of resistance'?

1   🎧 **8.9** Work in pairs. Listen to four men talking about their experiences of different cultures, and complete the table.

2   Compare your answers with your partner and and explain the reasons for your choice. Were you mainly influenced by what the speakers said, or by how they said it?

	R. Norton	M. Gandy	L. Gregory	T. Southern
Australian, English, or Indian?				
Approximate age?				
Interesting or boring voice?				
Clear or unclear enunciation?				
Introvert or extrovert?				
Confident or insecure?				
Which photo?				

Understanding natural speech

4 You can help your listening skills considerably by preparing yourself beforehand for what someone is going to say.

Tom Southern, (the last speaker in **3**) is English, but he lives and works in Sydney, Australia, where he is Managing Director of a US company which has many clients in Japan, Hong Kong, and Singapore. Work in pairs and discuss these questions.

1 With which group (Australians, Americans, Asians) do you think he would have the most cultural similarities? Why?

2 With which group do you think he would have the most conflict? Why?

5 While you are listening you should be able to predict what someone is going to say next, and if necessary, revise your initial assumptions (i.e. break down your 'screen').

🔊 8.10 Listen to this extract from an interview with Tom Southern. At each pause, try to predict what Tom will say next, choosing the best option, (a), (b), or (c). Compare each answer with your partner before moving on to the next one.

1 … our attempts in those markets have been to try and focus on any aspects that we could that would:
   a cause problems
   b bring different cultures together
   c exploit cultural differences.

2 … and not really spending a lot of time worrying about things that were:
   a alien to us
   b very like our own culture
   c clearly quite different.

3 … people make the immediate assumption that Americans and British, and for that matter, Australians are essentially:
   a the same people
   b very very similar types of culture
   c completely different cultures.

4 … the differences, which might only be a relatively small percentage of the total picture, become the thing that you:
   a focus on
   b should not ignore
   c don't need to worry about.

5 … we actually find there is more conflict, or more potential for conflict, with:
   a Asian-Pacific groups
   b the Australian government
   c these American businessmen.

6 🔊 8.11 Now listen to someone talking about the Western and Japanese approaches to decision-making in meetings. At each pause in the recording, try to predict what he will say next. How accurate were your predictions?

7 Work in pairs.

Student A: choose one of the topics 1–3 and start to talk about your views or experiences.

Student B: listen and interrupt at a suitable moment to respond with your own views or experiences. Try to keep the conversation balanced. Then swap roles.

1 What kind of conflicts, if any, have you had when dealing with people from other cultures? Have you let your stereotypes of them 'screen' you in any way?

2 Think of a country you have visited. What impressions did you have of that country before you visited it? To what extent were these impressions confirmed?

3 When using the telephone, do you create a mental image of what the other person looks like? When you actually meet the person, is this image usually confirmed?

Review Unit D

Active and passive forms

1 Rewrite sentences 1–3 using the passive form (without an agent), and sentences 4–6 using an active, imperative, or personal form.

1 The IT support team are repairing the computer at the moment.
2 I'll do it by tomorrow.
3 You should have finished the report yesterday.
4 In the diagram, the relevant amounts regarding X, Y and Z are shown.
5 The two cars were bought by our company last year.
6 The form should be completed in black ink.

Have / get something done

2 Complete the second sentence so that it means the same as the first using *have* or *get something done*.

1 a Someone stole her wallet on the metro.   b She …
2 a Your teeth need checking before you travel.   b You need to …
3 a Someone is redecorating their house while they're away.   b They're …
4 a The wind was so strong it blew our fence down last night.   b We …
5 a The mechanic serviced my car last week.   b I …

Conditionals

3 Put the verbs in brackets into an appropriate tense, changing the word order where necessary. Then ask and answer the questions with a partner.

1 Which company you (join) if you (not decide) to join your current company?
2 If you (make) enough money by the time you are 50, you (retire)?
3 You (stop) working if you (win) the lottery?
4 If you (arrive) late for work, what (happen)?
5 What things you (change) in your company if you (be) the boss?
6 If you (do) this exercise before you (tell) the teacher?

Modal verbs – speculation

4 Underline the correct modal verb in *italics*. More than one may be possible.

1 It *must / can / could / may* not have been him you saw – he's left the country.
2 You shouldn't drive so fast – you *could / can / might / must* have had an accident.
3 You *must / can / could / may* be right, but it still seems strange to me.
4 You *must / can / could / may* have realized that you had got the wrong person when she told you that she didn't know what you were talking about.

Vocabulary

5 Underline the correct word(s) in *italics*.

1 Living with my grandparents as a child meant that I had a very strict *education / formation / upbringing*.
2 Football is my brother's favourite *subject / argument / topic* of conversation.
3 *Actually / Currently / Presently* there is a lot of media interest in food and health.
4 People always assume that we are a large company, when *in fact / instead / whereas* we only have twelve employees.
5 We agreed to the takeover because we were in a financial crisis, and *eventually / consequently / subsequently* we had no choice.

Apologizing

6 Complete the sentences with *apologize, excuse me, I'm afraid, please,* or *sorry*.

1 A _____ let me _____ for any inconvenience this may have caused.
  B That's all right. I'm sure it wasn't intentional.
2 A Is Mr Wood there, please?   B _____ that he's not in today. Can I help you?
3 A _____, could you lend me your newspaper a second?   B Yes, of course.
4 A Ouch, you're standing on my foot!   B Oh, _____, I didn't realize.

Prefixes and suffixes

7 1 Create the opposites of these words by adding or changing a prefix.

    a approve   c export   e pro-democracy
    b cover (verb)   d legal   f semi-automatic

  2 Look at these pairs of words. Does the second word have the same stress as the first word? Mark the main stress in each word.

    a commerce / commercial   f interview / interviewee
    b difficult / difficulty   g organize / organization
    c govern / government   h product / production
    d happy / happiness   i refer / reference
    e industry / industrial   j reliable / reliability

Getting more information, clarifying, paraphrasing, confirming

8 Write an alternative for each of these expressions.

1 OK, but I still don't see what you're getting at.
2 Can you be more specific?
3 Well, let me put it another way.
4 Yes, precisely.
5 That's not exactly what I had in mind.

Now work in pairs. Have a short discussion on one or more of these topics. You get one point for every phrase you use. See who uses the most phrases.

    Is it better to:
    – work for a small or a large company or institution?
    – have a boss of the same sex or the opposite sex?
    – work four 10-hour days or five 8-hour days?

Meetings phrases

9 Imagine you are participating in a meeting. Write down one phrase you can use to:

1 get a discussion going   5 ensure that other people get to speak
2 emphasize a particular point   6 move on
3 manage an interruption   7 resume
4 ask for clarification   8 summarize.

Interviews

10 Imagine you are interviewing someone for your own job (you are being promoted). Write down five questions to ask the candidate and five questions that you would expect the candidate to ask you. Make sure you write both general and specific questions.

Work in pairs. Take it in turns to interview each other and decide whether you would give each other the job!

Self-check box

	YES	NO	📕		YES	NO	📕
Active and passive forms	☐	☐	13	Apologizing: *sorry, excuse me*, etc.			
Have / get something done	☐	☐	8		☐	☐	28
Conditionals review: hypothesizing				Prefixes and suffixes	☐	☐	
	☐	☐	3	Getting more information, clarifying,			
Modal auxiliary verbs for speculation				paraphrasing, confirming	☐	☐	29
	☐	☐	12	Meetings phrases	☐	☐	34
Vocabulary: education, sequencing				Interviews	☐	☐	
	☐	☐					

Unit 9

Food and hospitality

OVERVIEW

● Permission, possibility, necessity, and obligation: present and past forms
● Food and drink vocabulary
● Verb – noun collocations
● Adjective – adverb collocations
● Making and responding to invitations, suggestions, requests
● Explaining menus and dishes
● Being a host/guest

LANGUAGE FOCUS | **Permission, possibility, necessity, and obligation**

❶ How are food-buying and eating habits in your country changing?

1 In general, do people in your country buy mostly locally produced food, or multinational brand names like Nestlé and Kellogg's?

2 Do most people prefer to eat at local, more traditional, restaurants, or large global chains like McDonald's and Pizza Hut?

3 Do you think that in the future there will be a monoculture of food, and that people all over the world will eat the same things?

❷ How much do you think multinationals vary the ingredients of the food they produce to suit different markets: (a) a lot, (b) a little, or (c) not at all?

1 Read the article and check your answer. Are you surprised?

TASTE A WORLD OF DIFFERENCE

Wherever you are in the world, it seems, the billboards and supermarket shelves are saturated with the same brand names. There are few places left on the planet where you can't[1] buy a Diet Coke, a packet of Kellogg's cornflakes, or Oxo cubes.

But just try tasting them. The packaging and the product may[2] look identical, but the flavour may[3] be far from familiar. Even the most famous brand names are specially formulated to appeal to individual national palates. Heinz, for instance, insists that its tomato ketchup is 'the same recipe worldwide', but admits that 'there may[4] be very subtle variations in the spicing'.

Even the ultimate global brand, Coca-Cola, accepts that not all its products are what they appear to be. 'We go to great lengths to ensure that Coca-Cola is the same wherever you drink it,' says a spokesman. 'But Diet Coke may[5] change slightly from country to country, because we use different sweeteners in different places.'

Americans prefer many products, particularly chocolate, to be far more sugary than Europeans do. The French perceive strawberry flavour in a different way from the British, so the artificial flavouring in France will not have a 'proper' strawberry taste to Britons. Preferences for saltiness and colour differ as well, and most Japanese consumers dislike the taste of milk.

The French in general prefer stronger, fuller-tasting coffee than the British. There is a higher cream content in a Magnum in Italy than in Britain, because the Italians expect ice-cream to have a much richer taste. Tea sold in Europe tends to be weaker than the strong tea preferred by Britons. Taste preferences can[6] vary even within countries: at least one well-known soft drink is made to a sweeter recipe in the southern states of the United States than that on sale in the north.

Local water and soil will affect the taste of home-grown natural ingredients. Some key constituents may not[7] be available, meaning that alternatives must[8] be found. Sometimes, especially in developing countries, premium-grade components, such as high-grade flour, are replaced with lower-quality equivalents.

Extremes in climate will require different additives and preservatives to be used. Chocolate calls for an alternative recipe in hot countries if it is to maintain its texture and taste.

And multinationals must[9] conform to national laws and regulations on additives, flavourings, colourings, and artificial low-calorie sweeteners. Mars and Snickers bars taste slightly different in Australia, since laws there state that vegetable fat must not[10] be used in chocolate.

Local religious sensibilities must[11] also be observed. Even McDonald's, which proclaims the homogeneity of its Big Macs around the globe, has to[12] serve lamb rather than beef burgers in India, because the sacred status of cows means that the majority of its Indian customers can't[13] eat beef.

The Guardian Weekly

2 Read the article again. What five factors can affect the manufacturer's choice of ingredients? What implications does this have for manufacturers developing a new product?

3 Work in pairs. Find out each other's attitudes to additives in food. Are you worried about *artificial additives*? Do you try to eat foods with *natural ingredients*? Do you read the packaging on foods you buy to find out what's in them?

Permission, possibility, necessity, and obligation   Present forms

1 **Focus on the words in blue in the article.**

1 Look at the use of *may* in 2, 3, 4, and 5. Which example refers to something that is actually true?

2 What is the difference in meaning between these sentences?
   a Consumer tastes **may** change.
   b Consumer tastes **can** change.
   In which examples in the article (2, 3, 4, or 5) could *can* replace *may*?

3 What is the difference between the uses of *can't* (1, 13), *may not* (7), and *must not* (10), in these sentences?
   a ... few places where you **can't** buy a Diet Coke.
   b ... its Indian customers **can't** eat beef.
   c Some key constituents **may not** be available ...
   d ... vegetable fat **must not** be used in chocolate.

4 Is there any difference between the uses of *must* in 8, 9, and 11, and *has to* in 12?

5 Is *don't have to* closer in meaning to *don't need to / needn't* or to *must not* (10)?

2 **Group these question forms according to whether they are asking if something is possible, permitted, necessary, or obligatory.**

Are you allowed to ...?   *Do you need to ...?*
Do you have to ...?   *Must I ...?*
Can I ...?   *Is it necessary to ...?*
Is it possible to ...?

📖 Pocket Book page 11

4 Underline the correct form or forms in these sentences.

1 There *can/may* still be some seats on the flight – I'll check for you.
2 I'm sorry, I *can't/may not* get you on to that flight – all the seats are booked.
3 It *can/may* rain a lot in Manchester – it's a very damp climate.
4 It *can/may* rain when you're there, so take an umbrella.
5 If you want to work in the US you *have to/must/need to* get the right visa.
6 You *can't/mustn't* work legally in the US without a visa.
7 You *don't have to/mustn't/don't need to* apply now, it *can/may* wait until tomorrow.
8 If you have time, you *must/have to/need to* visit the new Opera House – it's fabulous.

5 What information would it be useful for a visitor to know about your town or region? Think about things like the weather, food and drink, local customs and restrictions, travelling round, entertainment, working. Work in pairs, and ask and answer questions about what is possible, permitted, necessary, and obligatory.

6 Look at these photos. All of these creatures are regarded as food in certain parts of the world. Are there any of them that you can't / are not allowed to eat, or that you would never eat? Why?

7 You are going to listen to a radio discussion about food taboos. Before you listen, discuss these questions.

Why do food taboos exist?

What typical restrictions are there when people are fasting?

🔊 9.1 Listen to the discussion and answer the questions.

1 In early medieval times, what were monks allowed to eat?
2 In later centuries, where did their food come from?
3 How many fast days were there? What were they not supposed to eat on such days?
4 What did they do to enable them to eat rabbit?
5 Why do some Tibetan monks eat meat?
6 What foods were not allowed during Great Lent in Greece?

Permission, possibility, necessity, and obligation   Past forms

Look at these sentences from the radio discussion. Match each form in bold (a–h) with one of the explanations (1–6).

a The monks **had to** fast a lot.

b They **couldn't** eat any meat or fish.

c **Did they have to** go to a market?

d They **didn't have to** buy anything.

e They **weren't supposed to** eat meat, but they did eat rabbit.

f They **needed to** eat food that provided plenty of calories and vitamins.

g You **couldn't** get fresh vegetables for the same reason.

h In Greece during Great Lent people **weren't allowed to** eat meat.

1 it wasn't necessary
2 it wasn't permitted
3 it wasn't possible
4 it was what was expected from them but they did something else
5 it was what they were obliged to do and really did do
6 it was necessary for them to do it

 Pocket Book page 11

8 Complete this extract from an email to a friend from someone who has just come back from a 'health and fitness break'. Use appropriate phrases from the box.

were / weren't supposed to	could	needed to	had to
were / weren't allowed to	couldn't	didn't need to	didn't have to

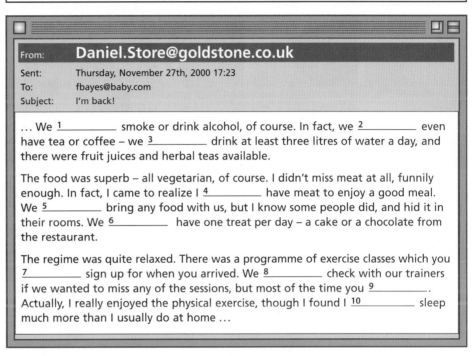

From: **Daniel.Store@goldstone.co.uk**
Sent: Thursday, November 27th, 2000 17:23
To: fbayes@baby.com
Subject: I'm back!

… We ¹_____ smoke or drink alcohol, of course. In fact, we ²_____ even have tea or coffee – we ³_____ drink at least three litres of water a day, and there were fruit juices and herbal teas available.

The food was superb – all vegetarian, of course. I didn't miss meat at all, funnily enough. In fact, I came to realize I ⁴_____ have meat to enjoy a good meal. We ⁵_____ bring any food with us, but I know some people did, and hid it in their rooms. We ⁶_____ have one treat per day – a cake or a chocolate from the restaurant.

The regime was quite relaxed. There was a programme of exercise classes which you ⁷_____ sign up for when you arrived. We ⁸_____ check with our trainers if we wanted to miss any of the sessions, but most of the time you ⁹_____. Actually, I really enjoyed the physical exercise, though I found I ¹⁰_____ sleep much more than I usually do at home …

9 Work in pairs. Ask and answer some of these questions in relation to some or all of the following: (a) your schooldays, (b) your home life as a child, (c) your military service, (d) your previous job.

1 Did you have to wear a uniform?
2 Were you allowed to smoke indoors?
3 What time were you supposed to get up?
4 Did you have to eat all your food?
5 Did you have to follow a certain timetable?
6 Could you organize your own time?
7 What things were you not allowed to do that you think you should have been allowed to do?
8 What things did you need to do that you felt you couldn't do?

Talking point

10 🎧 9.2 Listen to two women at a restaurant talking about the foods they can and can't eat because of the various allergies they have.

café noir lunch menu

| 2 courses | .... £12.95 |
| 3 courses | .... £15.95 |

excluding drinks

starters

Potato pancakes with smoked salmon and sour cream

Goat's cheese salad with grilled peppers

Paté campagnard

Carrot and coriander soup

main courses

Caesar salad with char-grilled chicken and garlic croutons

Roasted lemon chicken with noodles

Seafood and saffron risotto

Roasted Mediterranean vegetables with couscous

desserts

Summer fruit compote

Chocolate surprise pudding

Creme brulée

A selection of ice creams and sorbets

Coffee £1.95

1 Tick the items on the menu that they can't have, and note the reasons why.
2 Discuss any foods that you, your family, or your friends can't eat or don't eat. Explain whether these restrictions are due to allergies, concerns for health, ethical or religious beliefs, or other reasons.

🔲 Understanding natural speech

11 'Within five years 90 to 95 per cent of plant-derived food material in the United States will come from genetically engineered techniques.' (*Vegetarian Times*)

1 Should research into this area be allowed?
2 How can we ensure that scientists only conduct 'ethical' research?

1 How healthy is your diet? Work in pairs and discuss how many portions of these foods or units of alcohol you eat and drink in an average day.

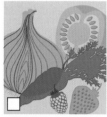
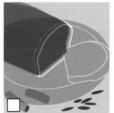
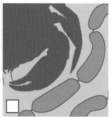

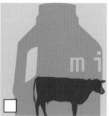

FRUIT & VEGETABLES   BREAD, PASTA, & RICE   MEAT & FISH   CAKES, SWEETS, & CHOCOLATE   MILK & DAIRY PRODUCTS   ALCOHOL (UNITS) a unit of alcohol = 250ml of beer or 1 glass of wine.

2 What is the best way to ensure you have a balanced diet? What effect do you think concerns for health have on the food industry?

1   Read the article and check your answers to the questions.

Healthy eating

If you thought healthy eating was simply about buying a balanced mix of meat and fish, fruit and vegetables, bread and pasta, and ensuring that less than one third of your calories come from fat, it is time to think again.

Soon, supermarket shelves will not only take care of our present state of health, but also guard against our future propensity to such conditions as high blood pressure, heart disease, arthritis, and diabetes. Already a huge range of products exists from which animal fat has been removed, lowered or replaced with less life-threatening substances. And there are also foods, such as milk, cereals, and salt, which have been added to, or fortified with vitamins and minerals or fibre.

In Japan, where functional foods are hugely popular, there are drinks with added 'polyols' to reduce the risk of dental cavities. Coca-Cola has also launched a controversial adolescent soft drink containing DHA, an essential fatty acid, which is said to promote learning ability. Meanwhile, scientists in Australia are trying to produce a low-cholesterol 'super egg' by feeding fish oils to chickens.

Not all the theories about functional foods can be proved. But it is useful to have some idea of what the foods contain. The healthiest approach, however, is still to choose a varied diet and to avoid too much sugar and fat.

Daily Telegraph

2   What are 'functional foods'? Find five examples mentioned in the article.

3   What do food producers tend to add to, or remove from, food? Do you think this is a good idea?

3 Work in pairs. Student A should turn to the information on page 114. Student B should turn to the information on page 118. Discuss what you've learned about the different types of food.

4 Complete the table with more examples from the texts, then add further examples of your own.

fish	meat	vegetables	fruit	dairy products	drinks	others
salmon	chicken	spinach	strawberries	milk	tea	pizza
sardines	beef	soya	cherries	eggs	Coca-Cola	flour

Tell your partner which are your favourite and least favourite foods. Do any of these include foods that are *good for you* or *bad for you*?

Verb–noun collocations

5 Look at both texts in **3** on pages 114 and 118.

1 Match each of the verbs/verb phrases with a suitable noun phrase. There may be several possible combinations.

Verbs/Verb phrases	Noun phrases
be rich in	the risk of heart disease/cancer
contain	blood pressure
destroy	cholestrol levels
have a high level of	vitamins and minerals
increase/lower/reduce	cancer cells
prevent	anti-oxidants
protect against	blood clots forming

2 Make sentences explaining the benefits of different foods using the verb–noun collocations. For example:

*Eating plenty of fruit and vegetables can help **reduce the risk of heart disease**.*

6 🔊 **9.3** Listen to a Japanese woman, an American man, and an English man talking about some of the foods in the table in **4**. Tick the items that they mention.

7 🔊 **9.3** Listen again and answer the questions.

1 How many glasses of red wine should you drink to stay healthy?
2 What is the effect of drinking a lot of coffee?
3 What kinds of food can you get in pill form?
4 Why is soya good for you?
5 What is bad about red meat and white meat?
6 What conclusion do the speakers reach?

Adverb–adjective collocations

8 Look at these examples from the listening.

*Fish oils as well, you know, keep you **very healthy**.*

*Meat is **absolutely packed** with fat and cholesterol.*

*We're **pretty lucky** to even be making these choices.*

Some adjectives are **gradable** (*healthy, lucky*) – they describe a quality you can have more or less of. We normally use adverbs like *extremely* or *very* with gradable adjectives.

Others are **ungradable** (*packed*) – they already imply 'a maximum amount'. We normally use adverbs like *absolutely* or *completely* with ungradable adjectives.

1 Divide these adjectives into two groups, gradable or ungradable. Then decide which adverbs they can combine with. Which combinations are not possible?

Adjectives			Adverbs		
angry	difficult	interesting	absolutely	pretty	totally
dangerous	disgusting	useful	completely	rather	very
delicious	effective	useless	extremely	really	

2 Work in pairs. Make sentences using the adverb–adjective combinations you thought of in 1. Compare your sentences with another pair.

9 Work in pairs. Think of a food. Describe it and explain its benefits to your partner without naming it. See if your partner can guess what it is.

10 Work in pairs and exchange information about the following questions.

How healthy is your own diet?

How important to you is eating healthily?

Which foods do you actively try to eat, and which ones do you avoid?

How do you think you could improve your diet?

Are there any other things you could do to improve your health?

❶ 1 Do you prefer to entertain guests at your home or at a restaurant? Abroad, would you prefer to be invited to someone's house or to a local restaurant? Why?

2 What is a typical eating or drinking experience in your town or region? What would you arrange for a guest who wanted to experience local hospitality? How much difference is there between home cooking and restaurant food?

❷ Read this text about eating out in West Africa. What does it tell you about:

1 the presentation of food?

2 table manners?

3 the influence of foreign cuisines?

4 the difference between home cooking and restaurant food?

WEST AFRICA FOOD

Cooking and eating in both **Senegal** and **The Gambia** are based on the tradition of hospitality. Meals are copious, geared to feeding a large family and to always having enough for the unexpected guest. Food is served on a large flat tray, rice underneath and vegetables arranged over the top, with careful attention to final presentation. (It must appeal to the senses of sight and smell as well as to taste.) This is placed on a mat on the floor and the family sits grouped around it.

Traditionally, eating is done with the right hand, so a bowl of water is provided before and after the meal for hand-washing. A little rice is rolled up in the fingers, squeezed into a ball, and popped into the mouth. If you feel you cannot manage this, a spoon will be provided. Succulent pieces of fish, meat, or vegetables are broken off by the hostess and tossed in front of the visitor because stretching is not good manners.

French influence in Senegal, though relatively unobtrusive in the cooking, has left the Senegalese with a taste for fresh French bread, dressed salads, and hors d'oeuvres. British culinary practices have fortunately not affected Gambian cuisine, but have regrettably left their mark on some modern hotel kitchens. These have a tendency to serve unimaginative meat dishes in bland sauces, chips with everything, and unseasoned garnishes.

Regrettably also, not enough traditional Gambian or Senegalese dishes find their way on to hotel menus. The gourmet visitor will have to seek out smaller bars and restaurants, or be lucky enough to be invited to a Gambian or Senegalese home for lunch.

The Gambia and Senegal, APA Insight Guides

Invitations and arrangements

❸ You are going to listen to three invitations.

1 🔊 9.4 Listen and in each case decide:

a what the invitation is for   b if the context is formal or informal.

2 🔊 9.4 Listen again and make a note of phrases used to:

a introduce an invitation   c respond to an invitation

b make an invitation   d suggest arrangements.

Which invitation was the most formal? Which was the least formal?

📖 Pocket Book page 32

4 Work in pairs. Practise making and responding to invitations. You should include at least one informal and one more formal invitation.

Student A	Student B
Introduce the invitation and invite B.	Respond positively.
Suggest a place and time.	Agree and respond positively.

Offers, requests, and suggestions

5 A visitor has been invited to a restaurant. Her host has already arrived.

1 During the first few minutes, the host says all of these things. In each case, decide whether she is making an offer, a request, or a suggestion.

a Can I take your coat?

b Shall we have something to drink before we order?

c Why don't you try the seafood pasta? It's really good.

d Shall I ask the waiter if there are any other vegetarian dishes?

e Excuse me, I'm just going to the bathroom. Would you mind ordering for me?

f Would you like to try some of this asparagus? It's delicious.

g Can I pour you some wine?

h Could you pass me the bread, please?

2 Decide how the guest might reply to each offer, request, or suggestion.

6 1 🔊 9.5 Listen to some extracts from the conversation. Match the guest's answers to the questions in **5**.

2 🔊 9.6 Listen to the complete exchanges. What phrases does the guest use to accept or reject her host's offers, requests, and suggestions? What else could she say?

📖 Pocket Book page 33

7 Look at the script on page 136. Work in pairs and practise reading through the extracts. Then close your books and re-enact the scenario. Include appropriate phrases for making and responding to offers, requests, and suggestions.

Explaining food

8 Here are some typical items that you might find on a menu in an international hotel. With your partner, put them in the order that you would expect to eat or drink them. Group some of them together into courses, and decide what name to give each course.

bread	cheese	digestif	ham	meat	pasta	sorbet	whisky
cake	coffee	fish	ice-cream	melon	salad	soup	wine

9 🔊 9.7 Listen to someone explaining a typical Senegalese dish, Chicken Yassa.

1 What does he say about the dish?

2 Make a note of phrases used to: (a) say how the dish is prepared, (b) say you don't know the word for something, (c) express appreciation.

10 Work in pairs. Think of a local speciality from your town or region, or your own particular speciality that you like to cook. Describe it to your partner. Alternatively, one of you should look at page 114, the other should look at page 118.

11 Work in pairs and improvise a conversation in a restaurant.

1 Before you start, think of a short but typical menu for a meal in your country, or a country you are familiar with. Limit it to two items per course.

2 Hold the conversation. Student A should look at page 115; Student B should look at page 119. When you have finished, change roles.

❶ Work in pairs. Think of three characteristics of the perfect host and the perfect guest. Then share your ideas with another pair.

The perfect host	The perfect guest
1	1
2	2
3	3

❷ Read the text about being a guest in Russia.

1 What kind of tone is it written in? If you were Russian, how would you feel about it?

2 Is there any information which surprises you? How different is this from advice to guests visiting your country?

Meals in Russia, whether in homes or restaurants, are often grand occasions. Nothing is too good for a guest, even if it means financial hardship for the host. The food seems never-ending (and full of garlic) and the vodka flows like water (which, if it comes from the tap, is more hazardous than the alcohol). Toasts are still the norm, but never propose a toast before the host – it's the height of *nyekulturny* (bad manners).

There are a few ground rules to keep in mind:

ф Often you'll be expected to leave your shoes at the door. The host will provide you with a pair of slippers.

ф It's all right to dress casually in a colleague's home, but avoid blue jeans and T-shirts.

ф Never arrive empty-handed. Lavish gifts aren't expected, but flowers for the hostess and a mid-to-expensively priced bottle of wine or a box of chocolates will be appreciated.

ф If you're offered second helpings of food, don't refuse, even if you take only a small amount. It's considered an insult to your host.

C Mitchell, *Passport Russia*

❸ Imagine a friend from abroad is going to visit your country.

1 Write them an email with some general advice about social habits and manners in your country. Use the text in ❷ as a basis. Begin with some general observations and then note down a few ground rules.

2 If you are in a class with people of your own nationality, compare what you have written and see if you agree. Do habits vary from region to region? If you are in a multinational class, form small groups, and ask each other questions about your traditions and ground rules.

Arriving

❹ A guest from abroad has been invited by a colleague to dinner at their home.

🔊 **9.8** Listen to the first extract as the guest arrives and note the phrases used to:

1 welcome the guest

2 apologize for being late

3 put the guest at ease

4 compliment the host

5 offer a gift

6 accept the gift.

What other phrases could they have used?

 Pocket Book page 32

5 Work in pairs. One of you (Student A) has invited the other (Student B) for a pre-theatre drink. The host arrives at the bar on time to find the guest already waiting. Make up a short conversation using the framework below.

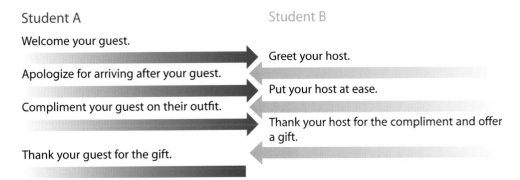

Student A

Welcome your guest. →

Apologize for arriving after your guest. →

Compliment your guest on their outfit. →

Thank your guest for the gift. →

Student B

← Greet your host.

← Put your host at ease.

← Thank your host for the compliment and offer a gift.

For more practice, look at the information on page 123.

During the visit

6 9.9 Listen to the second extract from the dinner party in **4**. Note the phrases used to:

1 offer the guest more
2 ask the host if it is acceptable to smoke
3 ask for the bathroom
4 offer the host help.

What phrases are used to respond to these offers and requests?
What other phrases could they have used?

 Pocket Book page 33

7 Work in pairs. Take it in turns to do the following. For example:

Ask for water.
    A *Could you pass me the water, please?*
    B *Yes, of course, here you are.*

1 Ask if your guest is ready to eat.
2 Offer to help with something.
3 Ask if you can make a phone call.
4 Refuse coffee.
5 Offer your guest more to drink/eat.
6 Check if your guest is OK.

Departing

8 Work in pairs. Think of phrases to use in the following situations:

1 a guest is preparing to leave
2 a guest is complimenting a host on the evening
3 a host is thanking a guest for coming
4 a host is saying goodbye.

Pocket Book pages 33, 37

9.10 Listen to the third extract from the dinner party in **4**. Did the speakers use any of your phrases? Note down the phrases they used.

9 Work in pairs. Student A is the host and Student B is a visitor from another country. You are at a restaurant. Improvise a conversation for the evening, using the information on page 123. Before you begin, read your role carefully and decide which phrases from **4**, **6**, and **8** you could use.

Unit 10

Looking ahead

OVERVIEW
- Future Continuous, Future Perfect and *will*
- *job/work* + *make/do*
- *bring/carry/take*
- Word-building (2): prefixes
- Concluding a conversation
- Thanking
- Wishing someone well
- Discussing ethical issues

LANGUAGE FOCUS   Predicting the future

1. Which decade were you born in? What difference has technology made to the lives of you and your contemporaries compared to people of your parents' generation?

   Between which consecutive generations do you think there has been, or will be, the most and the least change? Those born in:

   a   the 1890s and the 1910s

   b   the 1920s and the 1940s

   c   the 1950s and the 1980s

   d   the 1990s and the 2020s?

2. Read the article on page 101 about the technological future.

   1   Which generations have seen, or will see, the greatest changes?

   2   What two areas of technological change will have the biggest impact on our lives in the future? Find examples of each.

3. Read the article again. Work in pairs and discuss these questions.

   1   What does the author mean by the phrase 'Computers are over'? Do you agree?

   2   The author wrote this article in 1995. Which of his predictions are now a reality? Do you agree or disagree with his other predictions?

Predicting the future   Future Continuous, Future Perfect, and *will*

1. **Look at these sentences from the article.**

   a   By then we **will have succeeded** in connecting everything to almost everything else.

   b   Every product we make, ... **will contain** enough intelligence to communicate with other products. Your car **will know** where it is, ...

   c   By 2020, **we'll be making** vegetables and fruits that don't rot ...

   Which sentence:

   1   refers to an action in progress at a certain point in the future?

   2   refers to something completed or achieved by a certain point in the future?

   3   makes a general prediction about the future?

2. **Why can't the Future Continuous be used in (b)?**

3. **What is the difference in meaning between these pairs of sentences?**

   a   **I'll speak** to her tomorrow for you if you like – it's no problem.

   b   **I'll be speaking** to her tomorrow anyway; we've got a meeting.

   c   What **will you be doing** this time next week?

   d   What **will you have done** by this time next week?

   e   **I'll have been** here for six months in May.

   f   **I'll be here** for two weeks in May.

4. **In which sentences in ❸ can *will* be replaced by *may* or *should*? What effect would this have on the meaning of these sentences?**

   📖 Pocket Book page 6

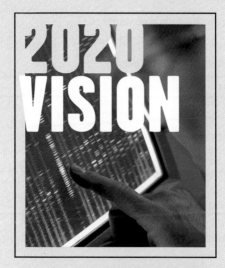

2020 VISION

IT IS OFTEN SAID THAT CHANGE IS SPEEDING UP.

I'm not so sure. I was born in 1952, my father in 1927 and my grandfather in 1895. The difference between my grandfather's world and my father's was profound: my grandfather had no TV news, no motor car, no jets, no antibiotics, few telephones and no power tools. His typical day was 12 hours of manual labour. My father's world, by contrast, was shaped by the escalating influence of electricity and automation. His typical day – filled with instant news, air travel, office work – was almost indistinguishable from mine. In this sense, the rate of change in the daily pattern of a modern person's life has plateaued. All the great disruptions made by the automation of industry and the miniaturisation of computers have already occurred.

Computers are over. The main influences on social change in the near future will be communications and biotechnology. Ubiquitous telecommunications via wire and wireless, and neobiological techniques of gene manipulation, promise to speed up the rate of change again. I expect my daughters (born in the 1990s) to lead lives in 2020 that will be significantly altered in everyday detail from mine.

By then we will have succeeded in connecting everything to almost everything else. Every product we make, from book, to doll, to truck, to door, will contain enough intelligence to communicate with other products. Your car will know where it is, what kinds of roads it has been on lately and when a repair is likely to be needed. Your stereo will turn itself down when the phone rings. The book you are reading will indirectly let you know when its movie will be premiering on the Book Channel.

Retailing and customer service will have changed beyond recognition. Imagine all retail products implanted with a chip, updating their shelf price according to daily demand. Imagine all manufactured items – a vacuum cleaner, a drill press – linked together, calling for parts when broken, feeding wear-and-use information back to the designers, tracking sales dates directly to the factory floor, letting customers dictate options so that every product is custom-built.

Privacy, or lack of it, is a legitimate concern in this future. There are ways to protect privacy with unbreakable encryption, and ways to extract data so individuals are protected. But we can look forward to privacy becoming a major issue in the future.

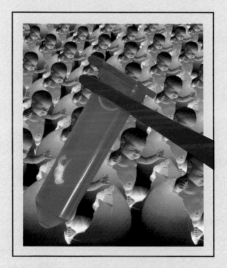

Equally powerful (and equally worrying) are neobiological technologies. Gene therapy, gene counselling, embryonic clones, ethnic biotreatments, gene databanks. DNA fingerprinting and bioengineered food are about to explode on society. We can be whatever we want to be – so what do we want to be?

Biotechnology is too powerful to suppress. It can and will cure heritable diseases, instead of just infectious diseases. By 2020, we'll be making vegetables and fruits that don't rot in stores if we want to. We will be able to pinpoint late-onset diseases (cancer at age 55) in a human foetus if we want to. But do we want to?

In the future, the distinction between technology and biotechnology will disappear. As everything connects, living things, from bananas to humans, will have become things we can engineer. Machines become biological and life gets engineered, but of the two forces, life is the more powerful. If we want greater complexity in our constructions, life is the model. The future we are headed toward, therefore, is a grand neobiological one.

GQ

---

4 Put the verbs in italics into an appropriate future form. Change the word order where necessary.

1 By next summer my parents _____ (*live*) in the same house for thirty years.

2 You _____ (*call*) us when you know what your plans are.

3 If things go to plan, this time next year I _____ (*run*) my own business.

4 Will they _____ (*finish*) by the time he gets back?

5 Call me on Saturday – I _____ (*work*) at home all weekend.

6 Have a great holiday. We _____ (*think*) of you there lying in the sun, doing nothing.

5 What do you think will happen in your life in the next five years?

1 ⏯ 10.1 Listen to what three people say about changes to their lives over the next five years. Make notes in the left-hand column of the table.

	Changes over the next five years	Future forms
Julia		
Stefan		
Judy		

2 Listen again and note down the future forms they use in the right-hand column.

6 Complete these sentences about your hopes, plans, or expectations for:

- your own personal future
- the future of your area of work, or profession
- the future of your country.

1 By the end of this week …
2 This time next year I hope …
3 In the next five years …
4 In ten years' time …
5 By the time I retire …
6 In the long-term future …

Work in pairs. Use your sentences as a basis for asking and answering questions.

Talking point

7 How do you think everyday life will be in fifty years' time. Work in pairs and discuss these questions.

a What will we be doing healthwise? _____ _____ _____
b Will more people be working from home? _____ _____ _____
c Will we be having holidays in space? _____ _____ _____
d Will we have more free time? _____ _____ _____
e How are we going to get around? _____ _____ _____
f Will there be less pollution? _____ _____ _____

8 1 Now choose three words from the box that you associate with each question, and write them in the spaces beside each question.

air traffic	fresh water	hotel	planet	television
careers	greater percentage	leisure	professions	trees
cars	herbs	medicine	progress	
drive	homeopathy	oxygen	robot	

2 ⏯ 10.2 Listen to two groups of people talking about the questions in **7** and check your answers to 1.

3 ⏯ 10.2 Listen again and make brief notes about what they say. Were their ideas similar to yours?

1 Readers of a Sunday magazine were asked how they thought people's lives would change over the next few years. Read some extracts from their replies. Do you agree with them?

1 There are already signs that we won't be doing our shopping in real supermarkets any more. We'll be buying directly from the web, making our choices with a click of the mouse. What we order will be **brought** directly to our house so we won't have to **get** things from the shops or **carry** heavy shopping bags any more, which suits me just fine as it will save me a lot of hard work.

2 Increased technology will **lead to** more and more databases on our private lives and I think this will **bring** with it a considerable reduction in privacy. However, I also expect that the biggest threat to society will be **brought** about by electronic terrorism, creating new jobs where people are employed to hack into their own company's computer network.

3 About ten years ago they predicted that in the first decade of the 21st century robots would be doing all kinds of things. You know, **taking** our children to school in the morning and **bringing** them back in the evening; doing all kinds of jobs around the house – the cooking, the cleaning, making cakes, **getting** the clothes from the laundry, doing the ironing. They'd even be doing our children's homework for them, and not making any mistakes either! Well, where are these damned robots? I need them now!

His homework has been done, miss.

But the dog ate it.

4 They're always saying that we'll be doing less work in the future, but I just don't see that happening. It seems to me that we have made a whole load of time-saving machines, which simply enable us to have more time for work, not less. And we should take advantage of that. I hope the time will come when we realize that we shouldn't be spending so many hours at work. I hope we actually go backwards technologically and re-discover the joys of life before …

Job vs *work, do* vs *make*

2 Underline all the examples of the nouns *job* and *work* in the extracts in **1**. Circle all the examples of the verbs *do* and *make*.

1 Do we use *job* or *work* to talk about:
   a individual tasks?
   b a mass of general non-specific activities?
   c a profession or occupation?
   d a place of employment?

2 Do we use *do* or *make* with:
   a domestic and academic activities (the cleaning, the shopping, an assignment, research)?
   b products, anything created or manufactured?
   c business-related activities (arrangements, decisions, plans, suggestions)?
   d non-specific activities?

📖 Pocket Book pages 22–23

3 Complete the dialogue with *job* or *work* and an appropriate form of *do* or *make*.

A I hear you've got a new teaching **1**_____. What exactly will you be **2**_____?

B Well, my main **3**_____ is to create new materials for online courses; it should be interesting **4**_____.

A How did you **5**_____ in the aptitude test? Did you **6**_____ a good **7**_____ of it?

B It was pretty hard **8**_____, but I think I managed OK.

A Great … So, are you **9**_____ anything at the weekend?

B Well, I haven't **10**_____ any plans yet. I've got a lot to **11**_____ today. I've got to **12**_____ a start on my course material – and it's my turn to **13**_____ the cleaning at home!

④ Look at the different uses of *bring, carry, get, lead to*, and *take* in the extracts in **①**. Which uses of these verbs mean:

1   to accompany (to a place)? _____   4   to go with? _____
2   to deliver (to a place) ? _____   5   to result in? _____
3   to fetch (from a place) ? _____   6   to transport by hand? _____

📖 Pocket Book page 22

⑤ Complete the sentences with *bring, carry, get, lead to*, and *take*. More than one word is possible.

1   Will you _____ us the menu, please?
2   This might _____ considerable problems.
3   Shall I _____ this to reception on my way out?
4   Marc doesn't seem to be here – I'll go and _____ him.
5   Sorry, I forgot to _____ my notes – do we need them?
6   The number 48 bus will _____ you to the city centre.
7   You can _____ my car if you want – I'm not using it today.
8   Would you like me to help you _____ your cases?

⑥ 1   🔊 10.3 Listen to four people talking about how their lives will be very different in the future. What has happened to each of them to change their lives?

2   Listen again and make a note of any phrases with *bring, carry*, and *take*.

bring	carry	take
about unexpected changes	*on working*	*advantage of that*

⑦ Match the phrasal verbs in italics with the verbs in the box which are closest in meaning. Work in pairs and ask and answer the questions.

begin	continue	employ	perform	succeed
cause	educate	look/act like	produce	

1   Does your company/department currently need to *take on* new staff?
2   Have you *taken up* any new hobbies recently?
3   What factors *brought about* the need for a single European currency? Has the Euro *brought about* the expected changes?
4   If you were asked to make a presentation in English, how well do you think you would *carry it off*?
5   Will you *bring up* your children in the same way as your parents *brought* you *up*?
6   Which member of your family do you most *take after*?
7   What is the most interesting type of research that is being *carried out* at the moment?
8   Have any of your favourite musicians *brought out* any CDs recently?
9   Are you going to *carry on* studying English after the end of this course?

What other uses of any of these phrasal verbs do you know?

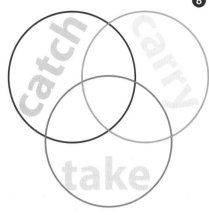

8 Put the words in the box into the appropriate circle in the diagram. The same word may belong in more than one circle.

advantage	an exam	passengers	a size
advice	fish	photos	a suitcase
care	flu	a risk	a test
credit cards	goods	a road	a thief
a decision	a gun	the shopping	a train
a driving licence	identification	a shower	weight

Now invent questions to ask your partner. For example:

*Should traffic wardens be allowed to **carry** guns?*

*What forms of identification do you **carry** with you?*

Prefixes

9 These words appear in the article on page 101.

antibiotics	biotechnology	neobiology	telecommunications

1 What do you understand by the prefixes *anti-*, *bio-*, *neo-*, and *tele-*?

2 Match each of these prefixes with the appropriate meaning.

a	anti-	f	pre-
b	ex-	g	pro-
c	non-	h	re-
d	over-	i	semi-
e	post-	j	under-

i	before	vi	not
ii	half, partly	vii	too much
iii	against	viii	previous, former
iv	not enough	ix	after
v	again	x	for, in support of

3 Match the prefixes and words in the boxes to make as many combinations as you can.

anti-	pre-
ex-	pro-
non-	re-
over-	semi-
post-	under-

arrange	graduate	school	war
democracy	immigration	skilled	weight
developed	paid	smoker	work
estimate	partner	smoking	
existent	resourced	use	

4 Choose ten combinations from 3 and make questions with them. For example:

Are you a non-smoker?

Do you ever under-estimate your abilities?

Which words do you over-use?

Work in pairs. Ask and answer your questions.

sensible /'sensəbl/ *adj* **1** (*approv*) having or showing the ability to make sound judgements; reasonable: *a sensible person/idea/diet/suggestion* ○ *It was sensible of you to lock the door.* **2** [attrib] (of clothing, etc) practical rather than fashionable: *wear sensible shoes.* **3** [pred] ~ **of sth** (*dated or fml*) aware of sth: *Are you sensible of the dangers of your position?*
▶ **sensibly** /-əbli/ *adv* in a sensible(1) way: *eat sensibly* ○ *be sensibly dressed* ○ *They decided, quite sensibly, to postpone the broadcast for a few months.*

NOTE The noun **sense** can mean your ability to experience things in the world through different organs of the body: *the five senses of sight, smell, hearing, taste and touch.* It can also mean the ability to think in a practical way and make good judgements based on reason:

She talks a lot of good sense. The adjective **sensitive** relates to the first meaning and to how easily you feel or experience something: *a soap for sensitive skin* ○ *He's a very sensitive child and gets upset easily.* **Sensible** relates to the second meaning and to making decisions based on reason: *She gave me some very sensible advice* ○ *It wasn't very sensible to go climbing alone in such bad weather.*

sensitive /'sensətiv/ *adj* **1** ~ (**about/to sth**) easily offended or emotionally upset: *a frail and sensitive child* ○ *He's very sensitive about his baldness, so don't mention it.* ○ *A writer mustn't be too sensitive to criticism.* **2** ~ (**to sth**) (*approv*) having or showing intelligent awareness or sympathetic understanding: *an actor's sensitive reading or a poem* ○ *be sensitive to the needs of others.* **3** needing to

Concluding a conversation

1 Read these telephone tips. Who do you think they were written for? Are they relevant to the phone calls you have to make (either with foreigners or people of the same nationality)?

When having a transcontinental conversation over the phone, or during video-conferencing, whether speaking through an interpreter or not, there are a few tips to follow.

first...
speak slowly, clearly and distinctly.

second...
avoid idioms and slang.

third...
say numbers slowly, and repeat them.

fourth...
at the end of your conversation, summarize the key points.

finally...
repeat them in writing and either fax or send them by email as back-up confirmation of your discussion.

R E Axtell, *Do's and Taboos of Using English Around the World*

2 🔊 10.4 Listen to these telephone conversations. Do they all follow the suggestions outlined in **1**? What phrases do the speakers use to:

1 show that they wish to draw the conversation to a close?
2 summarize the key points?
3 say goodbye?

📖 Pocket Book page 37

3 Work in pairs. Student A should turn to page 115, Student B should turn to page 119. Act out the scenarios. Then write a short email confirming what you have summarized.

Thanking

4 🔊 10.5 Listen to these extracts from four short conversations. Which of these phrases for thanking and responding to thanks do the speakers use?

a *It was really very kind of you (to ...)*
b *Thanks very much (for ...)*
c *Thank you very much indeed (for ...)*
d *I don't know how to thank you (for ...)*
e *I'm very grateful.*
f *I just wanted to say thanks ...*
g *I really appreciate ...*

h *You're welcome.*
i *Don't mention it.*
j *Not at all.*
k *It was a pleasure.*
l *That's all right / OK.*
m *I'm glad it was a help / you enjoyed it.*

📖 Pocket Book page 37

5 Work in pairs. Improvise short conversations for thanking your partner in the following situations. You decide the exact context.

– for taking you out for a meal
– for giving you some advice

– for giving you a present
– for helping you find a job

6 Write a thank-you letter or email to a friend or colleague. Use one or more of the situations from **5**.

Wishing someone well

7 Look at these phrases for saying goodbye and wishing someone well at the end of a conversation or communication. Can you think of other similar phrases?

a	All the best.	i	It was good to see you again.
b	Best of luck.	j	Keep in touch.
c	Best regards.	k	Look forward to seeing you soon.
d	Bye for now.	l	Our best wishes for the future.
e	Goodbye.	m	See you later.
f	Have a safe trip.	n	See you soon.
g	Hope to see you again some time.	o	Take care.
h	It's been really nice talking to you.	p	Well, that's all for now.

1 Which phrases would be most appropriate:
  – in a letter or email?   – in conversation face to face?   – on the phone?
2 Which ones are informal?
3 For which ones can you think of a suitable reply?

📖 Pocket Book page 37

8 What might you say to a colleague who is leaving to start a new job elsewhere?

🔊 **10.6** Listen to two people talking. Which expressions from **7** do they use?

9 Work in pairs. Use the script of the conversation on page 138 as a model, and act out the following situations. Take it in turns to be Student A and B.

Student A is saying goodbye to Student B who:
– is leaving to work in another country
– is going to get married this weekend
– has been visiting your company and is returning home
– is leaving for a holiday abroad
– is going to take an exam tomorrow
– is going away on a two-day business trip.

10 Work in pairs. Choose one of the scenarios, 1–3. Improvise a dialogue for your scenario using appropriate phrases from **2**, **4**, and **7**.

Context	Reasons for concluding	Reasons for thanking	Wishing well
1			
2			
3			

1 How often are heart or organ transplants carried out in your country? Are they routine, or still quite rare? Is there generally public support for, or opposition to, transplants?

2 Work in groups. Decide the approximate dates that the following transplants and implants were, or will be, carried out for the first time.

		a	b	c
1	human-to-human heart	1967	1977	1987
2	animal-to-human heart	1964	1974	1994
3	artificial heart	1962	1982	2002
4	brain	2010	2050	2100
5	kidney	1950	1960	1970
6	lung	1953	1963	1973

Check your answers on page 123.

3 How much do you know about transplants? Work in pairs and see if you can answer these questions.

1 When was the first heart transplant done in the UK?
2 What's the maximum number of hours between switching off the life support machine of the donor to getting the heart into the recipient?
3 Have animal-to-human organ transplants already taken place?
4 Do doctors in the UK have the knowledge to carry out an animal-to-human heart transplant?
5 Why would pig's hearts be suitable for humans?
6 What do you think are the concerns about this procedure?
7 Why do you think there is a shortage of human donor organs?
8 Will animal-to-human transplants become more common in the future?

4 10.7 Read this article and listen to an interview with Jim Quick, one of Britain's first heart transplant patients. Check your answers to the questions in **3**.

Understanding natural speech

Pig organ transplants much closer

The time when a human is kept alive by a pig's heart may not be far away. Scientists are now able to produce cloned and genetically-modified pigs, which will be important in the future.

What is more, they understand the few steps they need to take to genetically modify pig tissue so that it will not be rejected by the human immune system after transplantation.

But there are still major problems and it will be years before we know if it will be possible to use pig organs this way. There is also the fear that viruses that only affect pigs may cross into humans.

The British Government gave the go-ahead for research on the use of pigs for transplants because of a shortage of human organs. As yet, no licence for the transplant of a pig organ into a human has yet been granted in the UK, but doctors in the US have already performed successful operations using pig cells.

Cloning at the level of individual cells offers great promise and could revolutionize medicine. In twenty years' time, we may not be thinking of cloning animals at all, except to save endangered species. Instead, if you need a new heart, liver, lung tissue or even brain tissue, it will be cloned from your own cells and grown in the laboratory.

Metro; BBC News Online

5 Match each of these predictions with a suitable ending by writing a letter in the box. You can write more than one letter in each box.

a   Some direct control of individual thought processes …

b   The ability to choose the sex of unborn children …

c   Human hibernation for relatively long periods (months to years) …

d   Direct input into human memory banks …

e   Life expectancy increased to more than 150 years …

f   Lifetime immunization against practically all diseases …

g   Laboratory creation of artificial live plants and animals …

1   ☐   will have happened before 2050.

2   ☐   will be happening soon.

3   ☐   will never happen.

4   ☐   has / have already happened.

5   ☐   would be very useful if it happened.

6   ☐   should never be allowed to happen.

6 🔊 10.8 Listen to these extracts from people discussing some of the points in **5**.

1   Which points do they discuss?

2   Do they sound certain or undecided in their views?

3   What expressions do they use to indicate how they feel?

7 Work in pairs or small groups. Discuss when you think the predictions in **5** were made (the 1940s, the 1960s, the 1980s, or the 1990s), and with reference to which year (2000, 2050, or 2100). Check your ideas on page 123.

Compare your answers to **5** with another pair or group. Decide what other big ethical issues there are likely to be in the next fifty years.

Review Unit **E**

Modals of obligation, possibility and permission

① Underline the correct words/phrases in *italics*. If two words/phrases are possible, underline both.

1 I'm sorry, but I *may / can* not have enough time to finish it today.
2 I'm sorry, but I *may / can* not come tomorrow – I have to go to Rome.
3 I *had / was* supposed to go to Paris yesterday but there was a strike.
4 You *don't have to / mustn't / don't need to* do it now, it *can / may* wait.
5 We *didn't have / hadn't / didn't need* to buy anything – they paid for it all.
6 They *couldn't / weren't allowed to* go in because they were too young.
7 We *couldn't / weren't allowed to* find our way home.

Future Continuous, Future Perfect, and *will*

② Put the verbs in italics into an appropriate future form (the Future Continuous, the Future Perfect, or *will*). Change the word order where necessary.

1 Next year we *live* here for forty years.
2 Next year we probably *live* a life of luxury – if we win the lottery that is!
3 When I come back, you already *finish*?
4 Don't call us at 8.00 because we probably *eat* then.
5 You *call* me when you've done it?
6 Have a great holiday. I *think* of you next week, lying there in the sun.

Gradable and ungradable adjectives

③ Match the adverbs with the adjectives. Several combinations may be possible. Make sure you use all the words.

Adverbs					
absolutely	almost	fairly	quite	rather	slightly

Adjectives					
better	embarrassing	empty	expensive	fantastic	hopeless

Vocabulary food and drink

④ Write down your two favourite and two least favourite:

1 vegetables   2 fruits   3 drinks   4 meats   5 fish.

Work in pairs. Discuss what other kinds of food you like or don't like to eat, and what foods you or members of your family can't eat or are allergic to.

Invitations and suggestions

⑤ Work in pairs. Take it in turns to make invitations and suggest arrangements for these situations.

1 invite a colleague you don't know very well for lunch at a restaurant
2 invite a friend to a concert
3 invite a colleague you know well for dinner at your house
4 invite a client for drink after a meeting

Hosting and being a guest

⑥ Work in pairs. What would you say in these situations?

1 You have been invited for lunch at a client's house and you arrive late because your train was delayed.
2 You have had a very enjoyable evening with some colleagues, but you are tired and would like to go home.
3 You have been offered some wine by a client, but you don't drink alcohol.
4 A visitor from another country has given you a beautiful gift.
5 You are having lunch with some visitors and you receive an urgent phone call.

Prefixes

7 Work in pairs. Match the prefixes in list 1 with an appropriate word in list 2 to form a new word. Make sure you use each prefix at least once.

1	anti-	post-	semi-
	ex-	pre-	under-
	non-	pro-	
	over-	re-	

2	active	historic	time
	clockwise	husband	write
	final	statement	
	graduate	stop	

Vocabulary

8 Complete the sentences with an appropriate form of the words in the list. Use each word only once.

bring	carry	do	get	job	lead to	let	make	take	work

At the moment I'm working for a large company in the city as Sales Manager. It's interesting ¹_____, mainly because it involves a lot of travel and I meet lots of different people. It's good experience and I hope it will eventually ²_____ an even better ³_____. My normal working day means arriving at around 8.30 a.m., often by car, as when I'm visiting clients I need to ⁴_____ a lot of files and documents. I spend the first part of the morning ⁵_____ routine things like answering emails and ⁶_____ phone calls. I ⁷_____ my secretary open and answer most of my mail, and she normally just ⁸_____ me the urgent letters. If there's time mid-morning I ⁹_____ cakes for everyone, which makes me very popular! I ¹⁰_____ my own sandwiches for lunch, which I tend to eat at my desk. I'm normally out of the office all afternoon and my day finishes at around 6.30 p.m.

Concluding, thanking, and wishing someone well

9 1 Write suitable replies to these expressions of good will.

    a Best of luck for the exam.
    b Have a safe trip.
    c It was good to see you again.
    d Keep in touch.
    e Say 'hello' to Martha for me.
    f Take care.

2 Work in pairs. Take it in turns to be the main speaker in each situation.

    a You are given a ride to the airport by a friend in their car. You won't be seeing them again for a few months.

    b You are having dinner with two visitors from another country who are returning home tomorrow. You are tired and would like to leave early.

    c You are in a meeting with a colleague who has given you some useful advice. You need to end the meeting as you have another meeting in ten minutes.

    d A friend has given you a present for helping them revise for an exam. The exam is tomorrow.

    e You are holding a training event. You need to bring it to an end and thank people for attending.

Discussing ethical issues

10 Work in groups. Choose one or more of these topics and discuss whether they should be legal or illegal in your country.

a prostitution	c cannabis	e euthanasia
b guns	d human cloning	f abortion

Self-check box

	YES	NO	📖		YES	NO	📖
Modals of obligation, possibility, and permission	☐	☐	1	Hosting and being a guest	☐	☐	32
				Prefixes	☐	☐	
Future Continuous, Future Perfect, and *will*	☐	☐	6	Vocabulary: *bring, carry, do, get, job, lead to, let, make, take, work*	☐	☐	22–23
Gradable and ungradable adjectives	☐	☐		Concluding, thanking, and wishing someone well	☐	☐	37
Vocabulary: food and drink	☐	☐		Discussing ethical issues	☐	☐	
Invitations and suggestions	☐	☐	32				

Pair work file

UNIT 2 | **Focus on functions** page 18

Conversation 1

Improvise a phone conversation with Student B, who wishes to talk to Richard Chambers. You begin the conversation by answering the phone.

- Answer phone.
- Ask caller how to spell their name.
- Inform caller that Mr Chambers is not in (give reason).
- Inform caller that Mr Chambers cannot be reached.
- Inform caller that all colleagues are at lunch.
- Take a message.
- Conclude the conversation.

Conversation 2

Your name is Alex Delacroix, from JKC Associates, telephone 001 819 2088. Improvise a phone conversation with Student B. You wish to talk to Madeleine Hogan. Student B will begin the conversation by answering the phone.

- Announce who you are and what you want.
- Ask where Ms Hogan can be reached.
- Ask if you can speak to someone else.
- Ask to be called back (say when and where).
- Conclude the conversation.

UNIT 4 | **Focus on functions** 8 page 41

Your name is Jan Gugurevic. You work for ECI Trading, and you want to speak to Student B (on the phone). Student B's name is Andrea Rigobon and he/she works for Soft Systems. You want to speak to Andrea about ordering some new software called MIS. His/her name was given to you by someone in the production department at Soft Systems. Student B will answer the phone.

- Announce who you are (without giving spelling) and who you want to speak to.
- Repeat and spell your name when requested.
- Give the name of your company when requested.
- Explain why you're calling.
- Explain where you got Student B's name from.
- Improvise any other information Student B requires.
- Check all details and conclude the phone call.

You work for a multinational company. You have invited two management consultants from the US to visit your offices for a series of meetings next week. Your schedule for next week is below, but it is incomplete. You have highlighted the items you are not sure of.

Telephone your colleague (Student B) to check the information you are unsure about. Your colleague will also have some questions for you.

Take turns to ask and answer questions, and discuss any items which are not clear.

You can improvise and invent as much information as you wish. Confirm that you have understood your colleague's answers. Make a note of your colleague's answers and correct any mistakes on your schedule.

You begin. Remember you are on the phone, so use appropriate greetings, etc.

MONDAY

Flight arrives at 13.30? From New York or Boston?

I'll meet them.

Meeting with HR Director at 16.00.

One visitor is Thomas E Harris – check name of second person.

Hotel – the Bristol or the Astoria?

Dinner – where? What time?

TUESDAY

Morning – meeting with project team at 10.00.

Lunch – working?

Afternoon – on-site inspection of work practices at main site.

Dinner at my house?

WEDNESDAY

Pick up at hotel 9.30.

Meeting with legal advisors – where?

Legal advisors' email address?

Agenda for meeting?

Check-in at airport 16.30 – I'll drive them.

1   Interview the students in group B for one of these jobs. Their task is to guess which job they are being interviewed for. Prepare ten questions to ask, and see how quickly the interviewees guess the job. Make sure your questions are not too easy or too obvious.

Jobs			
lighthouse attendant	priest (or equivalent)	prison warder	hairdresser
film director	politician	astrologist	optician

2   The students in group B will interview you for some different jobs. Your task is then to guess which job you are being interviewed for.

❶ Read this information about several different types of food. Use a dictionary to check any words you don't know. Prepare to explain the information to your partner, who will ask you questions.

BRAZIL NUTS	A daily helping of Brazil nuts provides a rich source of selenium. Low levels of this mineral reduce the risk of heart disease, cancer, and thyroid problems. The mineral is also contained in meat, especially kidneys, as well as oily fish, bread and rice.
FRUIT AND VEGETABLES	Studies that have linked the low intake of vitamins C, E, and beta carotene in Scotland with its particularly high rate of heart disease provide important evidence that fruit and vegetables should be eaten every day. They are full of anti-oxidants. An intake of five to seven helpings a day is recommended.
GREEN VEGETABLES	Broccoli, sprouts, cabbage, cauliflower, turnips, and kale all have anti-cancer properties. Sprouts contain so much sinigrin, a natural anti-cancer chemical, that according to a food scientist at the institute of Food Research in Norwich, even an occasional meal could destroy cancer cells in the colon. According to a recent study reported in the British Medical Journal, the most effective vegetable to counteract cataracts and other vision impairments is spinach.
BERRIES	Cranberries, strawberries, blueberries, and raspberries are rich in anti-oxidants and vitamin C. Strawberries contain more vitamin C by weight than oranges. Like cherries, they contain ellagic acid, said to block an enzyme used by cancer cells.

❷ Find out from your partner about these types of food:

     a   tomatoes   b   garlic   c   green tea   d   oily fish   e   soya.

Ask questions about what healthy substances they contain, and what positive effect they can have on our health.

Read this recipe for *Jansson's Temptation*, and make brief notes. Prepare to explain the dish to your partner.

Jansson's Temptation

A traditional Swedish supper dish made with anchovies (small salted fish).

6 medium-size potatoes

2 onions

50g butter

2 cans of anchovy fillets

250–300 ml cream

Pre-heat the oven to 200°C.

Peel the potatoes and cut them into very thin slices. Chop the onions finely. Drain the anchovies and save the liquid from the cans. Cut the anchovy fillets into two or three pieces.

Butter a baking dish. Put a layer of potato on the bottom, then a layer of onion, a layer of anchovies, and another layer of potato. Continue like this until everything is used, finishing with a layer of potato. Pour over the liquid from the anchovies and half the cream. Put a little butter on top.

Bake for about 20 minutes, then add the rest of the cream, and continue cooking until the potatoes are tender. Serve with crispbread and cold beer.

You are hosting Student B at a restaurant where the menu is the one you have just created. You meet inside the restaurant. Make sure you do the following:

- Greet Student B.
- Ask about their journey to the restaurant.
- Suggest a table.
- Explain the menu, and suggest particular items.
- Offer wine, or mineral water.
- Ask B if they like the food.
- Suggest that B tries your food.
- Ask if B would like a dessert (you have now finished the main course).
- Offer to share a taxi home.

Scenario 1

You have been talking to Student B about arranging a dinner to celebrate the end of the English course. Together you have agreed to:

- invite your teacher and their partner
- have a pre-dinner drink at 7.30 at the English pub
- meet at a restaurant at 8.15.

You have a meeting to go to and you need to conclude the conversation. Summarize the arrangements. Get Student B's mobile phone number so you can tell them about any changes to the arrangements. Conclude the conversation.

Scenario 2

You have been talking to Student B about arranging a meeting. You have decided to:

- have the meeting at 9.00 on Tuesday at their office
- discuss the next English course and possible improvements.

Student B will begin the conversation by summarizing what has been arranged.

Pair work file

UNIT 2   **Focus on functions** page 18

Conversation 1

Your name is Lindsay Cartwright, from CBA Promotions, telephone 020 7999 6776. Improvise a phone conversation with Student A. You wish to talk to Richard Chambers. Student A will begin the conversation by answering the phone.

- Announce who you are and what you want.
- Ask where Mr Chambers can be reached.
- Ask if you can speak to someone else.
- Ask to be called back (say when and where).
- Conclude the conversation.

Conversation 2

Improvise a phone conversation with Student A, who wishes to talk to Madeleine Hogan. You begin the conversation by answering the phone.

- Answer the phone.
- Ask caller how to spell their name.
- Inform caller that Ms Hogan is not in (give reason).
- Inform caller that Ms Hogan cannot be reached.
- Inform caller that all colleagues are at lunch.
- Take a message.
- Conclude the conversation.

UNIT 4   **Focus on functions** page 41

Your name is is Andrea Rigobon and you work for Soft Systems, a software house. Student A will telephone you. Deal with their enquiry.

- Answer the phone.
- You didn't catch Student A's name – ask.
- Ask for name of Student A's company.
- You are not sure what Student A is talking about – interrupt and ask for clarification.
- Explain that the software Student A wants no longer exists – ask if there is any other way you can help.
- Check all details and conclude the phone call.

You work for a multinational company. You have invited two management consultants from the US to visit your offices for a series of meetings next week. Your schedule for next week is below, but it is incomplete. You have highlighted the items you are not sure of.

Your colleague (Student A) will telephone you with some more questions about the schedule.

Take turns to ask and answer questions, and discuss any items which are not clear.

You can improvise and invent as much information as you wish. Confirm that you have understood your colleague's answers. Make a note of your colleague's answers and correct any mistakes on your schedule.

Remember you are on the phone, so use appropriate greetings, etc.

MONDAY

_____

_____

Visitors (Thomas A Harris and Carl

Washburn) arrive at 13.00 from Boston.

Who is going to meet them?

_____

Meeting with HR Director today or

Tuesday?

_____

Booked into the Hotel Bristol – 2 nights.

_____

Dinner – where? What time?

_____

TUESDAY

Morning – meeting with project team?

What time?

_____

_____

Probably have working lunch.

_____

_____

Afternoon – on-site inspection of work

practices – which site?

_____

_____

Dinner at my house.

WEDNESDAY

Pick up at hotel 9.30? Or earlier?

_____

Meeting with legal advisors at their

offices.

Legal advisors' email address?

_____

Agenda for meeting to be discussed with

visitors.

_____

_____

Check-in at airport 16.30 – have we

arranged a car?

_____

1   You are going to be interviewed by the students in group A. Your task is to guess which job you are being interviewed for.

2   Interview the students in group A for one of these jobs. Their task is to guess which job they are being interviewed for. Prepare ten questions to ask and see how quickly the interviewees guess the job. Make sure your questions are not too easy or too obvious.

Jobs			
astronaut	army general	babysitter	headhunter
psychologist	fashion designer	website manager	head of the United Nations

1 Find out from your partner about these types of food:

   a Brazil nuts   b fruit and vegetables   c green vegetables   d berries.

Ask questions about what healthy substances they contain, and what positive effect they have on our health.

2 Read this information about several different types of food. Use a dictionary to check any words you don't know. Prepare to explain the information to your partner, who will ask you questions.

TOMATOES	Tomatoes are exciting growing scientific interest. In a recent survey of the eating habits of nearly 48,000 men over six years, researchers at Harvard Medical School in the US linked a high intake of tomato-based foods – more than ten helpings a week, including pizzas – with a reduction in the risk of prostate cancer of up to 45%.
GARLIC	Studies suggest that garlic can lower blood pressure and cholesterol, as well as thin the blood to prevent clots forming. As little as half to one clove of garlic a day lowers cholesterol by nine per cent, according to a major New York study.
GREEN TEA	Green tea, as enjoyed in Japan and China, is said to be a defence against cancer, especially pancreatic cancer, and ageing. Its anti-oxidant effect suggests protection against heart disease and strokes.
OILY FISH	The best sources of omega-3 fatty acids – which are said to help keep cholesterol levels low – are mackerel, sardines, herrings, salmon, pilchards, and fresh tuna. At least two portions a week are recommended. Fish is particularly recommended after a heart attack and for those with hardening of the arteries, as the oils prevent clot formation.
SOYA	Soya bean flour and curd protein are attracting increasing interest for their high level of calcium and a substance called genistein. Japanese women favour it to strengthen bones and even to lower the risk of breast cancer.

Read this recipe for *Aloo Chana*, and make brief notes. Prepare to explain the dish to your partner.

250g chick peas
soaked in water overnight and boiled for 2 to 3 hours

1 onion

1 teaspoon turmeric
a mild, yellow spice

2 teaspoons chilli powder
a hot, red spice

a piece of fresh ginger
grated

1 fresh green chilli
chopped and the seeds removed

2 tomatoes *chopped*

450g potatoes
cut into cubes and partly boiled

oil *for frying*

salt and pepper

Aloo Chana

Chick Pea and Potato Curry

A traditional family dish from Pakistan.

Heat the oil in a large, deep pan. Fry the onions for a few minutes until they are soft. Add 2 teaspoons of salt, the red chilli powder, and the turmeric. Continue cooking for a minute or two, then add the ginger, green chilli, and tomatoes. Cook for a few more minutes, then add the chick peas, potatoes, and about 200ml of water.

Continue cooking until all the water has gone.

Serve with rice or traditional bread (*naan*).

You have been invited by Student A to a restaurant. You meet inside the restaurant. Make sure you do the following:

- Thank A for inviting you.
- Respond positively to A's offers and suggestions.
- Answer A's questions appropriately.
- Ask relevant questions about the menu and the restaurant.
- Ask A to pass you things (e.g. bread, salt, water).
- Refuse politely anything you don't want.
- Thank A for the meal.
- Say you'll make your own way home.

UNIT 10   Focus on functions ❸ page 106

Scenario 1

You have been talking to Student A about arranging a dinner to celebrate the end of the English course. Together you have agreed to:

- invite your teacher and their partner
- have a pre-dinner drink at 8.30 at the English pub
- meet at a restaurant at 9.15.

Student A will begin the conversation by summarizing what has been arranged.

Scenario 2

You have been talking to Student A about arranging a meeting. You have decided to:

- have the meeting at 9.00 on Thursday at your office
- discuss the next English course, and possible improvements.

You are in a hurry to get home. Summarize what has been arranged. Get Student B's home number so you can tell them of any changes to the arrangements. Conclude the conversation.

Information file

UNIT 2	Skills focus ② page 20

Answers

Good topics		Bad topics	
1	England	6	the UK, Ireland
2	Israel	7	Finland, France, Hungary, Ireland
3	Brazil, Italy	8	South Korea
4	Thailand	9	Jordan, Lebanon
5	Kenya, South Africa	10	Norway

UNIT 4	Language focus ⑤ page 36

The mobile phone he was using was not real. He was pretending to speak to someone to impress the other passengers.

UNIT 4	Skills focus ④ page 43

Suggested answers

a We hope to have all the reports back by the end of this financial year, or by the start of the next year at the latest.

b If you paid by cheque I will need to confirm with the bank that it has cleared before we investigate further.

c To improve the efficiency and professionalism of the department, please deal with all enquiries and correspondence within five days of receiving them.

d If you are updating a file with EDITMENU, and that file is also currently being used by STARTSYSTEM, any changes you make will not affect STARTSYSTEM until you terminate STARTSYSTEM and then start it up again.

UNIT 7	Skills focus ⑥ page 77

This table was prepared by the business journal *People Management* for human resource departments within companies, following the introduction of the Data Protection Act 1998 and the Human Rights Act 1998.

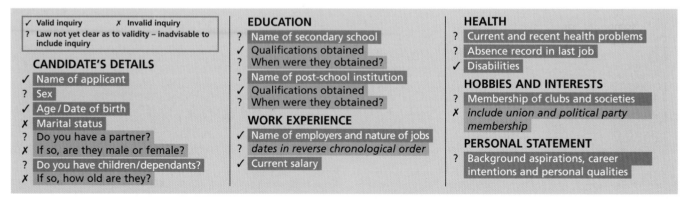

✓ Valid inquiry   ✗ Invalid inquiry
? Law not yet clear as to validity – inadvisable to include inquiry

CANDIDATE'S DETAILS
- ✓ Name of applicant
- ? Sex
- ✓ Age / Date of birth
- ✗ Marital status
- ? Do you have a partner?
- ✗ If so, are they male or female?
- ? Do you have children/dependants?
- ✗ If so, how old are they?

EDUCATION
- ? Name of secondary school
- ✓ Qualifications obtained
- ? When were they obtained?
- ? Name of post-school institution
- ✓ Qualifications obtained
- ? When were they obtained?

WORK EXPERIENCE
- ✓ Name of employers and nature of jobs
- ? *dates in reverse chronological order*
- ✓ Current salary

HEALTH
- ? Current and recent health problems
- ? Absence record in last job
- ✓ Disabilities

HOBBIES AND INTERESTS
- ? Membership of clubs and societies
- ✗ *include union and political party membership*

PERSONAL STATEMENT
- ? Background aspirations, career intentions and personal qualities

The Apology Game

Play this game with a partner. The first person to complete the day's work is the winner.

At the start of the game you are on the underground in London, travelling to visit a client. You arrive at your client's office, have a meeting / presentation, go out for lunch, and then leave to go home.

Toss a coin to move: heads = move one square, tails = move two squares. Follow the instructions on each square as you land on it, using the statements as the basis for a short, polite dialogue with your partner.

You call someone by the wrong name.	Your English isn't very good and you are about to give a presentation.	You don't understand someone's question.	You want to know where you can make a phone call.	At lunch you spill wine on someone's suit/dress.	
You arrive at the office late.				You accidentally offend someone by criticizing their country.	You embarrass someone by referring to something they'd obviously prefer not to talk about.
You want to know where to get off the tube.	You sit in someone's seat by mistake.	You tread on someone's foot in the tube.			It's time for you to go.

▲ Student A

START

FINISH

FINISH

▼ Student B

It's time for you to go.			Someone pushes in front of you in the ticket queue.	You want to ask what time it is.	You want to ask for directions to Market Street, where the host company is.
You have to ask someone to repeat something for the third time.	You want to know where the bathroom is.				You arrive at the office very early.
	Your mobile phone rings.	You realize you've forgotten to bring some documents/data.	You realize you have misinterpreted what someone has said.	You can't stop coughing or sneezing during the meeting.	You meet someone and immediately forget their name.

As a group, select one or more items to discuss from the following:

- health   - the arts   - taxation.

By the end of the meeting you need to have agreed to implement at least two people's ideas.

Look at the briefing notes below and choose one role each. Before you begin your discussion, spend some time preparing what you are going to say. Prioritize each set of proposals on the agenda. During the meeting, try to argue in favour of your top two proposals, giving reasons for rejecting the other two. Think about the consequences of what you are going to propose.

Student A	Student B	Student C	Student D
Your brief is to ensure that everyone has a chance to speak and that no one is left out.	You represent interest groups who want to introduce radical policies. Your brief is to stress the importance of these ideas.	You have been given the responsibility of ensuring that everything is understood and the objective of the meeting is achieved.	You are the time-keeper – you need to make sure that the meeting keeps moving and finishes on time.

Objectives   To discuss one or more of the following policy areas. Try to reach agreement about the implementation of at least two of the proposals.

Agenda

Policy area – Health

Proposals

1 Drug companies should no longer be allowed to make large profits from selling drugs to developing countries.

2 There is no longer a need for so many doctors. People can learn to diagnose their own health problems via special computer programmes.

3 No private health care insurance, hospitals, clinics, or schemes should be allowed – taxes should be increased to allow state health provision for everyone.

4 People who smoke should not be able to receive free health care, but should be obliged to take out private health insurance.

Policy area – The arts

Proposals

1 Entry to all museums and galleries should be free.

2 The study of music should be compulsory at school and all pupils should have to learn an instrument.

3 The government should make grants available to theatre projects for the unemployed.

4 State funding of the arts should be supported by an 'arts tax' on business.

Policy area – Taxation

Proposals

1 People should be taxed according to the real contribution that their particular profession makes to society (i.e. the more 'really useful' they are, the less tax they pay).

2 On the last day of the financial year, a random tax on the ownership of certain goods should be declared. People would have to pay a flat rate of tax, for example on the ownership of any of the following items: a red sports car, country music CDs, an untidy garden, designer clothes, etc.

3 People and businesses should be taxed according to how environmentally friendly they are. The more resources they consume, the more tax they should pay.

4 Families should be allowed to decide how much tax they should pay and the amounts should be published annually.

	Richard Norton	Martin Gandy	Lyndam Gregory	Tom Southern
Age	early 30s	early 50s	mid 30s	early 40s
Nationality	Australian – spent childhood in Australia, now in the UK	British – always lived in the UK	British – spent childhood in India, lives in the UK	British – spent childhood in the UK, now living in Australia

Student B has invited Student A to watch an outdoor sports event. You both arrive at the stadium at the same time. Make up a short conversation using the framework below.

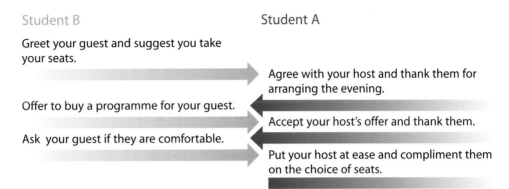

Student B

Greet your guest and suggest you take your seats.

Offer to buy a programme for your guest.

Ask your guest if they are comfortable.

Student A

Agree with your host and thank them for arranging the evening.

Accept your host's offer and thank them.

Put your host at ease and compliment them on the choice of seats.

Host

You want to impress your client and make sure they have an enjoyable evening. You have pre-ordered a meal for you both and a bottle of champagne. Your train is delayed on the way to the restaurant and you arrive late, after your guest.

Welcome your guest and apologize for being late.

Offer your guest some champagne.

Thank your guest for the gift.

Direct your guest to the bathroom.

The food arrives: roast beef.
Apologize and offer to order different food.

You've finished eating. Ask if you can smoke.

Offer your guest coffee.

Offer to ring for a taxi and get your guest's coat.

Thank your guest for coming.

Client

You have been travelling all day, and you're very tired. You don't want to offend your host but you would like to leave early. You don't eat meat or drink alcohol. You arrive at the restaurant before your host.

Greet your host and put them at ease for being late.

Refuse offer of champagne and ask for a soft drink.
Offer your host a gift.

Ask for the bathroom.

Refuse the food and explain why.

Put your host at ease.

You've finished eating.
Tell your host you don't want them to smoke.

Refuse coffee. Tell your host you want to leave.

Accept the offer of a taxi.

Thank your host for the evening and apologize for leaving early.

Answers   1 a   2 a   3 b   4 ?   5 a   6 b

Answers   All the predictions come from a book published in 1967 and concern the year 2000.

Listening script

 1.1 Authentic

A I think the biggest thing is, is that men are being asked to do new stuff, shall I, dare I say, feminine stuff, as well as hold on to all the traditional masculine things, so it's kind of like, I mean, if you don't mind me using the characters, it's kind of like you're supposed to be Arnold Schwarzenegger [Yeah.] as well as some very soft Alan Alda all at the same time as the new American male and … Well, it's not fair, that's too many jobs.

B So you think you're getting a bad deal, you think men are getting a bad deal?

A I think lately, yeah. I think I'm held up to two opposing standards sometimes, and it gets really difficult in a relationship when you're trying really hard but it turns out you're holding up the wrong standard on the wrong day.

B OK, here's a question for you. Do you think that men yet have the option not to work? Like and to stay at home, and do you think that …

A Yeah, just barely, yeah, I think actually they do, but do you know they got to do a lot of explaining for themselves still, whereas women who step out into the work world don't have to do as much explaining for themselves.

B Well, except that they do in the sense that we still have a big debate about whether or not women should work full time when they have children, you know, who does the childcare, should women try to be home when the kids are home, should they feel guilty?

A Nobody questions them saying, is it right? I mean, they may question themselves but men have to defend themselves greatly if they said they wanted to be a househusband.

B Mm-hm. So you still think that it's, it's, men have to justify themselves if they decide to stay home or if there's a man in the playground, with …

A Yes, or if they hold up a singularly masculine role of only, you know, a provider [Yeah.] which twenty years ago back in the, you know, or back in the fifties say when that was, what a male was, after the war, was supposed to do. If a man tries to hold on to that now he's not really a modern guy and he has to defend himself quite a bit, whereas if a woman wants to quote, unquote, have it all, well, that's almost expected, really. I mean that she's allowed to have a fulfilling career, be a perfect mom, and have a lovely tended home.

 1.2

I = interviewer, A = Andrea

I Andrea, you have your own company. How successful have you been?

A Well, I've been running my own business for just over two years, now, and in that time we've attracted about a hundred and twenty client companies, which is one a week on average. So, I would say pretty successful. I mean, well, the business has been successful right from day one, but for the last six months it's been growing really fast … I've taken on three new staff members, and recently I've been looking for new offices – there just isn't enough space here any more … And we, we've also just started up a new web-based recruitment service, which is doing really well, it's very popular …

I So it's definitely worth making the move to working for yourself?

A Well, yes, yes for me, because I've always wanted to be my own boss. And, and it's great, you know, you have the freedom and the independence to do what you want, you, you make all the decisions … but, well, it is, it is incredibly hard work. You know, it's very hard to ever switch off completely – I mean, I really do work twelve hours a day, six, seven days a week. There's very little free time. Everything else just has to fit in around work, really. Um …

I You have an understanding husband, though?

A Oh, yes, I'm very lucky that he's extremely supportive, yes, yes. It does help.

 1.3 Authentic

Timothy Mitchell

One of the *tactics* I would use, I guess, would be the 'learning ten new words a day' tactic, which basically in *itself* would be the, I would select ten words, they could probably be more than ten. But what I would normally do is, I would go into, like, the *kitchen*, or go into, like, a *bedroom*, and just select ten *objects* out of that bedroom and try to learn those words so that I would get a *better* idea of how to use those words in *sentences*, just regular text within the Italian *language*, of course. And I would try to use those words *during* the day. And, I would do this every, day, and after a while what I would do is, every day you add ten new words and I would, after you've accumulated x *amount* of words, it can be like ten days, so there'd be like a *hundred* different words, I would go back and review those words so that I would have a better understanding of the Italian language.

Ruth Glassock

I think of it in terms of *pictures*. I looked at the Arabic alphabet and I just learnt it like the Arabs learnt it which is basically seeing a *letter* and writing it and repeating it and repeating it and repeating it *across* the page. How I personally learnt it, I was told by *someone* if you think of an Arabic word or you speak an Arabic word, try and imagine it in letters going across your head, your *forehead*, *because* that way you get a pictorial idea of what Arabic is like and it will automatically come, so if you, if you remember things in terms of experience, in terms of sound, and also in terms of *visual*, what the letters physically look like, what the words physically look like and represent, you can actually learn it more easily. And I think at the start it was, it was just sitting down rote learning. You had to learn things and just get used to it and also just put it into *practice* so that it actually seemed *something* relevant.

James Lewin

I read somewhere quite recently, I would say in the last year, that you can't learn a new word unless you hear it at least eight times, it won't stay with you. I mean, obviously up to a year ago I didn't know anything about that so I must have remembered lots of words and not used that *technique* … I learned them from writing lists, vocabulary lists, and learning the lists, putting a mark against the ones that I didn't remember that first time round, making a smaller list, putting a mark against the ones I didn't remember the *second* time round, until I got it down to one word and hopefully no words … but I think the words that I have learned are words that either I've seen, then I've seen them again, and I've seen them again, I've seen them again, I've used them, which I think is really important, that if you're learning and you've got a chance to use them then that is going to establish them *somewhere* in your subconscious anyway … So either use them if you can, if you get an opportunity to use them, or to somehow either relate them to other words that are similar, even words in another language that are similar, or put them in a *context* maybe because of their sounds, so that they trigger off some kind of meaning, or rather some kind of other word that will bring you back to that meaning.

 1.4

1 Hi, Bill, how are *you doing*?
2 How *are you*?
3 Pleased to *meet you.*
4 Hi, Kate. Good to *see you* again.
5 May I *introduce myself*?

 1.5

Hello. How *are* you?
And *you*, how are *you*?
I *gave* it to her.
I gave it to *her*, not to *him*.

 1.6

1 **A** Hello.
 B Hi, could I speak to Andrea Matthias? This is Paul at CPMD.
 A I'm afraid he's not here at the moment. Have you got a number he can call you back on?
 B Yes, I'll give it to you right away. It's 020 7346 2642.
 A … 2642. OK. I've got that.
 B Great. Thanks. Bye.
 A Goodbye.

2 **A** How do you do, Mr Schroeder? My name is Rachel Flynn. We spoke on the telephone.
 B Of course. How do you do, Mrs Flynn? It's very nice to meet you. I hope you had a pleasant journey.
 A Yes, it was fine, thank you. Mr Schroeder, may I introduce my colleague, Anthony Edwards? He'll be working very closely with us on this case.
 B Pleased to meet you, Mr Edwards. Welcome to Strasbourg.
 C Thank you, Mr Schroeder. I'm very pleased to meet you.

B And if I could just introduce my assistant, Johanna Dietmeyer? This is Mrs Flynn and Mr Edwards from Sackerby Hunter in Boston.

D Hello, pleased to meet you …

3 A Hello, Geraldine Cotton, please.

B I'm sorry she's out at lunch. Can I take a message for her?

A She doesn't know me. My name's Miranda Richards and I'm calling from a company called CPMD – we're in discussion with Ms Cotton about the possibility of doing some work together.

B Can you give me your number, please?

A It's 020 7346 2642.

B And can I ask what it's about, exactly?

A We're waiting for a quotation.

B OK, I'll get her to call you as soon as she comes back.

A Great. Thanks very much for your help. Bye.

B Goodbye.

4 A Hello, Suzanne. How are you? I haven't seen you for ages.

B Hi, Darius. How are you?

A I'm fine … fine … yeah. What about you? How was your trip to the States?

B Oh, it was great … [Yeah?] … yeah, really great.

A You were in California, right?

B Yeah, mostly … it was, it was amazing.

A How was the food? And the wine?

B Oh, amazing. Just so much of it, you know … Oh, sorry, Darius, this is Martina, from our Italian office. She's going to be looking after all the European accounts.

A Hi, Martina, nice to meet you.

C Hi, you too.

B Darius is our Creative Director. He has all the brilliant ideas. We just sell them.

A Well, in theory … So, you're coming over later this morning?

B Yeah, 11.30 in your office. Is that still OK?

A Yes, absolutely.

B OK. See you at 11.30, then.

A Nice meeting you, Martina.

C And you. See you later. Bye.

 1.7

A Hello.

B Hello.

A My name is Sandra. Nice to meet you.

B I'm André.

A I'm a bit nervous, you know. It's my first time I've been on a, like this, on a course.

B Uh-huh.

A I was sent by my company. I work in the city, here in London. What about you?

B I arrived in London this morning.

A Oh, really?

B Yes.

A So are you staying somewhere here in London?

B I'm staying in a hotel just around the corner.

A Oh, really? Oh, what's it like?

B It's fine.

A Have you got everything you need?

B Yes.

A Well, that's good.

 1.8

A Hello.

B Hello.

A Hello. Is there coffee in the pot?

B Oh, would you like some?

A Oh, yes, please. Thanks.

B My name is Akemi. Nice to meet you.

A Oh, hello. I'm Stefan Grothgar. Have you just arrived this morning?

B Yeah, yeah.

A Yeah, me too.

B I'm a bit nervous, you know. It's my first time I've been in a, like this, in a course.

A Yeah, yeah? Oh, I've done, I've done some others before. Yeah. Very good.

B Oh, good, yeah.

A Yeah, they're great.

B Yeah, not too, not too much pressure I hope.

A No, no, no. No, it's really nice and we do get to know each other very well over, you know, the week.

B Good, yeah. Well, I was sent by my company. I work in the city.

A Oh. Are you from round here then?

B Yes, yes.

A Ah, right, you live here in …?

B Yes, well, it's a Japanese company but I'm a local staff, I live in London, so yes …

A I see, I see.

B I've been there for, well, not too long, so, but they sent me here, so, yeah. How about you?

A Oh, I've come straight from Germany, you know.

B Oh, really?

A Yeah, yeah this morning.

B I see.

A Yeah, I'm staying in a hotel just around the corner.

B Oh, really? Oh, what's it like?

A Oh, it's nice, you know, it's, it's sort of, simple but clean and breakfast, you know, everything you want.

1.9

Oh, are you?

Oh, is it?

That's excellent.

Oh, really?

OK, right.

How interesting.

1.10

A Hi.

B Hey.

A How are you doing?

B I'm fine.

A Are you on this?

B Yeah, yeah.

A Excellent.

B I haven't seen you for a long time.

A How are you?

B I've been fine, been busy …

A Working?

B Yeah, yeah, yeah a lot of stuff came up so …

A And your man?

B Fine, he's he's great, that's all.

A Yeah? Give him my best, give him my best.

B I will do. Are you qualified to do this 'cause I'm … ?

A Sort of, sort of, I've actually done this before, years ago, and I'm just coming back to take it again.

B OK. And do you know who's teaching this one, 'cause I really don't know that much about it?

A No, no idea.

B You don't? How did you get here today?

A I came by the tube.

B Oh, right, OK, 'cause when I tried to get on this morning where my stop was closed, so, yeah, I just made it, I can't believe it.

A Now we got plenty of time to get coffee and find out who's teaching this thing.

B Yeah, I'd like to know that because it sort of depends on whether I'm going to do the three days or the two days …

A I'm here for the whole time.

B Oh, you are. So you're … OK.

 2.1 **Authentic**

I = interviewer, B = Sir Bobby Charlton

B When I first got involved with football, footballers were just as important as they are now, maybe more so. Maybe there was more of an affection towards the footballer because they really in a way were just working, working class people like everybody else, they were not getting any more money than anybody could get in a decent job elsewhere. [Oh, really?] Well, I mean, when I first started, I was on, my first wage was twelve pound and ten in the summer, you know, even just after the war I think the wage was about eight pound, you know, so it's changed in as much as, but, but peo, but footballers were famous, you know. You went down the main street, you know, just as today, you were inundated with people wanting to talk about the game, etc.

I But were the pressures the same?

B No, no people left you alone. If you played bad, if you played bad there was no sort of recriminations or anything like that, you waited till the next match. No, there was no sort of detailed insight into why it was all wrong, and there were no supporters' bodies, you know, who wanted to know how this was done, and why, and this is wrong, etc. I remember when I used to go to watch Newcastle United play, when I was a young lad, and I remember just after the war, it must have been in the late forties when they put the price of admission up, from two-and-six, from two shilling to two-and-six. You know, and it was like questions in the House of Parliament, you know. But there were no supporters' associations that actually went and complained to the club, etc. [Right.] – it was a government thing.

I And did the media kind of hound players like they do today? [No, not at all.] Their private lives were their private lives?

B Not at all, it's nonsense. I mean some of the players today, they've got, as soon as they go home they've got to pull the sheet, pull the curtains, you know, it's a nonsense really, it's outrageous really, in a way. But it's because they're acknowledged now as film-star type people, you know and what you used to read about in Hollywood – the glitzy stars – it's now about football … And the more people want the players, you know, the more difficult it is for the players to give it. You know, we give I don't know how many thousands of footballs a week, a year, away. We give them away but they all have to be signed, you know. [I see.] And that was never the case in the old days. You used to finish your training, you would go home, and you would do a little bit of some recreation, whatever you wanted to do, and you'd play the game on a Saturday. But you were never hounded by the media like you are now, you know. But that's, that's one of the big things, really, and I think because of that, the public don't look on the footballers with affection, … it's curiosity now. Really.

I I see. What was your, what have been your best and worst moments, would you say, during your career?

B Well, worst moment was Munich without any question, there was just at the beginning of a great era for Manchester United, and it was, suddenly it's gone …

I What about your best moments, what are you most proud of?

B Er, many, many, I'm, I mean, every footballer dreams of achieving things, winning an FA Cup, even just becoming a footballer, you know, and I was lucky, I had all sorts of aims like everybody else, and I fulfilled most of mine. I wouldn't like to have finished a career without winning the European Champions Cup, … and the World Cup, when you beat the best. … But it's nice, it's nice that I've, I'm still involved, and still, people still want to see me and ask me about things, and I'm still very much involved in football, which after all this time, you know, is very satisfying, yeah …

🎧 2.2

1 I remember going fishing with my older brother when I was a child – we used to go a lot in the summer. But then I became a vegetarian and it just seemed cruel, so I stopped going. I hated to see the fish with hooks in their mouths. I remember being quite upset about it, but I certainly don't regret giving it up.

2 Every year we used to go on a walking holiday in Wales. My parents really enjoyed walking, but the problem was that my father always liked to keep going. We never used to stop during the walk, even if it was raining. Sometimes we didn't even stop to have lunch. My father would try to entertain us with stories and jokes, he tried hard, you know, but it didn't really work. I haven't been back to Wales since I was about fourteen. I always hated walking – I still do.

3 Well, when I was a teenager I really used to enjoy dressing up to go out with my friends. I really liked going to parties and clubs, and I would borrow my sister's clothes or jewellery – she was older than me and she had some really lovely things. But I always remembered to put them all back exactly as I'd found them. I don't think she ever found out what I was doing.

4 I remember having to do a lot of sport at school. I wasn't very athletic, and in particular I couldn't stand cross-country running. I always used to make up an excuse not to have to do it. Sometimes I would try pretending I was ill, but I regret to say it never worked. Funnily enough, I really enjoy running now; in fact I'd like to do it more often, but now that I've got my own kids, I don't know, I don't seem to have the energy.

🎧 2.3

A I didn't really know what to expect, you know, when you hear the word 'security' you think of things you've seen in films, like, you know, like James Bond or the secret service. [Yeah.] I looked around the house thinking about how I might come across … the ornaments I had, the colour of things, bottles of alcohol, the pictures on the walls, [Right.], my CD collection, and my books. I thought some of these might seem suspicious to a complete stranger, 'cause I thought he must be looking for signs of subversion in my character, you know.

B I know, it can make you paranoid, that kind of thing.

A I even considered removing everything personal and putting it all away, but then I thought that would look really odd. But I did remove three books and hide them in a cupboard – they were *Vice: An Anthology*, er… *The Kama Sutra*, and *The Book of Blue Verse* – because I thought they might make me seem like someone who I wasn't really, you know… I didn't want to risk creating the wrong impression. And then, then I made it look like they'd never really been there by moving the other books together.

B That was clever of you.

A And then I couldn't decide how I should be when he arrived. You know, should he find me listening to some intellectual programme on the radio, or watching a documentary on TV? Should I offer to show him round the house? When he finally came I could actually hear my heart beating, I was so nervous. I was expecting him to look at all the things around the house and to watch every move I made. Instead he just sat down, and I managed to make him coffee, even though my hands were shaking. My voice sounded really nervous, and he must have seen that I was sweating. But in the end, all he did was ask me a few questions about my previous experience, and I never noticed him looking at anything. But then I suppose they're trained to be like that.

🎧 2.4

A I think it sounds fantastic and it's just what we've been looking for.

B Well, it certainly looks like a lovely place but it seems really expensive.

🎧 2.5

a It looks like a really interesting job and it's very well paid.

b She seems very nice but there's something about her I don't quite trust.

c It sounds like the perfect house for us and it's got lots of space and a huge garden.

🎧 2.6

B Hello.

A Good morning. Could I speak to Roberta Lee, please?

B She's not in today but she should be in tomorrow.

A Well, do you think you could tell me where I could reach her?

B I don't know where she is, but I could find out from a colleague.

A Has she got a mobile phone?

B I'm not sure, let me just check – no, I'm afraid she hasn't.

A Is there anyone else I could talk to?

B Everybody is at lunch, but if you give me your name and number I'll get someone to call you.

A Well, can I leave a message?

B Yes, of course.

A Could you tell her that Gavin Milsom called. That's M-I-L-S-O-M. From Mediatech in Dublin. And if she could ring me after ten o'clock your time.

B OK. So that's Gavin Milsom from Mediatech in Dublin, and you want her to call you after ten o'clock our time.

A That's it. Thank you for your help.

B You're welcome. Bye.

🎧 2.7

a … I could find out from a colleague.

b … let me just check – no, I'm afraid she hasn't.

c … if you give me your name and number I'll get someone to call you.

d … and you want her to call you after ten o'clock our time.

🎧 2.8

1 A Mediatech, good morning.
  B Could I have extension 2131?
  A Who's calling, please?
  B Louisa Jordan from Scott Financial.
  A One moment, please, I'll try to connect you.
  C Peter Andersson.

B Good morning. This is Louisa Jordan speaking. I'm calling about the arrangements for the project meeting, and I believe that you are the project manager at Mediatech.

C Yes, that's right. Did you have any particular day in mind?

B Well, I was thinking about next Wednesday, in the afternoon if that would suit you?

C Mm-hm. Yes, that would be fine.

B Shall we say two o'clock here at my office?

C Excellent.

B Right, well, I look forward to meeting you next Wednesday, then. Goodbye, now.

C Goodbye.

2 A Hello, Mediatech.
  B This is Louisa Jordan. Could I have Peter Andersson, please?
  A Sorry, what did you say your name was?
  B Louisa Jordan.
  A OK, just a moment.
  C Peter Andersson.
  B Hi, Peter, it's Louisa. How are things?
  C Fine. You?
  B Yeah, great. Listen, about the project. We really need to meet. Would next Wednesday after lunch be OK?
  C Just a moment … Yeah, sounds fine.
  B Two o'clock at my office?
  C Fine.
  B Brilliant. Thanks, Peter.
  C No problem. See you then.
  B Bye.
  C Bye.

🎧 2.9

A Good morning. Can I help you?

B This is Ralph Kinnock from Mediatech. Could you put me through to Maria Delosantos, please.

A Sorry, the line's really bad. Could you speak up a bit, please?

B Yeah, sorry, I'm on a mobile. It's Ralph Kinnock from Mediatech. Maria Delosantos, please.

A I'm afraid she's on the other line at the moment. Would you like to leave a message?

B Yes, could you tell her I called and that …

A Sorry, sorry, could you spell the name of the company?

B It's M-E-D-I-A-T-E-C-H. Mediatech.

A And what was your name again?

B Ralph Kinnock. Could you tell her that I've made the addendum to the joint venture agreement, but that in any case the meeting's been postponed till a week on Friday.

A … Meeting a week on Friday, sorry, I didn't quite get the first part.

B That I've made the addendum to the joint venture agreement.

A You've made a what, sorry?

B An addendum.

A Oh, an addendum. Sorry, the line's so bad, I can hardly hear you.

B That's all right.

A OK. I've got all that. Does she need to call you?

B No, I don't think so. Thanks for your help.

A You're welcome. Bye.

B Bye.

🎧 2.10 Authentic

Paddy Glynn
I think it's good to start on a safe subject at a dinner party. It's generally OK to comment on the food nowadays. Broadly speaking. [But then, sometimes …] It's also, I think, OK, to make little light comments about people's appearance which used to be absolutely taboo, it was considered very rude to comment on a lady's dress, say thirty or forty years ago. [Really?]

Lyndham Gregory

Well, in India, in formal situations, it's not the done thing to talk about politics or religion. Ironically enough, if you do know the people very well then those are quite often the two subjects you will talk, sometimes quite heatedly, about.

Richard Norton

Another topic I found in Australia which is probably equally as taboo or causes a lot of, you know [Yes], heated discussion is racism, and 'cause a lot of, there's a cultural divide in Australia between generations of what they believe, [Oh, yes.] and it's, you know, that can cause a lot of problems even in the same family.

Stephan Grothgar

Yeah, it's funny, conversations. You know what I find interesting is that when you're, sort of, at dinner parties with friends something that gets more and more acceptable these days is talking about sex. [Oh, yes?] But you don't talk about it personally, you never say, like, I like to do this or that. It's always very informal and general [Yes]. It's very strange, there seem to be certain rules to it.

 2.11

Conversation 1

A You know I told you we were getting a new research assistant?

B Yes …

A Well, they've finally appointed someone. He starts next week.

B Mm. And what's he like?

A Well, his name is Michel and he's from France, obviously, and …

B Oh, really? OK. Have you actually met him yet?

A Not exactly. I was away when the interviews were happening.

B Uh-huh. Oh, talking of France, you know we're going skiing there in January?

A Are you? Whereabouts?

B Val d'Isère. We went there last year – the skiing was fantastic.

A Oh, that sounds great. How can you afford to go every year?

B It's not really that expensive. I mean, the price includes, let's see, hotel accommodation, ski rental …

A Anyway, I was telling you about Michel. He's been working in London, he has three children, a lot of experience …

Conversation 2

A … and all being well, I'm hoping to visit East Africa for the first time in the autumn.

B That's great. How long are you planning to go for?

A Well, it depends how the project develops …

C By the way, did anyone see that story in the news about Ethiopia? It's so awful, what's going on there at the moment.

B Yeah, things are really bad again, aren't they? The war and famine, it just seems to go on and on, doesn't it?

C And it doesn't seem to matter how much aid goes in, you know, it's not enough …

B No …

A Anyway, as I was saying, I'm probably going to Kenya in the autumn, and then Tanzania and possibly Uganda.

B Wow! Sounds really exciting. What are you doing there, exactly?

A Well, I haven't been before, so I need to meet people, get to know how things work. I've planned my visits and I've got some good contacts.

B Yeah, you can never have too many contacts.

C You know, talking of contacts, did I tell you I met this really interesting guy in London last week? He was telling me about this website where, if you're looking for a new job overseas, you can post your details and say what you're looking for. And then people contact you directly. It's like a kind of online employment agency.

B Mmm … sounds an interesting idea.

A I think it sounds a bit suspicious, actually …

B So, anyway, we were talking about your trip to East Africa.

A Yes, well, as I was telling you, it's Kenya first, then Tanzania, possibly Uganda, and then after that …

Unit 3

 3.1 **Authentic**

I = interviewer, M = Mark Ellingham

I What countries have particularly fascinated you?

M Well, I suppose really the ones that I've personally written books about, because you have to get completely inside a country when you, when you write about it. When you write a guidebook, you have to, you have to become interested in just about every aspect of the country, whether it's the ancient monuments, the ancient history, the beer, the football teams, I mean, just every aspect of the culture which … Normally when you're travelling, or when you're on holiday, there are two or three things you're really interested in seeing, but you just have to become a kind of polymath. So I suppose the ones that have interested me most have been Morocco and Greece, which were two of the books I've written most of, and also Spain which I've had a sort of a long relationship with Spain over the past twenty years. I had very close Spanish friends at university, so I've been going back and forth for for a long time.

I And of the countries that you haven't visited, but the Rough Guides do guides on, which ones would you like to visit?

M Well, I think almost all of them, I don't think I've been put off by reading anything that we've published so far. I'd like to do some travelling in Latin America if I get the chance, and I'd like to travel more in Asia as well.

I And this year are you planning any trips?

M This year I'm probably going to Morocco in a month or two … My wife is actually, her family's from Sri Lanka, so we're probably going to Sri Lanka again, either towards the end of the year, or probably more likely early next year …

I Are there any countries that you'll never visit, or you'll never have time to visit, do you think?

M I'm sure, yes. I'm never quite sure how many countries there are in the world. I think very few people get around much of the Pacific, for example, it's just too time-consuming and too remote for most people. There are actually countries that we don't, you know, we deliberately don't publish guides to. The obvious example is Burma, where the democratic opposition, if one calls them opposition since they were actually elected, have asked for a tourism boycott of the country, so we wouldn't publish a book on Burma, just as we in apartheid days wouldn't have published a book on South Africa.

I In the next ten years or so do you think the places where people will be visiting are going to change? I mean, what are going to be the really popular places, do you think?

M Just looking at Europe, obviously Croatia's going to be coming back very soon as a major destination, having been a kind of huge package destination, and then gone to sort of no tourism at all, that's going to come back. I think it's just a sort of steady process of everywhere becoming easier and more popular. Certainly, you know, if you're living in Europe, southern India has become much much more accessible than it used to be, and non-stop flights to Goa and Kerala, you know, has led to this extraordinary thing of people actually going to southern India for a week, I don't think that could possibly have been the case, you know, five or ten years ago. So I guess that will, will escalate.

I And at Rough Guides here, what plans do you have for the future?

M We're producing about, I think about twelve or fifteen new destinations each year … And we're also doing quite a number of sort of general reference guides. We see Rough Guides as a kind of brand that applies not just to travel but to accessible popular reference. So we've moved into popular cultural areas. We've produced a series of music reference guides. We also produce a hugely best-selling little guide to the Internet, that sells about 300,000 copies a year … We're looking at a weather guide, a health guide, possibly a book about magic … [So all kinds of things.] All kinds of things, yeah but again trying to sort of bring a very accessible popular kind of slant to it and explaining things in a straightforward language without in any way kind of dumbing down and being too simplistic.

 3.2

1 I guess the number of visitors to southern India will escalate.

2 I think Croatia is probably going to become a major destination.

3 We'll definitely see a rise in the number of business travellers.

4 Look! The flight's leaving – if we don't hurry we're going to miss it.

5 I think it's likely that prices are going to go up.

6 I'm not totally convinced that these climate changes will happen.

7 I'm quite sure that business travel is going to get cheaper.

8 I think it may well get more expensive.

3.3

A I think possibly the worst journey in my life was when I went to Italy for the first time. I was going there to live.

B To live?

A Yes, and I wanted to take as much luggage with me as possible, so I decided to go by train. I was living at my brother's house about thirty kilometres from London at the time. So I decided to go on the underground to Victoria station, where I had to get on a train for Dover, and then I went by ferry to Calais.

B So this was before the Channel Tunnel, then?

A Yes, they hadn't finished building it then. Anyway, so I got off the ferry at Calais and got on another train to Paris, where I had to change stations. I had to take a taxi from the Gare du Nord down to the Gare de Lyon, I think it was. But I was travelling with a couple of other people and we couldn't all get into the taxi with all our luggage, so we actually had some of it hanging out of the windows.

B You're joking.

A When I got out of the taxi and had to pay, I realized I'd lost my wallet, at least I thought I had. In fact, I wasted so much time trying to find it that I missed my train.

B No.

A I finally arrived in Milan about thirty-six hours after leaving London. What about you? Have you had any disastrous journeys?

B Well, I was just trying to think. I once had to fly from Mumbai to London. I'd decided to fly with Air India because it was quite a bit cheaper. The flight there was fine, but coming back it was a nightmare. I had to wait in the airport for over twelve hours, then we flew from Mumbai to Delhi rather than going direct to Heathrow. Well, I thought the problems would be over when we landed at Heathrow, but there'd been a bomb scare …

A No.

B … and it took ages to go through customs, and then of course I'd lost my luggage. I didn't get home till three o'clock the next morning.

3.4

When I got out of the taxi and had to pay, I realized I'd lost my wallet, at least I thought I had. In fact, I wasted so much time trying to find it that I missed my train.

3.5 Authentic

M = Mustapha, C = Clare

M In Morocco I think time is not the most important thing, it's actually eventually being there that's the most important thing. Dinner parties or weddings obviously with family and friends, people often turn up late and turn up when maybe an hour or two later than they're supposed to, but that's not considered impolite or rude, it's just a generally widely accepted thing, but I don't think in the States that would be well looked upon, would it?

C No, I think that people tend to want you to be where you're going to be on time. And expect you to call if you're not going to be on time. And that's pretty much every, you know, kind of business meeting, or lunch or, or even social. If it's a dinner, an arranged dinner at someone's house, you're expected to be there roughly on time if they give you a time, because the meal will be planned a certain way. People are very planning-conscious. And whereas if you, a party is very flexible, and of course the earlier you are to a party the less fashionable it is, so it's customary to just show up, whenever. The later the better.

M It's not to do with fashion in Morocco, I think it's just the way people are, it's almost kind of a genetic thing, that you just turn up a couple of hours late, knowing that everybody else will be doing the same.

C Yeah, no, I think that definitely Americans, you know, you need to be on time or with an excuse. I mean, if I were meeting friends at a restaurant, and, if I was ten minutes late I wouldn't worry, if I was fifteen minutes late I wouldn't worry, twenty minutes late I would call the restaurant and leave a message and tell my friends I was late and to start without me.

M But that's what you're like in the States, you know, everything has got to be on time, you've got to to get things done, you know, it's almost …

C Time for some flag-waving now.

M No, it's almost the pleasure of letting things happen, and sort of letting it just, the evening or the party or whatever rolling on and taking its own course is somewhat inconceivable in the States.

C Yeah, probably, I mean, you know, everybody has to be, because there's always the next thing, do you know what I mean, if you've scheduled a lunch, then you presumably have scheduled the rest of your day and so you have to be at lunch because then after lunch you have to be back at the office and then have meetings, and then you have this person blocked in for a certain amount of time. Everything is sort of put in blocks.

3.6

A Hello, design group.

B Paola Ferrara, please.

A Speaking.

B Hello, Paola this is Daniel Ferlin.

A Hi, Daniel, how are you?

B Fine, thanks. How are you?

A I'm fine, thank you. It's nice to hear from you. So, what can I do for you?

B Well, I was wondering if you'd got my email about our meeting next week.

A Yes, I'm just writing a reply to you.

B Well, perhaps we could arrange the time of the meeting now, and then some of the points for the agenda.

A OK, that sounds like a good idea.

B So, would Wednesday morning at nine o'clock suit you? There's an early flight from Stockholm.

A Ah, I'm afraid Wednesday's going to be difficult. The problem is, we have a group of visitors from the UK. I think, you know, Tuesday would be better for me.

B Oh, sorry, no, I can't make it on Tuesday. I'm afraid I have to be in Frankfurt all day. Now, let's see … Well, could you manage Thursday morning?

A Just a moment, I'll look in my diary … I'm sorry, it looks as if I'm going to be busy all morning. Could you make it in the afternoon?

B Well, the problem is that doesn't give us very much time.

A Well, yes … perhaps we could just continue into the evening, or do you need to go back to Stockholm?

B Yes, that'll be fine, that's no problem. Shall we say two-thirty, then?

A If it's OK with you, I think I'd prefer to make it a little later, because I have a working lunch with the marketing director, and these lunches, you know, they go on and on. What about three-thirty?

B OK, that's fine. So that's three-thirty on Tuesday.

A Thursday.

B Sorry did I say Tuesday? I meant Thursday.

A Yes, OK, but actually I'll need to check with Gianni and the others first. I'll email you later this afternoon to confirm.

B OK, fine. Now about the agenda points …

3.7

B So, would Wednesday morning at nine o'clock suit you? There's an early flight from Stockholm.

A Ah, I'm afraid Wednesday's going to be difficult. The problem is, we have a group of visitors from the UK. I think, you know, Tuesday would be better for me.

B Oh, sorry, no, I can't make it on Tuesday. I'm afraid I have to be in Frankfurt all day. Now, let's see … Well, could you manage Thursday morning?

A Just a moment, I'll look in my diary … I'm sorry, it looks as if I'm going to be busy all morning. Could you make it in the afternoon?

3.8 Authentic

Extract 1

A There seems to be a perception, well, in Britain anyway, that because a lot of American women work outside the home, that this has a sort of a bad effect on family life there. I mean, do you find that people say this to you, or do you think it's true?

B I think a lot of people presume that it happens, I don't necessarily think that there's a connection [Yeah.] but, yeah, everybody presumes that about America and our economy in general.

A Yeah, because also, I mean, America is also perceived to be a very violent culture, you know, we're all terrified of going to New York because we're going to get held up at gunpoint, and so on. I mean, do you object to that view?

C Yes, oh, certainly today because a lot, well, just use your example …

Extract 2

C You know, you were asking me earlier about how it feels when people make enormous generalizations about America and about American culture, and it's very tough because sometimes those generalizations are based in truth.

A Does that irritate you when people have this idea of Americans really being very insular, of only caring about America?

B Especially if you're the traveller, I mean if you're being hosted in a country and somebody asks you these questions, you can't seem to respond too truthfully because you're a guest, but at the same time they're saying, oh, well, Americans never go anywhere and you're sitting in their front room and have a full passport and you can read the Chinese characters on their tea set and stuff, so you sort of want to say, well, most of us who have passports have been to university and, you know, we got a little schooling behind us and stuff.

Extract 3

A It seems to me as an outsider looking at American politics that everything is stage-managed for the camera, for the press, that the press are all the time looking for little bits of scandal and so on, and then building on what they get, that really politicians are behaving for the cameras.

C I think that that's an unfair accusation really. For one thing television in most countries, especially in Europe, I think, is one of the major reasons why certain politicians get elected and others don't.

A Yes, yes, I think that's true, but on the other hand in the States it seems to be so much more so, I mean, on the Clinton business, I mean every single bit of that was televised, everybody knew everything about it and I can't believe that here in Britain that it would have had the coverage that you gave it in the States.

B I don't know, I mean, it may not have shown up on the television screen but some of the coverage in the newspaper here is pretty much the same thing. I mean, I don't condone it either way but what shows up in the newspaper here about politicians' nights out isn't too different from what shows up on the television, just 'cause we seem to be rather efficient at getting it.

C That's true, actually, we certainly don't have a monopoly on scandal, some of your newspapers seem to thrive on scandal and in much greater detail than we did.

A Oh, yes, no, no, I agree with that totally, yes, I mean, I don't approve of it, but I agree with it. But it seems that in America everything is dressed up for the media, everybody is packaged the … I mean when Hillary Clinton had her makeover job, you know, she was … .

B Oh, we don't do anything halfway you know, I mean we try to do, you know, I think that Americans really do try to do their best at anything and that's why you find overly …

3.9

1 A ... And there seems to be a perception that the political system here is basically corrupt. Is that really true?

B Well, actually, I don't think I'm the best person to answer that. I don't know very much about politics.

2 A ... Yes, I mean, it seems to me as a visitor that the British don't really like foreign tourists, and don't really want them here. Why is that?

B That's a very good question. What do you think?

3 A So, Holland is seen as a very liberal sort of place, I mean, very tolerant in its attitude to drugs and things like that. Do you think that's a good thing?

B Actually, I don't really want to go into that now, if you don't mind.

4 A ... And I've heard that this is a really dangerous city, that there's a lot of robberies and muggings, and all that, that you shouldn't go out after dark.

B Well, it's the same everywhere, I think. All major cities have their dangerous parts.

5 A Everything seems so expensive here, and I've heard that taxes are very high. Why do you put up with it?

B Mm, yes, you know, I'd quite like to know what the situation is in your country.

Unit 4

 4.1

A So the answer to the first one is the US and Great Britain. Did you get that right?

B Yes, I did, actually, but it was just an educated guess.

A And for number two, the answer is by gestures. What did you get for this one?

B For me this was quite easy to make a guess at. Mainly because I have a university friend who's Italian and she gestures an incredible amount.

A OK ... The answer to number three is San Juan 180, Paris 110, Gainsville, two and London zero.

B Yep, there's no doubt that for me, this was the easiest one. But still, I was surprised at the actual numbers. I mean, the question says it was in the space of an hour and 180 times is a heck of a lot.

A OK, so moving on to the next one. The answer to four is Italy 35.3%, the US 18%, UK 22%, and Germany 17%. How did you find this one?

B Well, I would have said the US or even Australia. I didn't realize mobile phones were such a European thing.

A Oh, yes. Mobiles are definitely the accessory to have.

B The interesting aspect is that they're not as common in Germany, but I suppose if they repeated the study on a regular basis rather than just doing a one-off, the figures would change again.

A No doubt. So number five, the answer is the Quakers.

B Really? That's an unusual thing, isn't it? I mean, I have heard of them but I didn't know they had this thing about silence.

A Did you know that Richard Gere was a Quaker?

B What? The Richard Gere?

A Yes.

B No, he isn't, he's a Buddhist!

A Oh, right. I thought he was ... well, never mind. OK, and the final answer is an old woman and a young woman.

B Gosh, you know, I find an old woman very difficult to make out. But overall I think answer four is the one I find the most surprising.

 4.2

an educated guess
a university friend
an incredible amount
an hour
a European thing
a one-off study
an unusual thing
an old woman

4.3

a So the answer to the first one is the US.

b This was the easiest one.

c Oh, yes. Mobiles are definitely the accessory to have.

d The interesting aspect is that they're not as common in Germany.

e I think answer four is the one I find the most surprising.

4.4

A You know we were talking about the possibility of using video-conferencing facilities?

B Uh-huh.

A Well, there was a report about it on TV last night.

B Oh, really?

A Yeah, and it made some interesting points that I think we might find useful.

B Oh? So what did they say in particular?

A Well, they looked at how people are using it – as an alternative to meetings, mainly, as you'd expect. And there was one woman, a woman executive that they interviewed. She lives in Arizona and she said that she conducted most of her meetings from home, via her computer. She said she'd flown over a hundred times in the previous year, travelling to meetings all over the States. And now she doesn't need to fly anywhere.

B Yeah, well, I guess that's always the main benefit – time-saving.

A Yeah. And space, too ... you know, where office space is very limited.

B OK, so savings on time and space. And cost-saving must be a factor too.

A Yes, absolutely. They talked to a British lawyer. He said it allowed him to take on cases that would otherwise cost him money because of the time involved in travelling. He reckons he can now have four meetings in the same amount of time he used to take for one. He wondered how he'd managed without it. And he also made the point that it's much more flexible – you know, you can break off and resume a meeting whenever you want. And another interesting thing is, he admitted that it makes people more polite. He said that a colleague had told him that he could now stare at a client without seeming rude.

B That's interesting. Any other tips?

A Yes, they had a consultant on the programme who explained that you should make sure the lighting is OK, and not sit with your back to a window, so you can be seen. And according to him, it's important to sit up straight and smile a lot [Oh, no ...] ... Yes, I know, but apparently subtle body language just gets lost on screen. And for meetings with more than two people, he thought it was important to have a strong chairperson, so people have to take turns, and raise their hands when they want to interrupt. You know, he admitted that it made things more formal, but even so, it's a good idea ...

B Mm, yes, it's all important. So did they touch on the technology? Is it going to get cheaper? Are we going to be able to use it?

A Well, they asked a software expert when the relevant technology would be available. And it seems that the software already exists for PCs and laptops, and it's not expensive. You need a digital phone line for home use, but those are getting cheaper. And he predicted that the next generation of mobile phones would allow video-conferencing on the move – he said it would become a normal part of daily life.

B Well, I guess we really should start looking into it ...

4.5

Message 1

A Sue Lindley's office.

B Could I speak to Ms Lindley, please?

A I'm sorry but she's out at lunch.

B Right, could I leave a message for her?

A Certainly.

B Could you tell her that Chas Zentnir telephoned? She was going to send me a quote for some ventilators. That was about a week ago and I was wondering if I could expect it soon.

A Has she got your number?

B Yes, I think she's got my number but I'll give it to you again. It's 0161 929 2519. If she could call me back this afternoon that would be good.

A Can I just check the spelling of your name. Chas – C-H-A-Z.

B No, A-S. And it's Z-E-N-T-N-I-R.

A OK. So you're expecting a quote for the ventilators.

B That's right.

A OK. I'll see that she gets your message. Thanks very much. Goodbye.

B Goodbye.

Message 2

B Hello.

A Hi, can I speak to Sue?

B No, I'm sorry she's in a meeting at the moment. Can I take a message?

A Yes, this is her friend Sian. Could you tell her I'm going to book tickets for the theatre tonight and I want to know if she wants to go next Tuesday or Friday.

B OK, I'll get her to call you.

A Well, I'm not going to be at home but she can get me on my mobile.

B Does she have your number?

A I'm not sure. It's 07569 320 986.

B So that's 07569 320 986.

A That's right.

B And what did you say your name was?

A It's Sian, S-I-A-N. I'm her flatmate, actually.

B OK, I'll make sure she gets your message.

A Brilliant, thanks. Bye.

Message 3

A Could you get her to call me? She's got my number.

B Yes, of course. Could I ask what it's about?

A Yes, I was wanting to come to your new warehouse next Thursday and I also need a copy of the new brochure.

B Perhaps you'd like her to post it to you.

A Yeah, that would be great. She could send it to me, Karen Ridehalgh, that's R-I-D-E-H-A-L-G-H. And the company is R. D. Coe Limited.

B C-O-E?

A That's right. Number 30, that's three zero, High Street, Measham, Swandincote DE12 7JR.

B Sorry, could you spell the place names?

A Measham. M-E-A-S-H-A-M

B A-M. Right.

A And Swandincote. S-W-A-N-D-I-N-C-O-T-E.

B And it's DE12 7JR.

A Right.

B OK. So that's a copy of the new brochure, and you also want to arrange a meeting to see the warehouse, next Thursday, that's Thursday the sixth.

A That's right. Great. Thanks a lot.

B You're welcome. Bye.

 4.6

I = interviewer, B = Dr Burrell

I … and there have been some surprising discoveries made concerning the ability of animals to acquire language. Joining me is Dr Harold Burrell who's responsible for the Department of Animal Behaviour at Ventura University. He's here to discuss some of his views with us and explain some of the recent discoveries. Dr Burrell, thanks for taking part in the discussion today.

B My pleasure.

I So how do scientists know that certain apes can acquire language? Can you tell us something about the type of research that's been carried out?

B Well, for many years now, researchers have studied chimpanzees in different ways with varying results. For instance, in the 1960s and 1970s studies focused on their ability to learn sign language, so that they were able to follow instructions, answer questions and make requests, and so forth. Their linguistic abilities appeared to be like those of, say, a two-year-old child.

I Well, this must have been an exciting discovery.

B Absolutely. However, some scientists were not entirely satisfied with the way some of these studies were carried out. You see, it was felt that the researchers had failed to be objective in their enthusiasm for their subjects. Video recordings showed how the researchers had unconsciously given the chimpanzees non-verbal prompts which enabled them to respond correctly but without really understanding.

I So should we not get too carried away with some of the more recent findings?

B Well, there is certainly still room for a degree of scepticism. However, I think many studies have benefited from past criticisms and have made definite improvements in terms of the methodology. Much more care is taken now to make sure that there is no unconscious prompting or scoring bias on the part of the researchers.

I And can the chimps learn to communicate with each other using sign language?

B Well, one of the most exciting discoveries is that signing chimps have been filmed passing on their skills to other chimps without any human intervention.

I Yes, I also heard that some projects have been working in a way which is much more like how children acquire language. Can you tell us something about this?

B Oh, yes indeed. Instead of slowly building up a vocabulary of signs with the chimps going through rote learning, they are given a large vocabulary of signs from a very early age. And then, the language is used around them to see if they can pick it up like children do.

I So you mean the emphasis is on comprehension?

B Exactly.

I And the results have been successful?

B Oh, very. Without training, one chimp has developed a vast comprehension of spoken words.

I And in what sort of conditions?

B Well, they have time off for play with other chimps, a fifty-acre forest with plenty of food,

interesting places to visit, and time set aside for structured testing. Routines include getting ready to go outside, bathing, riding in the car, looking at books, visiting other apes, playing games …

I As you would with any two-year-old child! Tell me, will the day come that a chimp will call me on my mobile and tell me to bring him a banana?

B Well, I don't know about that, not in the near future at least …

A Thank you, Dr Burrell.

 4.7 **Authentic**

Andy Crisp

I'm a client systems engineer working for my current company for, er, four months, primarily with foreign employees. I speak fairly quickly and they have trouble understanding me because of where I come from – Essex, London Essex area, so we do tend to speak quicker than a lot of other English people. I think I speak considerably slower than some of my friends. But the problems have really been speed, pronunciation of words because we do tend to, we're lazy really with our pronunciation, so we drop letters and things. So they have problems with that. And using slang terms as well, we use terms that are almost English language now, that aren't proper English. Things like using 'quid' for money, and stuff like that, that they don't pick up on or know about, which is understandable. It's like American, some Americans terms we don't know. Exactly the same.

 4.8 **Authentic**

I = interviewer, T = Tim Mitchell

T He's still difficult for me to understand, even though I'm with him, you know, every day, I'll, during the day I'll ask him probably, like, seven or eight times if he could just repeat what he just said because it's very difficult to understand.

I And how do you feel about that, does it make you, does it embarrass you that you have to ask him, how does he feel?

T No, normally when he'll start doing this, I'll start speaking in Texan, and so he doesn't understand what I'm saying, so it's kind of a game that we play with each other, I guess. No, it doesn't bother me at all.

I What advice would you give to, for example, your Italian colleagues when dealing with him?

T If you don't understand don't be afraid to tell him you don't understand what he just said. Ask him if he'll please speak a little bit slower, speak correct English.

 4.9

B Yes, hello.

A This is Paul Gold from Sachs. Could I speak to Jacqueline Rymell, please?

B Speaking.

A Your name was given to me by Leanna Ilvic from …

B By who, sorry?

A Leanna Ilvic.

B Oh, yes, right.

A She said you might be interested in some new technology we're developing. It allows people to see on their computer screen what's being said to them on the phone.

B So, you're talking about some speech recognition system. Is that right?

A Yeah, that's right.

B But I thought that kind of technology was already available.

A It is if you want to talk to your computer, but there's nothing doing that from an external source. And not only that, it automatically

translates what's being said into the language of your choice. It would be particularly useful, for example, with people who are …

B I'm not really with you.

A Look, so, basically what I'm saying is … look, let me give you an example. It's like if I were a secretary in Bulgaria, or wherever, and you called me, I'd see what you said on my screen both in English and Bulgarian.

B OK, I've got you. Sounds fantastic.

A Exactly, which is why Leanna thought you …

B Sorry, can I just interrupt you for a second? [Tell him I'll be with him at eleven, OK?] … Sorry about that. Where were we?

A I was just saying that Leanna thought you might be interested and I was wondering if I could come over to you and arrange a demo.

B Sure, when did you have in mind?

A Tuesday next week, that's Tuesday the fifth?

B OK. It would have to be in the morning.

A That's fine.

B Can I just have your number?

A It's 0127 781 324, extension fifteen.

B … 324, extension fifteen. That's one five, yeah?

A That's it. OK, well, thanks for your help, and I look forward to seeing you.

B Right. See you on Tuesday.

A Goodbye.

B Bye.

Unit 5

 5.1 **Authentic**

I = interviewer, M = Martha Lane Fox

I You've been described as a young and funky company. I just wondered actually what's the average age of the people working here.

M That's a good question, it's changed. When we started, when we launched the site, we worked out the average age was 24. I think it's gone up a bit now. We've had a couple of people over 40 creeping in, but I think it's still under 30, the average is about 29.

I What bizarre things can I get? Supposing I want to get married this evening by doing bungee jumping off the Tower Bridge or something like that, I mean can you, what can you do?

M We can do pretty bizarre things. We can send you on a MiG fighter jet with the Russian army, we can let you adopt a donkey, … we can get you an island in Fiji, we can get you travelling around the place. We haven't got weddings sorted quite yet, but it's on the cards. We can do pretty much a lot of unusual things and that's what attracts the attention, and what makes the site unusual. But we can also really help with a lot more fundamental kind of travel plans, hotel plans, holiday plans and watch this space because lots of new categories will be coming out in the next two to three months as well.

I Did you have any idea that this was going to be so successful?

M It's funny, I don't think we really thought about it. Brent is brilliant at thinking big. I'm quite good at completely overestimating everything. But to be honest when we wrote our original business plan, you're so focused on the next step and on the next, getting the cash in, launching the site. I mean, standing now and looking at the valuation of the company today and the amount of people that are working here and the markets we're about to branch into, I can't believe it on one level, and on another level I just think, 'cripes, we've still got so much to do'. So, I think that you have to think very big and act very fast. That's part of being successful.

I Do you manage to sleep at night?

M I didn't sleep before and I doubt I'll carry on, I won't sleep any more or less now. I don't not sleep because I'm worried, I don't not sleep just because I have, I only need very luckily about four hours sleep a night, so a bit like Mrs Thatcher, I hope the comparisons end there, frankly, but, yeah, there's a lot to do and I can safely say I've never worked so hard in my whole entire life, and if you're not physically in the office you're thinking about the business, and always on call obviously, so sleep varies.

I One last question: in ten years' time, how do you see yourself?

M Ha ha! Ten years! My God, ten years ago I was sixteen. I can't possibly answer what I'll be doing when I'm thirty-six. I have no idea. I mean, ten years in Internet lifetime, I could be in outer space by then. We've got lots of things in the next eighteen months that we want to make happen on the site: a lot more functionality, a lot better products, a lot more countries, a lot more distribution channels, a lot more fun for the people in this office, and a lot less working hours, I would hope. So that's the first thing to achieve. Ten years down the line there's lots of other things I want to do with myself, with my life. I think I will always have a role at lastminute and I hope I will, but ten years seems like a long way off.

 5.2 **Authentic**

A So, you use email a lot, right?

B Well, not a lot, but yeah daily, I mean, I check it just like your regular post, snail mail, you know, it's the same thing, I look every day to see if I've got any.

A Really? So you'd use it as though, let's say, you come home, you check your answering machine, you check your post and then you [Exactly] check your email?

B Yeah. Get online, check the mail. Usually respond online, you know, they're often really short, so…

A So, but who, for example, who writes you or who do you write to?

B International friends, you know, well, even as far as, I mean, London to Bristol sometimes too, but mostly it's a cheap way to keep in touch with people who live everywhere [Right.] and it's almost instant, and for me that's, you know, most of my friends are abroad, so …

A What about family?

B They're not on yet.

A Really?

B Yeah. My mum's, you know, in her seventies. I don't think she's going to jump online anytime soon, so, but I can send attachments like photos and stuff back to mum through other people and they print 'em out.

A Oh, right, so people scanning in photos?

B [I'm not too clear on how that happens.] Scan in photos, send them across on the email and then people print 'em out for other people and they're there the same day.

A Do you ever use it for work?

B No. [Right.] Not yet. So do you surf the Web as well?

A Yes I do. I'm not brilliant at it yet, I spend a lot of time finding what I need to find rather than just going right, I'm sure there are faster ways.

B Any favourites, you go anywhere, always?

A New York Times. [Yeah.] I get to read that … fantastic [Newspapers, isn't that funny, we're logging on to look at, to read newspapers?].

B Same, I do the same and I listen to radio stations.

A Oh, really?

B Yeah, like you can plug in, you can listen to your home radio station. It's just over the computer and stuff but [Yeah.] I love hearing those accents back home and them sports talk shows and stuff.

A And would you do that for an hour or two maybe?

B Not even. [Right.] Yeah, it's the half-hour, top of the news, like national public radio from PBS [Fantastic.] back in the States I do that [Yeah.]. I've never logged in to like a chat room or anything, I can't imagine what that, it's kind of like a version of that instant messenger. You go in and you meet strange people, don't you?

A I think so. I think you go, let's say, if you're interested in, you know, hiking in Tibet or something, then [There's a room for hiking in Tibet people?], I think so, yeah.

B Wow, a chat room.

A A chat room to do that.

B Never done it.

A But I know people who have met people through the Internet.

B You mean like they met 'em in person, they found out about [Yes, yes.] them first and then they met in person?

 5.3

a I went to Paris first.
  Oh, not to Rome?

b I went to Paris first.
  So you went, not Elena?

c I went to Paris first.
  So you went to Paris before you went to Rome?

 5.4

1 Let me explain what I mean. I think that many of these online companies are seriously overvalued. To give you an example, at one time this company, the world's biggest bookseller, was valued at an astonishing 22.5 billion dollars. And that was despite losses of 125 million dollars. The thing is, they are supposed to be cutting out the intermediary by selling direct to the public. Yet they themselves are really just another bookshop, so what's the difference? So, essentially, I think the next logical stage is going to be the publishers themselves selling direct to the public.

2 … But this is just the same crimes in a different context. What I'm trying to say is that people talk about Internet crime as if it's something completely new, but of course it isn't. For example, there's forgery. By 'forgery', I mean forgery of emails. There's assault, that is people hacking into your website. There's fraud, or rather, cyberscams as people call them. And there's robbery, or more specifically, people stealing information from your computer system. But the point is, the four most common online crimes are really just variations on conventional crimes. And the people who commit them are still criminals.

Unit 6

 6.1

I = interviewer, E = expert

I So, what do you think? How many billionaires are there in the world?

E Well, it's hard to say exactly – things change so quickly. There are still very few compared to the number of millionaires, but the number is growing all the time.

I And who are the super-rich? Who's the richest person in the world?

E Well, Bill Gates certainly is at the moment. At the turn of the century the value of his shares in Microsoft was worth, I think about 80 billion dollars. But the first dollar billionaire was John D. Rockefeller who lived from 1839 to 1937, and of course in those days, and this is the early part of last century, there were hardly any millionaires, never mind billionaires.

I Are there any billionaires who are women?

E Not many. There are currently none in the world's top ten richest people, though there are some pretty wealthy women in the US, and several outside the US. Queen Beatrice of the Netherlands, for example. And the Queen of England is extremely wealthy, too, but a lot of it is not personal wealth, you know, it's assets held in trust for the British people.

I So are you saying that most billionaires are in the US?

E The vast majority of billionaires are still in the US, yes, but there are a lot in the Middle East, and quite a few in Europe and the Far East, as you'd expect. For example, there's Francois Pinault in France, and Hasso Plattner in Germany. Hasso Plattner is like Bill Gates, he made nearly all his money in computer software.

I Well, that seems to be, like, the popular one, computer software, but generally, where does all the money come from?

E Yeah, well, in the US, most of the billionaires have made their money in either retailing, or finance, or in the computer industry. And in the oil industry, of course, that's worldwide it's a major source of wealth.

I You know, though, one billion dollars is a huge amount of money. I mean, how much money can one individual really use or need, or … ?

E Well, it depends on what you mean by 'need', I suppose. I mean, to most people it probably seems like plenty for one individual. But if you're one of the super-rich, well, there's a huge responsibility that goes with that territory. A lot of these people give away millions to good causes. And there are always more and more causes in need of help, so in fact even a billion is not nearly enough. In reality, you know, you can never have too much.

I So who is the greatest philanthropist of them all?

E Well, in recent years probably Bill Gates, who's donated about 6.5 billion to his various foundations. Apparently he plans eventually to give away the vast majority of his fortune.

I What, all of it? Give away everything?

E Well, no, not all of it, obviously. But another interesting case is the financier, George Soros. He was born in Hungary and he's donated millions to causes in Central and Eastern Europe.

I But he's now an American citizen, isn't he? [Yeah.] So does he give away money in the US?

E Certainly he does, he does, and to some quite interesting causes, too. He set up a $50 million fund to help legal immigrants, and he provided $12 million to improve maths education in the inner cities and rural areas. [That's amazing.] Then there was the $15 million 'Project on Death in America' which was a programme aimed at helping the terminally ill.

I It's interesting how they sort of choose …

 6.2 **Authentic**

Extract 1

James So, would you say the States has become more materialistic over the years or, or has it stayed just the same old materialistic culture that it ever was?

Laurel That's a really interesting question. I would say that it's stayed the same because if you think about what America's supposed to stand for, it's supposed to stand for the fact that you can come from nothing and do extremely well, and I think that's always included having material possessions, 'cause otherwise I think they think you have nothing to show for your new status, you know, if you come in as a penniless immigrant and you end up owning a big corporation you should have a few things to show that you've done really well.

Extract 2

Richard In Australia, I think in the city centres, it's a cosmopolitan western, more you know, ideology to be talking about money and jobs and success because so much of Australia is rural, you know, money's a big issue because farming's, you know, not as successful as it used to be, and …

Alan Do people tend to ask you how much you earn?

Richard No. I mean, yeah, they do but it's not, I don't feel it's out of, you know, like a class struggle, you know, I think it's more out of interest to say, oh, I wonder what that job's like, and can you earn a lot of money from that job? You know, oh, that's good, you know. Maybe in Sydney, perhaps in Sydney because it's, you know, that's sort of somewhere where people rise.

Extract 3

Lyndham Well, I think in India people have become, a lot of people have become more concerned with wealth and material possessions. It seems that there is this big divide between the middle class and people who just don't have access to that, people who don't have access to that, then it's just completely out of their remit, so getting enough to eat is the most important thing, not what you might be wearing or driving a car for goodness sake. [Survival.] That's completely out. Yeah.

 6.3

Good morning, ladies and gentlemen, if I may have your attention, please? *Thank you* very much for coming along today. *My name's* Nathan Morse and I'm going to be outlining some research we've *been doing* at the University of Arkansas on the *working week* in *twentieth-century* America. *First, I'll* be looking at the situation at the beginning of the *last century*. Then I'm going to *show you* how the *general trend* has *not always* been to work less and less, *and finally* we'll be looking at some *startling predictions*, some made in the 1930s and others more recently.

So, *first of all*, let's look at how many hours people were working last century. Data on the *annual average workweek* tends to vary enormously, *one reason being* that it depends on whether we are *talking about* agriculture or industry. For instance, in agriculture they worked just under seventy hours at the beginning of the twentieth century, compared to *sixty hours* in industry. *What is interesting* is that at the end of the nineteenth century the *highest paid workers* worked substantially fewer hours than the lowest paid, a situation that was *gradually redressed* over most of the twentieth century and has now almost completely been reversed.

Now, let's look in more detail at the situation for industry. In 1900, people were working an average sixty-hour week, which fell quite rapidly down to fifty by about 1920. It then went down steadily, but not quite so rapidly, to forty-five hours over the next twenty years. The Second World War meant that industry was working overtime, so there was a sharp rise in the number of working hours during the war years, reaching a peak of about fifty-five hours in 1943, before dropping rapidly back to forty-five in 1947. Between 1947 to 1970 there

was a gradual decline toward a forty-hour week. If we turn to studies made in the 1930s it's interesting to note, as you can see in this slide, that they forecast that the trend in the shorter working week would continue far beyond forty hours. This has not happened in the US, though in some European countries they were pushing for thirty-five hours at the end of the last century. Instead, in the US the total number of working hours has been going up since 1970 by an average of 163 hours per year. If the present trend continues, the average white collar American will be working over sixty hours per week by the year 2020.

So, to summarize, the idea that we will have more and more leisure time seems to be in total contradiction to today's working hours. In fact, more and more skilled workers and professionals are finding ways to keep themselves at work rather than at home.

OK, well, thank you very much your attention, and if you have any questions perhaps you'd like to ask them over coffee. Thank you.

Unit 7

 7.1

Extract 1

B So, Adriano, what about your research trip to the Himalayas? How is the preparation going?

A There's so much to do before I can even start. The problem is, I've been so busy.

C Yes, it's that time of year.

A There are thirty-five student projects from last term on my desk. I have all the assignments marked externally, so that needs to be arranged. I need to collate all the research data, and then get it programmed into the system – I have to pay someone to do that.

B It sounds like a lot of work.

A It's a huge amount of work. I have to have all the field equipment serviced and properly checked out before we can go anywhere. I have to finalize all the travel arrangements … and I mustn't forget to go down to the hospital and get myself vaccinated. I don't know how I'm going to get it all done.

C You'll be fine. There's three weeks before you need worry about that.

Extract 2

C So how does it work in Japan, then, if you're a student? Do your parents pay for your tuition?

B Yes, because there are no grants or study loans, or anything like that. Your family normally pays. You can have your study fees paid by a scholarship, but that's not very common. So quite a lot of students have part-time jobs as well.

C Is that the same in Italy?

A Yes, more or less. If your family is very poor, I think you can get your fees paid by a special grant, or something, but it's not usual. But most students live at home while they are studying, anyway.

C That's very different to here. I think most people in Britain, when they go to university, it's, well, it's an excuse to leave home, to be independent.

A But if you live at home everything is done for you. You have your meals cooked, you have a nice place to live, you have your washing done for you … I mean, why would anyone want to live away?

C Oh, come on, that's not what it's about. Going to university is about growing up, doing things for yourself, finding out who you are, that kind of thing …

Extract 3

A That was really bad luck, you know, what happened to you on the first day.

B Yes, it was.

C Why, what happened?

B I had my wallet stolen on the Underground, coming from the airport.

C Oh, no! Oh, I am sorry. That's awful.

B Yes. But, I only lost cash, not my credit cards, though, so I was lucky. So I had some more money transferred from my bank account in Japan. It's no problem.

C But even so, that's really bad luck.

A You know, it can happen anywhere. I mean, my sister had her bike taken in Milan, from right outside her flat. Anyway, Akemi, did you manage to get your accommodation organized?

B Oh, yes, everything's fine, everything in its place. I'm very happy with the flat. And I had all my books and personal possessions shipped over from Japan, too.

C It must be nice to have all your own things around you, you know all your …

 7.2

A French graduate who has taught for more than twenty-five years.
I'm doing a degree in languages. I'll graduate next year.

It'll take me a while to estimate the costs.
When I've finished I'll give you an estimate.

 7.3

Pupils now don't know the difference between past, present, or future.
She presented me with her new book.

Progress depends on memory.
He has progressed a lot this year.

7.4

I = interviewer, G = Mr Gonzales

I So firstly Mr Gonzales, why do you think English should be made the official language of the US?

G Well, currently in the United States there is a move towards multilingualism or 'language sensitivity' as it's called. This means that children in school can choose to take their classes in their own languages. Consequently, hundreds of teachers have been employed in schools all over the country as part of this bilingual programme, and many of them are not able to speak English themselves.

I But isn't that a good thing, that immigrants are being given the chance to have a voice? I mean, Hispanics are now the largest ethnic group in many of the major cities in the US, so shouldn't they be given the right to speak in their native language officially?

G Well, as an immigrant from Chile myself, I am obviously not against the idea of immigrants being powerful and successful in the US. And actually for me this is the whole point. An immigrant coming to the US, who doesn't learn to speak English, is ultimately going to end up doing some kind of menial job that no American wants to do.

I But is there any real proof that this is what happens? I mean, there must be a lot of people from immigrant communities who succeed without necessarily speaking good English?

G No, there is a lot of research to show that immigrants who speak English earn 30 to 40 per cent more than those who don't. There was a recent study conducted in New York which found that children in schools where they were taught in their own languages, did much less well than those children who were taught in English, but who were also given intensive support in English as a second language. Not being able to speak English in the US definitely leaves you at a disadvantage.

I But, OK, what about immigrant workers from, say, Mexico for example, who have no intention of staying in the US and becoming US citizens? For them it's more a question of being able to work, to send money home, and then eventually return to Mexico.

G I'm not saying that people shouldn't hold on to their native languages. This is about the government making better use of the resources. And I believe there are other negative consequences of this bilingualism. I think it promotes the idea of separatism and even segregation, and subsequently it may force different ethnic groups to compete with each other for funds to protect their own language rights.

I Wow, that's something you feel really passionate about. But, OK, finally, can you explain a little about 'US English'? It's said to be one of the fastest-growing interest groups in the US.

G Yes, the organization now has around one and a half million members and the support of many political figures on the left and on the right. The aim is to pass legislation making English the official language of government at all levels.

🔊 7.5

A Sorry, I don't really follow you.

B OK, what I'm trying to say is that the way we educate children needs to be radically changed along with the education system itself.

A What do you mean, exactly?

B Right, well, let's start with the education system. Actually, 'education system' is probably not the right term. It would probably be more accurate to say 'the education process'.

A Uh-huh …

B Well, at the moment, you normally go to school from the age of five or six, come out at eighteen, go to university, and get your first job in your early twenties.

A That is if you do the whole process.

B Yes, exactly. Now, we'd probably all agree that school and university are supposed to prepare you for the world of work and for life in general.

A Yes, OK, but I still don't see what you're getting at.

B Right, well, OK, let me put it another way. I believe that we've got the order of our lives completely wrong. We spend twenty years of our lives on theory and then the rest of our lives on practice. What we need is a process that would alternate these.

A Can you be more specific?

B Well, I'd suggest going to school for a few years and then at the age of maybe ten or eleven, beginning to work.

A Beginning to work at ten or eleven?

B Yeah. The idea would be that you would experience a series of different jobs, probably at that age basically manual jobs or ones that involve some hands-on experience.

A Well, can you give me some examples?

B Yes, I mean practical things like plumbing or carpentry, things that are going to be really useful in your life. But also more creative things, like dancing, making TV documentaries, or designing websites. Or even scientific subjects, medicine, geology, archaeology. In other words, things that would get children really interested.

A But would you then go back to school?

B Yes, that's right, you would, for a few years anyway, until you were eighteen or nineteen. Then you'd move on to the next stage and learn about different kinds of jobs, more intellectual, so-called professional jobs, such as lawyer, accountant, stockbroker, or architect.

A And I suppose this would also enable you to have a much clearer idea of what job would be suitable for you?

B Precisely. Then you'd choose a job, and then later, when you were in your late thirties, you'd go to university.

A That old?

B Well, not necessarily, it would depend on the faculty. If you were doing mathematics, for example, you'd probably want to start earlier, but in my opinion most humanistic subjects are far better studied at an age when you've had some experience of life, so that you can understand them much better. Going to university at such an age would also give you a break in your life, some time out to think about where you're going, and what you really want.

🔊 7.6

a I would hope to be working as Head of Marketing for a large well-known pharmaceutical company.

b I think that good communication skills are extremely important – to be able to get your ideas across easily and to bring out the best in your employees.

c It's all been very straightforward so far, so hopefully we should be ready well before the deadline.

d Yes, I had to resolve an awkward situation between two employees in my department who were not getting on, and it was really causing problems. I basically acted as mediator and got them to sit down and discuss the problem in a civilized manner.

e Well, I do quite a bit of writing in my current post. I am responsible for the annual report and quite a lot of our general promotional material.

f I think that my previous experience equips me really well for this post. I enjoy working under pressure and I think that my enthusiasm and flair will fit in perfectly.

Unit 8

🔊 8.1

A So what do you do if you find any errors in your statement?

B Well, usually if I ever get statements or letters like that, well, well, obviously not for twenty-one billion pounds, but I ring the bank up immediately and they generally solve the situation straight away. But in this case I'm not sure what I would have done. Laughed, maybe.

C I guess that if she had been an American she would probably have sued the bank for causing her stress.

B Right, yeah. Do you think she should have sued them?

C Well, …

A Well, let's look at this the other way round. What would you do if your bank inadvertently credited your account with a million pounds, or dollars?

C I think if it was a hundred dollars rather than a million, it would, well, there would probably be less chance of them realizing their mistake, but there's also a good chance that I wouldn't notice either because I never check my statements. But in any case I'd call the bank and let them know.

B Actually, it's interesting you should mention that, because in the same newspaper there was an article about this woman in France who found a bag of used banknotes and then anonymously took the bag to the police station. And it was a huge amount, half a million francs, or something.

C You mean she didn't even leave her name?

A No, she just left the money, walked out.

B That's amazing. Well, I mean, what would you do if you found all that money?

C Is that the proverbial million-dollar question?

🔊 8.2

a Well, I think she should have kept it.

b She may have simply wanted to expose the bank.

c I think she must have thought that someone had seen her. If I'd been her I would have kept the lot.

d It must be a bit of a shock, something like that happening.

e She must have known she could make a lot of money from the story – they must pay a lot for stories like that.

f She can't have known who the money belonged to – she could be just a very honest person.

g It may not have been because she was honest – she couldn't have kept that amount of money without someone finding out.

h Of course, she may be regretting it now. I mean, who needs that kind of publicity?

🔊 8.3

a If my bank gets it wrong I'll be very surprised.

b I'm not sure what I would have done.

c If my bank had made a mistake like that, they wouldn't have admitted it.

d What would you do if you found all that money?

e I think she should have kept it.

f She must have thought that someone had seen her.

g She can't have known who the money belonged to.

h It may not have been because she was honest.

🔊 8.4

1 Excuse me, but I think you've given me the wrong change.
  You're absolutely right. I do apologize.

2 I'm afraid I'm going to be late for dinner.
  That's OK, we'll wait for you.

3 Excuse me, please. Can I get through?
  Of course. Sorry about that.

4 I'd like to apologize for all the noise – we've got builders in.
  Sorry? What did you say?

5 I'm sorry, do you mind if I answer that?
  Of course not, go ahead.

6 Excuse me, I really have to go now.
  Are you sure you can't stay for one last drink?

🔊 8.5

analyse analytical
manage management
method methodical
organize organization
responsible responsibility
understand understandable

🔊 8.6

A So what do you think about it?

B I think in principle, it's a great idea. But I'd like to stress that the timing is extremely important. I mean, are we really ready for this kind of move right now?

C Can I just say that I'm not sure we know enough about the market.

A But think of the possibilities, it's …

C Yes, yes, but honestly, do we know anything about doing business in South America?

A Chris, I was in the middle of saying something.

C Sorry, do go on.

A Well, of course we'd need to do our homework and send someone over there to check it out. But surely it's worth exploring the possibilities?

🎧 8.7

C Would you like to say something about the timing, Ben?

B Well, I do think we should consider it, but I'm not sure we're operating well enough here yet to be ready to take such a big step now. By the way, did either of you see that Brazilian film on television last week?

C Can we just stick to this for a minute and try and come up with a decision?

B Sorry. It did seem sort of relevant, but anyway …

C OK, OK, tell us after, but I think if we're going to be considering this kind of thing, we need to come up with a country profile as soon as possible.

A What sort of profile? Can you be more specific?

C Well, like facts and figures on the lifestyle, eating habits, business culture, that sort of thing.

🎧 8.8

B Sounds sensible, yeah, but just going back to my earlier point. Don't you think we should be putting more effort into improving the set-up here?

A Yes, that's a fair point, but I'd assume we'd be doing that anyway.

C Yes, OK, but I think that's a separate issue. Why don't we come back to that later? So, next we need to decide who's going to do what.

A Well, I'm happy to put a presentation together from the stuff we already have in the office, if someone will help me sort it out.

C Yes, I'm happy to do that with you. Is there anything else?

A So, basically what you're saying is that we need to have another meeting and then maybe we'll make a decision!

🎧 8.9 Authentic

1 I really didn't believe that I would experience such cultural difference because (a) we speak the same language and I always believed that we had a very similar sense of humour, but we were living an American lifestyle sort of thing, so I figured that parts of me would be, would be a little bit different but I, I never thought that essentially we would be culturally different and when I came over here and I lived with my wife's family at the time I was making all sorts of mistakes and you know cultural *faux pas* and whatever, you know. But it's been a huge learning curve for me.

2 The main thing is not, not misleading anybody on each side of the equation, either the person in your own country who's doing business with you or with the person from the other country you're doing business with. And then you find the common ground in the middle and make things work from there and, and usually, in, in the case of most companies, there is common ground and it's a question of working at it at a methodical pace.

3 I had an impression that was what I thought England would be like and when I came here I expected tea at four o'clock with cucumber sandwiches *because* [Oh, really?] *that's what I'd had in India and* I hadn't realized that tea actually is dinner which is at something like six o'clock to eight o'clock in the evening and that's all you get, whereas *in India I used to have*, we used to have tea at four o'clock [Really?] which was just literally the drink and some sandwiches and then later on in the evening you'd have a meal.

4 I think there are situations where the Americans don't, they don't expect humour and they don't necessarily expect cynicism. What they expect is a very optimistic, enthusiastic approach, where everybody is eagerly sort of working together to produce some strong outcome. And I think that's very very different with the Japanese, for example, or Singaporeans and Hong Kong groups, because they don't come at it from that point of view. And therefore the, the experience with the Americans is more one of frustration, that they don't really understand and that a bit of humour might be a way of, sort of trying to lubricate the conversation and to, to get the parties comfortable with each other. To the Americans they may find that very frustrating, that they think somebody's being immediately negative.

🎧 8.10 Authentic

It's been very interesting because the, we've traditionally dealt with a lot of Asia Pacific groups, and those groups have usually been represented by natives of their own country and … And usually our attempts in those markets have been to try and focus on any aspects that we could that would *bring different cultures together*. So it was very much looking for small similarities and not really spending a lot of time worrying about things that were *clearly quite different*. What's happened with the Americans in many respects is that people make the immediate assumption that Americans and British, and for that matter, Australian are essentially *very very similar types of culture*, types of business approach. And that is often a pitfall because, what does seem to happen is that rather than understanding the similarities, that gets discarded and what we then find is that the differences, which might only be a relatively small percentage of the total picture become the thing that you *focus on*. And both sides then start focusing on things that could I suppose be seen as an annoyance or something that they don't particularly like, and that they feel that we do better or they do better. So, bizarre as it may seem, we actually find there's more conflict, or more potential for conflict, with *these American businessmen* than there probably is with any of our Asian experiences.

🎧 8.11

// = pauses

The Japanese don't necessarily enter the discussions or meetings expecting to // come up with an outcome or a solution. Whereas most of the western world is very // task-orientated. So the purpose of a meeting is usually // clearly understood and also the hierarchy of the people involved in the decision-making. Whereas the Japanese in certain instances still use a tradition that's probably got a lot of almost spiritual context in it, where they don't expect the individual to // necessarily come up with the answer. The answer will arise by the individuals participating in the discussions and in allowing time // to come up with the right solution, but they're not the ones who are necessarily expected to be sitting there delivering that solution.

Unit 9

🎧 9.1

I = interviewer, E = expert

E Food taboos are actually a fascinating part of history.

I You say 'history' – does that mean that they've varied a lot over time?

E Well, if you take the Christian faith, for example. Monks in early medieval times had a whole lot of restrictions on what they were and weren't allowed to eat.

I Were they basically vegetarian, then?

E Well, the idea was to reduce the appetite as much as possible, and this meant that they were only supposed to have dried biscuits soaked in broth, and occasionally some bread and wine. They couldn't eat any meat or fish.

I So how did they survive?

E Well, with difficulty. So later they started having two meals a day – fish, vegetables …

I And did they have to go to a market to get these things, or what?

E Actually, they didn't have to buy anything because most abbeys had their own fish ponds in the grounds and also vegetable gardens. In fact, there were around two hundred fast days, when they weren't supposed to eat meat. This meant that they had to reclassify certain animals as fish, such as frogs and rabbits.

I So a rabbit was considered like a fish?

E Well, it was classified as 'non-meat'. But this kind of thing goes on in other parts of the world, too. I mean, for example, although Tibetan monks are supposed to be vegetarian they sometimes eat meat, and butter and cheese.

I Why's that?

E Well, I suppose it's a tradition based on the need to survive, really. Tibet is a very cold place, and they needed to eat food that provided plenty of calories and vitamins. There's so much snow, so most fruits can't grow there. In the past, you couldn't get fresh vegetables for the same reason, so they just had to eat whatever was available. But even today, before eating meat they have to recite a mantra, then they blow on it so that the animal will have a good reincarnation.

I That's interesting. Going back to fasting for a moment, what kind of restrictions are still around today, in the Christian church, for example?

E Well, in Greece until recently during Great Lent, which is the seven weeks before Easter and Holy Week, not only was meat not allowed, but also fish and all animal products, you know, such as lard, eggs, butter, milk, and cheese. And you weren't supposed to drink wine or use oil either. Nowadays you don't have to respect all these rules.

I And are food taboos strictly connected to fasting?

E Not all, no. Many are connected with hygiene and what was considered good or bad for you. If you read the Old Testament in the Bible you'll find pages of food restrictions. In other religions there are even food restrictions related to the death of family members.

🎧 9.2 Authentic

A Right, well I don't know what I'm going to have. I can never make my mind up. It's going to take me ages to decide.

B And I'm a bit restricted because there's a lot of things on this menu that I can't have.

A Oh, really? What can't you have?

B Well, [Pancakes? What about the pancakes?] Yes, I can't have wheat. I mustn't have wheat so that means no bread, nothing made with flour, wheat flour so the pancakes are out.

A That must really restrict you, surely it restricts you a great deal not being able to eat …

B In restaurants, not at home because I use other flours, but I'm not supposed to have any dairy foods, so cheese, and milk things.

A What would happen if you were to have a dairy product or wheat product?

B Oh, I get puffy-eyed, I swell up. But I don't want to be difficult about this. Let's see. What can we find? I could have a salad. I'm not supposed to have mayo because that's got eggs, so I won't have that.

A What about the chicken, the caesar salad, the cos lettuce and the chicken crouton? Although bread, you see [Well, the crouton, yes] that would be no good 'cause there would probably be wheat, well there would be wheat in the crouton.

B The roast chicken would be nice except that's lemon chicken. I can't have citrus either. I do occasionally, I'm not supposed to, but I do sometimes.

A Would you have the same reaction eating something citrus?

B Yes, and very painful joints. [How long have you had these allergies?] Strange. Are you not allergic to anything?

A No. Oh, I am, actually. I'm allergic to crab, I must admit.

B So you mustn't have crab.

A No, I mustn't have crab and in fact shellfish, although I'm not allergic to shellfish, I can't have or I shouldn't have shellfish because the texture of it makes me want to be sick …

9.3 Authentic

A Well, you know what they say about wine.

B Especially the red one is good for you, that kind of thing.

C You're supposed to stop at a glass and a half though, to keep it healthy.

A Yeah, yeah.

B How about caffeine? Coffee and tea and stuff?

C I drink a lot of coffee.

A I'm sure that can't be good for you.

C No, it can't be. I'm sure in fact that it could plausibly be addicting because I wake up every morning in search of a hot cup of coffee.

A Really?

C Yeah. I would be the first to admit it. They say it can actually help you though because there are some purifying properties of coffee, but I can't imagine …

A Acid.

C Yeah, like acid. Terrible stomach acids.

A But apparently, I mean, I console myself with the fact that I drink a lot of tea instead of coffee [Me, too.] but actually, apparently it's just as bad for you because there's just as much caffeine [Oh no, really?] in tea.

C Fish oils as well, you know, keep you very healthy.

B Really?

A Right, yeah, that's what I …

C Things like sardines and salmon and stuff. Cold-water fish oils are good for your heart.

A But you can get, all these things you can get in pills now, can't you? I mean, I don't know if they're any better for you.

B No, I'm sure, I'm sure it's …

A They can't be as good for you as the real thing can.

B I'm sure it's the fresh food much better than a, yeah, pill form, I'm sure of that. How about spinach and stuff, you know it's, I heard …

C Full of iron and stuff.

B Oh, the Popeye, yes, of course it's simply good for you.

A Yeah, well, I'm not so sure about that one, but …

B Yeah? But I know in my country the really really good one is the soya, soya stuff, soya beans and stuff, you know.

A Why is it supposed to be good for you?

B Well, it's full of protein, and then there's no fat and no saturated, and, yeah …

A Beef.

B Beef. How about meat?

A Lovely red meat, juicy red meat.

C Not one bit good for you, is it?

A Oh, no.

C Well, definitely.

A Absolutely packed with fat and cholesterol, all the wrong kinds of fat.

C But it tastes great.

B I don't know about, you know, white meat like chicken and stuff, but about red meat, what I heard about it is that it's actually taking too much red meat is making you angry, is the anger, do you believe in that, do you think?

C Something to do with high blood pressure or something like that, they reckon from the red meat. I think it can be the same even, you know, like white meat can be bad for you too, just by the way they produce it.

A The point is you've got to live, haven't you? You've got to live and enjoy your life.

C We're pretty lucky to even be making these choices you know.

A That's right.

9.4

1 **A** If you're not doing anything later, would you like to go out for a meal?

B Yes, that sounds like a nice idea. Thank you.

A OK, I was thinking about, maybe a Thai or an Indian restaurant?

B Mm, yes, Thai food sounds good.

A Great. Why don't we meet at 7.30, outside the main entrance?

B Fine. I'll look forward to it.

2 **C** I don't know if you have any plans for tomorrow, but I was wondering if you'd like me to show you something of the city. We could go in my car.

D That's very kind of you. Thank you very much, I'd like that.

C Excellent. Shall I pick you up at your hotel?

D That would be good. What time?

C Shall we say ten o'clock?

D Ten o'clock. Yes, that would be fine.

3 **E** Are you doing anything later?

F Nothing special.

E OK, do you want to go out for a drink, or a coffee, or something?

F Sure, why not? Where shall we meet?

E How about six-thirty in the plaza?

F Fine. See you later.

9.5

1 Yes, please. If you wouldn't mind.

2 Yes, I'd love some.

3 Thank you, that's very kind of you.

4 Of course. Here you are.

5 Mmm. That sounds like a good idea.

6 Actually, I don't eat seafood. I think I'd rather have the goat's cheese salad.

7 Of course. Asparagus, and then the beef. Is that right?

8 No, thank you, I'm fine with this.

9.6

a Can I take your coat?
Thank you, that's very kind of you.

b Shall we have something to drink before we order?
Mmm. That sounds like a good idea.

c Why don't you try the seafood pasta? It's really good.
Actually, I don't eat seafood. I think I'd rather have the goat's cheese salad.

d Shall I ask the waiter if there are any other vegetarian dishes?
Yes, please. If you wouldn't mind.

e Excuse me, I'm just going to the bathroom. Would you mind ordering for me?
Of course. Asparagus, and then the beef. Is that right?

f Would you like to try some of this asparagus? It's delicious.
No, thank you, I'm fine with this.

g Can I pour you some wine?
Yes, I'd love some.

h Could you pass me the bread, please?
Of course. Here you are.

9.7

A So how is your starter?

B Mmm. It's absolutely delicious. What about yours?

A It's good. Would you like to try some? Here …

B Oh, thanks. Mmm … yeah, it's really tasty.

A You know, if you like this, you should really try something typical as a main course.

B OK, what do you recommend?

A Well, I'm going to have the Chicken Yassa. It's one of my favourites. It's a traditional Senegalese dish.

B Chicken Yassa. What's in it?

A Well, it's made with chicken, obviously. It's marinated in oil with onions, salt and pepper, red pepper, and the juice of … oh, I don't know the word in English, but it's like a lemon, only green.

B Ah, a lime.

A A lime. OK. So it's marinated in the juice of six limes for at least two hours. Then the chicken is grilled on a … like a barbecue …

B On a charcoal grill?

A Yes, or wood. Then you cook it in a pan with the onions and a little water to make a sauce. And it's served with rice.

B Mmm, sounds good.

9.8

H = host, G = guest

H Hello, nice to see you. Do come in. Did you find us OK?

G Yes, no problem at all. I'm sorry I'm a bit late – it was nothing to do with your directions!

H Don't worry, there's still a few people to come anyway. Can I take your coat?

G Oh, yes, thanks. Mm, I like your apartment.

H Thank you.

G It's really nice. Have you been here long?

H Er, about two years now. Have you been to this part of the city before?

G No, never. I haven't really had the chance to visit anywhere yet. By the way, this is something from my country for you and your wife.

H Thank you, that's really kind.

9.9

H = host, G = guest

G That was really delicious. I've never tasted anything quite like it.

H Thanks very much. Can I get you some more?

G Oh, no, thanks. I really enjoyed it, but I don't think I could manage any more. Let me give you a hand with those plates.

H It's kind of you to offer but really, you relax. This will take me two minutes.

G Do you mind if I smoke? I'm happy to go outside if it's a problem.

H Actually, I'd rather you didn't smoke in here, but I think there's someone else already outside if you want to join them.

G Thanks. And is it OK if I just use your bathroom?

H Sure, it's at the end of the hall on the left.

9.10

H = host, G = guest

G Well, it's getting late, so I think I should be going.

H Yes, of course …

G Thank you for having me.

H Well, thanks so much for coming. I'm really glad you could make it.

G I had a delightful evening. Both the food and the company were excellent. Thank you very much indeed.

H Let me get your coat. Now do you remember the way OK? Would you like me to go over it with you?

G No, really, thanks. I'm sure I'll be fine. Thank you again, and see you next week.

H Yes, see you then. Have a safe journey home. Bye.

Unit 10

 10.1 Authentic

Julia Brams

I've been rather stuck in my youth for a very long time and now being pregnant, five months pregnant, in four months' time, all being well, my life's going to dramatically change, so becoming a mother and my priorities will change, although I'll still very much want my career, being a mother I think will obviously be coming first and school runs and [it's an interesting, yes …] thinking of a child before, thinking of someone else before myself. [Yeah, there's nothing like having …], radical changes [… children to make you, to make you less selfish], absolutely [Nothing like having children] absolutely [to make you less selfish]. And not having as much sleep as well. I know in the next five years I won't be getting the sleep that I've been getting.

Stefan Grothgar

Well, in five years' time I think my professional life will be very different, because I'm planning on setting up my own company and … so it'll be much more creative, I can do what I really want to do. Personally, I think it'll be different as well because our children will have grown up and hopefully they'll be off to university and I can have a wonderful time with my wife, alone at home.

Judy Parfitt

Well, in five years' time I hope that my life will really be quite different from now. My husband will be about to retire and our plan is that we will have moved to the country by then. I plan myself to go on working, but actually living in the country would be wonderful and a huge change from living in the city where we are now.

 10.2 Authentic

Part 1

A What do you think we'll all be doing health-wise? How will we be? Will we be pill-popping or back to herbs, or will there be any herbs? What do you think?

C I think there'll be a mixture of modern medicine and, and, and [traditional remedies] homeopathic style and I think the complementary medicine will merge with modern medicine.

A What about work? I mean, will more people be working from home? I think probably there will be a greater percentage, and no doubt we'll be changing our professions more perhaps as well.

C We will need to be flexible, that's for sure, I'm sure we'll have several careers and I'm sure we'll be travelling into space.

A Oh, yes.

B In fifty years?

C Oh, yes. I'm quite sure that before I die I will be going to space.

B Oh, my lord.

C I mean, in fifteen years' time we're supposed to be able to have a little trip to a hotel, I forget which planet it's on, I mustn't get lost up in the universe.

A On the moon, probably, if we're lucky [Yeah] …

Part 2

B … I would presume we're going to have loads of, much more leisure time than we do now.

A But they've always been, they've been saying that for centuries, haven't they and it hasn't seemed to have happened.

B That is true. I'm still waiting for that robot to cut the lawn, they keep saying that's going to happen.

A Because the thing is that people do want to do things, they don't want to sit at home and …

C Well, presumably, but that's what, you know, we were talking about before, that is this progress to mean that we never have to leave our house for anything?

B To sit in front of the television, is that progress? Probably not. [Yeah, and what are we going to use our leisure time for?] And where do the fresh ideas come from if you're very passive in your life?

C That's right and your whole goal is not to have to work. And how are we going to get around? That's what I want to know. Are we going to drive, or is it going to all be air traffic?

B Well, that's why I always kind of hope sometimes that progress would come from somewhere else, because if we keep progressing down our own road we're going to have more cars, more pollution [Yeah], more, you know.

A But the pollution will be gone, I mean, that's got to be, in fifty years' time it's got to be solved, surely.

B Well, I hope but I fear not, I fear we're getting rid of the trees too fast, not enough oxygen, the lungs of the earth, always that concern about fresh water, I think those are all legitimate.

 10.3

1 I always said it wouldn't change me, you know, I'd still be the same person, do the same things. But actually, it does bring about unexpected changes, you know, how people see you, how you see yourself, and your life. I mean, it's a great opportunity to do new things, and I'm planning to take advantage of that. I'm completely free, I can just take off and travel the world if I want to.

2 I always expected to carry on working until I was sixty-five, another ten years, you know. But now I can do the things I never had time to do before. I've taken up gardening, because it keeps me outside in the fresh air. And I've always wanted to learn to fly, so I'm having flying lessons, and I'll be taking my pilot's licence in June.

3 It's quite scary, knowing that you'll be helping to bring up someone else's child. I mean, I don't have kids of my own, and the thought of taking responsibility for someone other than myself is terrifying, quite frankly. But hopefully it'll bring out the best in me, you know. Still, at least he won't be taking after me when it comes to looks.

4 I'm really excited. I'm ready to take on new responsibilities, and I love the idea of being completely in control of my life. There are quite a lot of changes I want to see carried out, and we may have to take on extra work initially. It's going to be a challenge, but I know I can carry it off. I'm looking forward to it.

 10.4

1 A OK, I think that's all we've really got time for. But before we finish, can I just summarize what I think we've agreed? We've drawn up a list of your requirements. We're going to use these requirements to build up a feasibility study, the results of which should be due on the first day of next month. We'll email those results to you. Does that all sound sensible?

B Yes, fine.

A OK, then we'll be in touch next month.

C We'll look forward to that.

A OK, then, goodbye, and thanks very much for agreeing to this phone conference at such short notice.

B No problem, it suited us very well.

A Well, thanks again. Bye.

B and C Bye.

2 A Listen, it's been really nice talking to you.

B Yes, you too, you've been really helpful.

A It's my pleasure. Anyway, I really have to go now. I have another meeting at eleven.

B OK, so I'll call you next week to confirm which restaurant we'll be going to.

A Great. Can I just give you my new mobile phone number?

B Yeah, sure.

A It's 07957 …

B 7, yes …

A 472 859.

B So that's 07957 472 859.

A That's right.

B OK, then. See you soon.

A Bye.

3 A Just one last thing.

B Yes?

A Would it be possible for you to give us a list of some of your other clients?

B I'd have to check that out first, but it should be OK.

A Well, I think that's just about it.

B OK. Can I just make sure I've got everything? You want a written statement of the work done so far, plus a summary of the expected extra costs. And you need it by the end of this week.

A That's right.

B OK, then, I'll send that to you as soon as I can.

A That'd be great. Thanks very much.

B You're welcome. Bye.

 10.5

1 A Well, thank you very much again.

B You're welcome. Thanks for coming.

A It was a really nice evening – I had a good time.

B I'm glad you enjoyed it.

2 A I don't know how to thank you.

B Oh, that's OK. It was nothing.

A Well, I really appreciate it.

3 A It was really very kind of you to come at such short notice.

B Not at all. I'm here to help in any way I can.

A Well, I am very grateful to you.

B Don't mention it.

4 A I just wanted to say, you know, thanks again.

B Well, it was a pleasure.

A OK, well … thanks.

B You're very welcome.

 10.6

A I hear this is your last day at work here.

B Yes, I'm starting a new job next week.

A So where are you going, if you don't mind me asking?

B I'm going to be working for DCL.

136 Listening script

A Oh, really? So what will you be doing exactly?

B I'll be working in their Sales Division.

A Oh, great. Well, best of luck.

B Thanks.

A I hope to see you again some time.

B Yeah, you too. Keep in touch.

A All the best. Bye.

B Bye.

10.7 Authentic

I = interviewer, Q = Jim Quick

I First of all, how many people actually have heart transplants, have you any idea?

Q I can give you only a rough idea. At Wynthenshawe we've done 450 transplant operations, of which about 250 are hearts, the others are heart–lung or lung … Since 1985, 1984 the first one was done in this country.

I Where do the hearts come from?

Q They come from literally all over the place, but bear in mind you've got four hours from when you switch off the life support machine of the donor to getting the heart into the recipient. [Right.] So. Which is why they use helicopters and fly people all over the place. So, the vast majority, well 99% of the hearts for Wythenshawe come from within this country.

I But they're all human hearts?

Q Oh, they're all human hearts. At the moment they're all human hearts, everybody's heart is a human heart. They've, they are working very fast on on animal hearts, particularly pig's hearts. They've been breeding pigs for a number of years now, because the pig's heart is very similar in size. They're ready to go with the pig's heart, they've actually had a monkey which has been alive for six months now with a pig's heart in it. But the ethics committee, the government ethics committee are under huge pressure. Because a lot of people say, 'Hey, you just don't know what you're doing, you don't know, when you transfer a pig's heart to a human, that may solve the problem for the patient, that his heart works and he'll keep on living, but, what, but you don't know just what else you're transferring.' We just don't know enough about the make-up of the pig, if you like. Antibodies and various other bits and pieces. So, there are, there are surgeons in this country who would do that operation tomorrow. Because there's a major shortage of donor organs, and surprisingly that's happened mainly because of seat-belt laws, people are not dying in car crashes, which is great, don't misunderstand me, it's great, but the number of donors has fallen hugely.

10.8

1 A Well this kind of thing is already going on, isn't it?

B Yeah, but it's hard to know where to draw the line. I know that the scientists who cloned that sheep have actually got a patent on that technique.

A Yeah, it's like having a patent on life. It's not an easy one, is it?

2 A They've been freezing people for a while now, haven't they? I think the first was in 1967. Do you have any strong feelings about it?

B I really wouldn't want to say. I suppose that people are entitled to do what they want with their bodies.

C Yeah, I suppose so, as long as the money to pay for the cryonic suspension is coming out of their own pockets.

3 A I don't really have any strong feelings about this. I mean in this post-modern world I don't think it really matters whether your children are male or female. You don't need strong boys to send out in the fields any more.

B I don't think it's that clear cut. If you can choose the sex, then next you're going to want to choose the appearance too. I think you're skating on thin ice if you start allowing that kind of thing.

OXFORD
UNIVERSITY PRESS

Great Clarendon Street, Oxford OX2 6DP

Oxford University Press is a department of the
University of Oxford. It furthers the University's
objective of excellence in research, scholarship,
and education by publishing worldwide in

Oxford New York

Auckland Cape Town Dar es Salaam
Hong Kong Karachi Kuala Lumpur Madrid
Melbourne Mexico City Nairobi New Delhi
Shanghai Taipei Toronto

With offices in

Argentina Austria Brazil Chile Czech Republic
France Greece Guatemala Hungary Italy Japan
Poland Portugal Singapore South Korea
Switzerland Thailand Turkey Ukraine Vietnam

OXFORD and OXFORD ENGLISH are registered
trade marks of Oxford University Press in the UK
and in certain other countries

© Oxford University Press 2001

The moral rights of the author have been asserted

Database right Oxford University Press (maker)

First published 2001

2010 2009 2008 2007 2006
10 9 8 7

No unauthorized photocopying

All rights reserved. No part of this publication
may be reproduced, stored in a retrieval system, or
transmitted, in any form or by any means, without
the prior permission in writing of Oxford
University Press, or as expressly permitted by law,
or under terms agreed with the appropriate
reprographics rights organization. Enquiries
concerning reproduction outside the scope of the
above should be sent to the ELT Rights
Department, Oxford University Press, at the
address above

You must not circulate this book in any other
binding or cover and you must impose this same
condition on any acquirer

Any websites referred to in this publication are in
the public domain and their addresses are
provided by Oxford University Press for
information only. Oxford University Press
disclaims any responsibility for the content.

ISBN-13: 978 0 19 457425 9
ISBN-10: 0 19 457425 3

Printed in China

ACKNOWLEDGEMENTS

*The author would like to thank the following people for
agreeing to be interviewed and recorded for the Student's
Book and Workbook:* Gabriele Azzaro, Chike
Azuonye, Staph Bakali, Sir Bobby Charlton, Andy
Crisp, Mark Ellingham, Martha Lane Fox, Martin
Gandy, Ruth Glassock, Clare Leavenworth-Bakali,
James Lewin, Timothy Mitchell, Hayat Mustofa-
Ibrahim, Jim Quick, Tom Southern, Richard
Smith, and Tau Pei Lin

Thanks to: Jean and Basil Wallwork for helping to
arrange the interviews, Richard Wallwork and
Angus Brogdon for their business expertise, Rupert
Burgess and Jackie Rymell for providing useful
articles and newspaper cuttings, and Caterina
Orlandi for preparing cartoons for my
presentations and for the picture stories in the
Teacher's Resource Book

*Big thanks also to the following teachers and email
acquaintances who sent me information regarding the
use of English in their various languages:* Jukka Korpela,
Filipa Plant dos Santos, Aleksandra Pazurek, Judith
Routledge, Leena Pihlava, and Sasa Segrt

A final thanks to: Anna Southern for helping me
to write many of the Focus on functions and Skills
focus sections of the book, and to Tommaso for
being a constant source of inspiration

The author and publisher would like to thank the
many teachers and institutions around the world
whose comments, feedback, and advice have
helped to shape this course, including Roger
Barnard, Brian Brennan, Anne Conybeare, Brian
Cross, Neil Deane, Liz Taylor, Don Ward, and Anne
Williams

*The author and publisher are grateful to those who have
given permission to reproduce the following extracts and
adaptations of copyright material:* p3 'Business
women leave jellies …' by R Scase and J Scales.
Appeared in *The Guardian* 22 July 1998; p4 'An end
to sec discrimination' by Laurette Ziemer. Appeared
in *The Mirror* 20 April 2000. Reproduced by
permission of Mirror Group Syndication; p16
'Mother Tongue' by Bill Bryson. Hamish Hamilton
1992. Copyright © 1990 by Bill Bryson. Reproduced
by permission of HarperCollins Publishers, Inc.
and Penguin Books Ltd; p8 'Passport Indonesia' by
G J Cole. World Trade Press 1997. Reproduced by
permission of World Trade Press; p10
'Sociolinguistics: An Introduction to Language and
Society' by Peter Trudgill (Penguin Books 1974,
revised edition 1983). Copyright © Peter Trudgill,
1974, 1983. Reproduced by permission of Penguin
Books Ltd; pp20, 32 'The Do's and Taboos of
Hosting International Visitors' by Roger E Axtell.
Copyright © John Wiley & Sons 1990. Reproduced
by permission of John Wiley & Sons, Inc.; p38
'The chimp who says just what she thinks' by
D Derbyshire. Appeared in *The Daily Mail* 26 July
1999. Reproduced by permission of Solo
Syndication Ltd.; p42 'Good Style: Writing for Science
and Technology' by John Kirkman. Reproduced by
permission of CRC Press, Boca Raton, Florida; p47
'I'm about as technical as a peanut' by Tim Hulse.
Appeared in *The Independent* 21 January 2000.
Reproduced by permission of Tim Hulse; p58
'A wealth of interests' by Richard Seven. Appeared
in *The Seattle Times* 14 June 1998. Copyright
© Seattle Times Company 1998. Reproduced by
permission of The Seattle Times; p62 'How family
spending has changed in the US' by Eva Jacobs
and Stephanie Shipp. Appeared in *The Monthly
Labor Review* March 1990. Reproduced by
permission of Monthly Labor Review; pp70, 120
'Don't ask, don't tell' by Professor Patricia
Leighton. Appeared in *People Management* 11 May
2000. Reproduced by permission of Professor
Patricia Leighton; p72 'Let's take leave of French'
by K Elliott. Appeared in *The Daily Mail* 26 July
1994. Reproduced by permission of Solo
Syndication Ltd.; p78 'Dear Madam, you are
£121,318,928.560 in the red on TSB account' by
Alistair Taylor. Appeared in *The Sun* 14 October 1998.
Reproduced by permission of News International
Syndication; p82 'Cross Cultural Conflict' by Duane
H Elmer. Copyright © 1993 Duane H Elmer.
Reproduced by permission of InterVarsity Press, P.O.
Box 1400, Downers Grove, IL 60515; p84 'Passport
Brazil' by E Herrington. World Trade Press 1998.
Reproduced by permission of World Trade Press;
p90 'Taste a world of difference' by J Hartley-Brewer.
Appeared in *The Guardian Weekly* 17-23 February
2000. Reproduced by permission of Guardian
Newspapers Ltd.; pp94, 114, 118 'Out of sorts?
Use your loaf' by C Doyle. Appeared in *The Daily
Telegraph* 14 February 1997. Reproduced by
permission of Telegraph Syndication; p96 'The
Insight Guide to The Gambia and Senegal.' Copyright
© 1996 APA Publications GmbH & Co Verlag KG.
Reproduced by permission of Insight Guides; p98
'Passport Russia' by C Mitchell. World Trade Press
1998. Reproduced by permission of World Trade
Press; p106 'The Do's and Taboos of Using English
Around the World' by Roger E Axtell. Copyright
© John Wiley & Sons 1995. Reproduced by
permission of John Wiley & Sons, Inc.; p108 'Pig
organ transplants much closer' by Dr David
Whitehouse. From *BBC News Online Sci/Tech* 14

March 2000. Reproduced by permission of BBC
Online; pp125, 126 Interview with Sir Bobby
Charlton. Reproduced by permission of Sir Bobby
Charlton; p127 Interview with Mark Ellingham.
Reproduced by permission of Mark Ellingham;
pp130, 131 Interview with Martha Lane Fox.
Reproduced by permission of Martha Lane Fox

Although every effort has been made to trace and
contact copyright holders before publication, this
has not been possible in some cases. We apologize
for any apparent infringement of copyright and if
notified, the publisher will be pleased to rectify
any errors or omissions at the earliest opportunity

Sources of information: p34 *Psychology* (second edition)
by Carole Wade and Carol Travis. Harper & Row
1990; p53 'Statistics on Internet use' from *The New
York Times Almanac* 1998 by J W Wright, and *The
Economist* 15 May 1999; p131 'Statistics on
billionaires' from *Fortune Magazine* 1 March 1999,
15 March 1999, and *Time* 28 April 1997; p86 *The
Manager's Book of Quotations* by L D Eigen and
J P Siegel. Amacom 1991; p86 *Listening Skills* by
I MacKay. Institute of Personnel and Development
1994; p93 *The Vegetarian Times* August 1999

Illustrations by: Katherine Baxter/Folio p107; Rachel
Oxley/Illustration pp60, 82, 94, 109; Pantelis Palios
pp3, 9, 10, 14, 16, 29, 36, 40, 51, 52, 70, 71, 74, 81,
98, 103; Gavin Reece/New Division p19; Technical
Graphics Dept/OUP p96

Studio photography by: Mark Mason pp24, 84

*The publishers would like to thank the following for their
kind permission to reproduce photographs and other
copyright material:* Allsport (UK) Ltd p12 (J Herbert/
B Charlton headshot, Hulton Deutsch/B Charlton
footballer, A Lyons/M Jones, D Beckham); Emily
Anderson p86 (man/top left); BBC Photo Library
p33; BBC Natural History Unit pp26 (J Foott/
glacier), 92 (B Castelein/frog, W Osborn/rabbit,
A Tabor/snail); Camera Press London pp12
(B Benkow/M Ali), 56 (I R Magneut/B Gates, S Mark/
Sultan of Brunei, A Tevner/G Soros); Collections
p17; Stuart Conway p38; Corbis Sygma pp34
(F La Guardia), 96, 108; Mary Evans Picture Library
pp28 (expedition), 35 (Quakers, illustration of
woman), 64 (factory, office), 100 (radio,
switchboard); GettyOne Stone pp8 (handshake),
26 (M Mehlig/Amsterdam), 30 (man), 32 (D Kitchen/
crime scene, J McBride/homeless, D Spiro/house),
34 (P Edmondson/mobile phones), 36 (S Peters/
video conference), 46 (M Mehlig/beach), 47
(D H Endersbee/theatre, M Mehlig/beach,T Wood/
donkey), 92 (Eastcott/Momatiuk/horses), 104 (M
Barraud/woman in Paris, R Ellis/father and son, C
Ledner/businesswoman); The Ronald Grant
Archive p2 (A Alda and Terminator); L Gregory p86
(man/middle left); Hulton Getty p64 (farming),
100 (TV); The Image Bank pp2 (shopping), 8 (kiss),
34 (J Silver/women), 50 (T Dosoyne/woman,
children), 64 (miners), 72 (E Lewin), 77 (Morrell),
92 (G K & V Hart/dog, G Ross/piglet, S Scata/fish),
101 (B Elsadle/circuit board); Katz Pictures pp62
(S Shepheard/McDonalds), 90 (E Perner);
Copyright © Kathleen King p58; Magnum Photos
pp8 (nose rubbing), 18, 21 (B Lewis), 74
(S McCurry), 91 (Buddhists); Mirror Syndication
p4; Network Photographers p50 (H Sykes/old
man); Panos Pictures p28 (M Sclossman/
backpacker); 'For God's Sake' by Chris Madden,
Paperlink Ltd 1999 p7; Ross Parry p78; Pictor
International pp2 (cooking), 65, 84 (businessmen),
86 (four men/bottom row), 99, 101 (man resting);
Pictures Colour Library p91 (floating market,
woman and child); Popperfoto Ltd pp13, 84
(restaurant); Rough Guides Ltd p25 (M Ellingham);
Science Photo Library pp92 (P Menzel/grubs), 101
(P Plailly/DNA, Tek Image/cloning); Frank Spooner
Pictures pp46 (E Mulholland), 56 (A Benainous/
Queen Beatrice), 130; Stone p30; The Sun p78;
Superstock Ltd pp2 (builder), 5, 34 (satellite), 62
(H Ford); Telegraph Colour Library pp94, 97
(T Howell), 100 (VCL); David Tolley p68–69